"In *Navigating Autism*, Drs. Temple Grandin and Debra Moore provide a 'circle of guidelines' that documents practical, strength-based information for supporting autistic children and adults. With reference to Temple's lifetime of experience, and multiple examples of children and adults on the spectrum from Dr. Moore's years of clinical practice, the guidelines address crucial issues such as diagnosis, associated conditions, clinical/educational assessments, and the need to build on strengths from a positive whole-child, whole-person perspective. This comprehensive work will be an invaluable resource for both families and professionals."

—**Barry M. Prizant**, Ph.D., CCC-SLP, Brown University, Author, *Uniquely Human: A Different Way of Seeing Autism*

"Temple Grandin and Debra Moore have made a valuable contribution to the body of literature for autism therapists and clinicians. As their book so eloquently states, autistic children are much more than 'packages of disabilities.' This book will help everyone see neurodiverse children in a different and better light, and open the door to better support."

—**John Elder Robison**, Neurodiversity Scholar, the College of William & Mary, Advisor to the Center for Neurodiversity, Landmark College

"Whether you're a therapist, physician, educator, parent, or caregiver, *Navigating Autism* is a must-read for all people who support and interact with autistic children/teens. The nine strength-based mindsets presented by authors Temple Grandin, Ph.D. and Debra

T0026440

Moore, Ph.D. encourage readers to look beyond the narrative and focus on what makes each child wonderfully unique. Teeming with professional experience and valuable anecdotes, this book energizes and empowers while providing a fresh approach to navigating autism."

—**Amy KD Tobik**, Editor-in-Chief/
CEO, *Exceptional Needs Today*

"This is an in-depth, essential resource for those helping clients on the autism spectrum who want to move beyond label-locked thinking and provide a whole-person approach that honors the rich lived experience of autism. From assessment that considers social-emotional, sensory, motor, medical conditions, and psychiatric comorbidities, to intervention that draws on a strength-based approach, this is an invaluable book for optimizing interventions to help clients feel and function at their best."

—**Lindsey Biel**, Occupational Therapist, author, *Sensory Processing Challenges: Effective Clinical Work with Kids & Teens*, coauthor, *Raising a Sensory Smart Child*, foreword by Temple Grandin

NAVIGATING AUTISM

A Norton Professional Book

9 MINDSETS
FOR HELPING KIDS
ON THE SPECTRUM

NAVIGATING
AUTISM

TEMPLE GRANDIN

DEBRA MOORE

W. W. NORTON & COMPANY
Independent Publishers Since 1923

This work is intended as a general information resource for teachers, mental health professionals, and parents. It is not a substitute for appropriate professional education or mental health training, peer review, and/or clinical supervision. Standards of clinical practice and protocol change over time, and no technique or recommendation is guaranteed to be safe or effective in all circumstances. For case-specific questions and guidance, if you are a teacher or mental health professional, please consult with your school and/or community mental-health clinicians, and if you are a parent, please consult the education and/or mental-health professionals who work with your child.

The names of all people presented in case studies in this book have been changed and potentially identifying details changed or omitted. Any URLs displayed in this book link or refer to websites that existed as of press time. The publisher is not responsible for, and should not be deemed to endorse or recommend, any website other than its own or any content not created by it. The author, also, is not responsible for any third-party material.

For information about permission to reproduce selections from this book, write to Permissions, W. W. Norton & Company, Inc., 500 Fifth Avenue, New York, NY 10110

For information about special discounts for bulk purchases, please contact W. W. Norton Special Sales at specialsales@wwnorton.com or 800-233-4830

Manufacturing by Lake Book Manufacturing, Inc.
Book design by Carole Desnoes
Production manager: Katelyn MacKenzie

Library of Congress Cataloging-in-Publication Data

Names: Grandin, Temple, author. | Moore, Debra (Psychologist), author.
Title: Navigating autism : 9 mindsets for helping kids on the spectrum / Temple
    Grandin, Debra Moore.
Description: First edition. | New York, NY : W.W. Norton & Company, [2021] |
    "A Norton Professional Book." | Includes bibliographical references and index.
Identifiers: LCCN 2021014663 | ISBN 9780393714845 (paperback) |
    ISBN 9780393714852 (epub)
Subjects: LCSH: Autistic children. | Autistic children--Services for. |
    Parents of autistic children. | Social work with children with mental disabilities.
    Classification: LCC RJ506.A9 G695 2021 | DDC 618.92/85882—dc23
    LC record available at https://lccn.loc.gov/2021014663

W. W. Norton & Company, Inc., 500 Fifth Avenue, New York, N.Y. 10110
www.wwnorton.com

W. W. Norton & Company Ltd., 15 Carlisle Street, London W1D 3BS

3 4 5 6 7 8 9 0

TWO NOTES
ABOUT TERMINOLOGY

The Diagnostic and Statistical Manual, published by the American Psychiatric Association, formalized the concept of a spectrum disorder in its fifth edition, which was introduced in 2013. Upon release of the DSM-5, the official diagnostic term for autism became Autism Spectrum Disorder. For purposes of smoother reading, however, we use the terms "the spectrum" or "ASD" throughout this book.

Both "autistic person" and "person with autism" are used by those on the spectrum and by professionals who work with them. Those who prefer "autistic person" hold an identity-based perspective, while those who prefer "person with autism" have a person-centered perspective. We're aware that some individuals have strong views on which term they would like authors and others to use. We use both terms throughout the book.

CONTENTS

ACKNOWLEDGMENTS

Debra Moore

This book emerged from and owes a debt to countless researchers, clinicians, writers, and families. Nuggets of insight and wisdom accumulated over the years shaped the mindsets presented here.

Authors with autism or the parents of autistic children contributed details and observations rarely found in academic texts or professional conferences. I'm grateful for their unsparing depictions of their personal lives.

Autistic clients and their families trusted me to accompany them on their journeys as together we searched for ways to make their trips smoother, more satisfying, and more enjoyable. I've appreciated their willingness to risk, to experiment, and to persevere. They are the true scholars of autism.

Students help teachers maintain a beginner's eye; a necessity for continued learning and growth. Many thanks to my trainees, and a special thanks to Kate Kramer for reigniting, decades ago, my interest in autism.

I'm awed by the generosity of spirit and time from others in the autism field. Rich conversations with occupational therapist Kelly Beins, special education teacher, blogger, and parent

Danielli Mini, and clinician, researcher, consultant, and advocate Yulika Forman, informed and enhanced this project.

Deborah Malmud, head honcho of Norton's Professional Books imprint, was a steady, responsive presence from the book's inception to publication. Her feedback made this a better book, and her ability to balance a multitude of tasks and demands in the midst of a pandemic was truly impressive.

Thanks, as always, to Cheryl Miller, assistant exemplar to Dr. Temple Grandin.

To my partner Gerard, who put down whatever he was working on to engage in yet another conversation about autism: your interest mirrors your heartscape—full, loving, and selfless.

Finally, it all goes back to Temple. It remains a rather bewildering surprise to find myself partnered with such brilliance. She is a model of authenticity, resourcefulness, and hard work. Collaborating with her is an honor and privilege.

PREFACE

When I was in elementary school, my ability in art was always encouraged. My mother always urged me to paint and draw many different things instead of creating a single horse head over and over. To determine what a child or adult is good at and likes requires exposure to a variety of activities. Today I am seeing too many kids who have never been exposed to using tools, playing musical instruments, or performing in a play. I get asked all the time what led me into a career in the cattle industry. The answer is real simple. I experienced the West and cattle when I visited my aunt's ranch at age 15. Both children and adults get interested in things they are exposed to. They may also try something new and find out that they hate it, but it is important to learn what a child likes and dislikes by trying many different things. My mother had a really good instinct on how to "stretch" me a little bit outside my comfort zone to try something new. She always gave me a choice. When the opportunity to go to my aunt's ranch arrived, she gave me a choice. I could stay all summer or stay only one week. I got out to the ranch and loved it and chose to stay all summer.

Too many kids with an autism label are overprotected by their parents. They are not learning basic skills such as shopping or handling money. Many grandparents have told me that they discover that they are on the autism spectrum when their grandchildren are diagnosed. In most cases, the grandparent had a job at young age, such as delivering newspapers. They learned how to work long before they graduated from high school. Teachers and parents need to find substitutes for the old paper routes. Some possibilities for 11- to 12-year-olds are volunteer jobs at a religious organization or farmer's market.

Autistic individuals will often have uneven skills. They will be good at one thing and bad at another. I am an object visualizer who thinks in pictures. This enabled me to understand animals and be good at design and building things. Another autistic person may be a pattern, mathematical, visual-spatial thinker. These people may excel at engineering and computer programming. A third type is the verbal thinker. Autism is a very broad spectrum ranging from a brilliant head of a major tech company to somebody with much more severe challenges. I love the Stephen Hawking quote, "Concentrate on the things your disability does not prevent you from doing well."

Temple Grandin
Professor of Animal Science
Colorado State University

INTRODUCTION

Temple and I share like-minded views when it comes to autism and children on the spectrum. We both put more value on potential than struggles. We emphasize the importance of strengths versus deficits. And when we see a child or teen with autism, we both see countless fascinating facets just waiting to be developed.

We decided to work together on *Navigating Autism* so we could share and more fully explain our views. We wanted to give you examples based both on Temple's own personal life and on my many years counseling individuals and families impacted by autism. We strongly believe that if the adults interacting with autistic children stay grounded in the mindsets presented in this book, each child has a much improved chance of reaching their fullest potential than otherwise.

In addition to our own perspectives, we've added the findings of scientific studies so that you can feel comfortable knowing our viewpoints are rooted in and confirmed by research. We've also included lots of checklists and practical suggestions to help you put the mindsets into concrete, tangible action.

We hope you already see each child with autism as more than a label. After reading this book, we hope you'll broaden that outlook and consistently integrate it into all of your evaluations and interventions. Whether you are an educator, medical provider, mental health counselor, or parent, you have the immense obligation and opportunity to change how others view autistic children. When you accept, embrace, and foster the uniqueness of each child you encounter, you shift that child's sense of themself. When you stay focused on strengths, passions, and possibilities, then they—and everyone around them—can, too.

NAVIGATING
AUTISM

Every Child is More Than Autism

We live in a world of labels. We use them—diagnostic and otherwise—to make the world more comprehensible. When we agree on criteria for a diagnosis, we have a way to talk to each other in shorthand. We know what we mean, for example, if we say a child has restricted, repetitive behaviors, because that is spelled out in the current *Diagnostic and Statistical Manual* (American Psychiatric Association, 2013).

Autism is an important part of who I am, but I won't let autism totally take over. I have to make sure 60% of my recognition is for my livestock work. I want to be recognized for cattle."

TEMPLE

But labels also have drawbacks. When we label someone, others start to see them through the filter of that label. When we use the term autism, some people have an accurate understanding of the word, but many others do not. Even professionals have their own notions of what autism looks like. Once the label is used, they will apply that image. This happens a lot to people with autism.

Once we label someone, we also risk creating an oversimplified snapshot of that person. Once a person gets labeled, people's opinion of that person may never change. But everyone—with or without a label—is always developing and evolving. Many of these changes are subtle and easy to miss. Seeing a child through the filter of a label may make it more likely we'll miss the small changes. No matter what role you play in the life of a child with autism—professional, educator, or parent—you should always look beyond labels and see all of their strengths and features.

People who realize that a diagnosis of autism describes only part of a child (by definition, only the deficits and impairments) are in the best position to help, teach, and nurture that child. They also have better odds of imparting helpful tools when they view that child as a complex, multifaceted person with unique interests, temperaments, and abilities.

> *Labels can hurt if they lower expectations for a child. Every kid needs to have high, but reasonable, expectations."*
> TEMPLE

The diagnosis of autism can sometimes help you better predict a child's behaviors, but it tells you nothing about their specific way of thinking, their idiosyncrasies, their strengths, or their individual personality. A wise clinician, educator, or parent must look beyond diagnosis and appreciate all aspects of the child so they can help them develop an identity based on more than just being autistic. An accurate view of any child's personality includes their talents and strengths. Their personality is not defined by autism. Every child is more than autism.

By the end of this chapter we hope you are quicker to recognize when you or anyone involved with an autistic child falls into the label trap. We'll help you get there by pointing out the many variables that shape a child, and we'll also introduce you to four tendencies that can limit or bias your understanding of them. Everyone, even well-trained professionals, can let unconscious biases skew their view of someone with autism. We'll bring these tendencies to life by giving you sample vignettes of children that illustrate how a professional (or parent) might see that child if the adult is trapped by any of these viewpoints. Then we'll give you suggestions to step outside each trap.

We'll also show you how the media has influenced our views of autism. One of the biggest factors that determines how a person views autism is their age. That's because their ideas about autism were shaped by the media images that were popular while they were growing up. If your first exposure to autism was the movie *Rain Man*, you may have a very different perspective than if you grew up watching the Netflix series *Atypical*.

We'll also share ways of viewing autism that go beyond the list of diagnostic criteria in the *DSM-5*. This will help you look for more than whether a child exhibits behavior necessary for a diagnosis. To really understand and help a child, you have to think about how their brain systems function and how they process information.

> *The problem with the label of autism is you've got a spectrum that ranges from Einstein to someone with no language and with intellectual disability."*
> TEMPLE

Your assessment of a child with autism is also filtered through your particular academic training. Specialists often overemphasize their own area of interest and minimize other contributions to a child's functioning. We'll detail how different groups of professionals tend to focus on different aspects of a child.

Even good approaches and interventions can fail if you don't appreciate all aspects of a child. By adding the mindsets in this book to your repertoire, you will be better equipped to maintain a broad perspective, conduct more useful evaluations, put interventions on concrete foundations, recognize obstacles unrelated to autism, and bring out a child's strengths. Using the nine mindsets will help you see more progress and bring out each child's unique and maximum potential.

Recognize the Difference Between Traits and Temporary States and Autism

We all have individual *traits*—innate, inborn reactions to stress, novelty, and people. When a person is labeled autistic, we may attribute their traits to their developmental condition, but this shouldn't be our automatic assumption. Their traits—be it shyness, fearlessness, curiosity, or lack of curiosity—might be equally strong even if they were not autistic.

We all experience *states*—temporary moods, reactions, and mindsets. We usually don't emphasize or dwell on the temporary states of people, but when someone has a label, we're more likely to attribute their temporary state to that label, even if it is unrelated. We don't realize we do this; it is an unconscious, automatic reaction.

Once someone is given a label, in fact, a cascade of events can happen. As described, those closest to the person, such as family or professionals, may filter their perceptions through that label. They may begin to mistakenly attribute traits and behaviors to the labeled condition, and they may being to organize their view of the person according to their understanding of the label. They may also begin to make the label the most important part of that person. When this happens, others in the child's environment tend to do the same. Here is one example.

> The first thing 14-year-old George's* parents announce when they introduce their son is that he is autistic. They know George comes across as "different," and they worry what others will think. They've had lots of experiences of George being misunderstood or bullied, and their intention is to prevent others from causing him further hurt. They have been his protectors for so long, it's become automatic.

They don't realize by putting George's label first—and not mentioning any of his other characteristics—they are shortchanging their son. The announcement of his label doesn't protect him; instead, it will often shift and restrict how others see him.

By leading with a label, George's parents imply autism is the most important part of him. They probably don't intend to do that. It is hoped that they see their son as a complex teen, with a variety of strengths and challenges, just like any other boy his age. Some of those challenges—and strengths—are related to autism, but some are not. By preempting the opportunity for others to get to know George by their own observations and interactions with him, they deprive both George and others of a fuller, richer experience.

---

* All names and situations used as examples are anonymized.

George's parents would never want him to be referred to as "The Smiths' son with autism," yet that might be what people tend to remember and even repeat to others. Because a label was their first framework for George, it may be how they think or speak of him from then on. His parents unwittingly spread an incomplete, distorted image of George.

Professionals, too, can fall into overemphasizing labels to the detriment of the person they are trying to help. Here is an example from the academic environment.

Mrs. Whittington is a talented high school guidance counselor. She has been with the school district close to 20 years. She has helped scores of children and families and is respected by her colleagues. She would never intend to limit or curb a child's potential.

When helping seniors plan for their futures, she often assists them in drafting letters to potential trade schools, colleges, and employers. She believes that when a child has a "disability," they should get all available resources, so she emphasizes their needs.

She wrote a letter of recommendation for Tyler, a student applying for a computer store job. She highlighted his autism. She wanted his prospective employer to be informed; she thinks it will help the company better understand his behaviors. While a worthy goal, she goes about it in a way that could limit Tyler's odds of getting hired.

The first sentence of her letter disclosed

(with his permission) that, "Tyler is autistic." She explained his challenges, and described how he may be misunderstood by others. Later in the letter she mentioned "how far Tyler has come" and says he would be a loyal, positive addition to their workforce.

By labeling Tyler right away, Mrs. Whittington made his autism sound like the biggest part of him. His punctuality, work ethic, and intense enthusiasm for all things computer-related were unintentionally relegated to secondary characteristics. Yet it is those qualities that Tyler has to offer. His autism is secondary.

She could have more appropriately included Tyler's autism within the larger context of a multifaceted young man, or she could have left it out entirely, while still describing his challenges and strengths accurately. There are valid arguments on both sides of the question of disclosing a diagnosis to prospective employees, but it rarely, if ever, should take center stage.

If you do want to disclose autism because you think it will help someone, embed the label within a full depiction of the person. Clarify why it is being disclosed and how the information can be put to good use. Here's an example of how you could go about this.

Dr. Moore once worked with Natalie, a young woman who wanted to get an apprenticeship as a brick mason. An interview was required as part of the application. Natalie did not interview well. In fact, she did quite poorly in these situations.

If an interviewer spoke fast, or in idioms or slang,

Natalie couldn't always grasp what was meant. She couldn't respond as quickly as most interviewers expected. She didn't pick up on subtleties of the social aspect of the interview, and she was lousy at small talk. She came across as too serious and awkward.

To help prevent Natalie from creating a misleading impression of her abilities, Dr. Moore sent a brief advance email to the interviewer. The email suggested Natalie had unique gifts to bring to the apprenticeship.

Dr. Moore listed this young woman's strengths: she was extremely detail oriented (which fit perfectly with this field), she spotted errors faster than most people (again, a critical skill), and she could anticipate problems that others didn't foresee. She could envision creative, novel, and simple solutions to problems that stymied others. She was loyal, punctual, and honest, and she had no interest whatsoever in workplace politics or drama.

Dr. Moore also wrote that Natalie often struck others as odd and was frequently perceived as aloof or uninterested. The email explained this was because Natalie focused so intently on her work that little else registered. If you wanted her attention, the email suggested, it was important to be clear, precise, and direct.

The email ended by noting that Natalie rarely made a good first impression in interviews. The interviewer was told that she might take longer than most to respond to questions due to her slower decoding and processing of information. The email explained that Natalie was methodical rather than impulsive (again, a necessary part of her chosen field) and that her brain digested data in a very linear, logical manner. Dr. Moore pointed out this was part of how Natalie's autism made her a uniquely well-suited applicant for the tasks involved in being a brick mason.

Natalie was accepted as an apprentice. Perhaps the letter helped. What the letter did not do was create an image of an autistic applicant. The average reader would instead have come away with a general sense of Natalie and how she might fit into the program. Her autism, obviously part of that, did not take the lead. The email may have helped prevent Natalie's interviewer from getting stuck in what Temple calls "label-locked" thinking.

> *Label-locked thinking can have disastrous effects. It can derail effective treatment. For instance, I heard a doctor say about a kid with gastrointestinal issues, 'Oh, he has autism. That's the problem'—and then the doctor didn't treat the GI problem."*
> TEMPLE

These three examples—of George, Tyler, and Natalie—illustrate the importance of always treating each person as a complex, multifaceted individual with unique challenges, strengths, and interests. This mindset is the most important first step for professionals and parents who want to really understand or help someone with autism. If you remember that a diagnosis of autism describes only part of a child (by definition, only the deficits and impairments), you will be in the best position to help, teach, and nurture a child.

Behavioral Diagnoses and Unconscious Biases: Four Tendencies That Skew Perceptions

Diagnostic labels exist to help clinicians and educators identify patients and students who exhibit common core features and thus benefit from similar interventions. Labels also give professionals and parents a way of talking to each other more easily; not everything has to be explained in detail. A diagnostic term also provides consistent guidelines for researchers.

Diagnoses can also restrict perception. This may be particularly true for diagnoses based on descriptions of behavior as opposed to medical markers. Although research is advancing our understanding of the genetic and biological underpinnings of autism, the current *DSM-5* diagnostic criteria remain based solely on observable behavior. When we focus on behaviors, particularly ones deemed *impaired* or *abnormal*, we selectively magnify these parts of the person and minimize other important aspects.

Social psychologist Solomon Asch conducted research with important implications for anyone working with autistic children (Asch, 1946). Asch wanted to find out what factors influence how we perceive and make sense of others. His findings have direct relevance for parents of autistic children as well as the children's clinicians and educators.

Asch found four tendencies that bias or limit our view of another person. We've paraphrased his language in order to make each tendency as clear and straightforward as possible. (You are probably most vulnerable to these tendencies when you are stressed, tired, or engaged in a behavior so routine that you've gone on autopilot.)

TENDENCY #1   We like simple explanations of a child's behavior, and we ignore contradictory data.

Jason, age 9 years, entered fourth grade at a new school after his family moved across town. He had been diagnosed with autism the year before, though his new teacher had not been informed. By the end of his first day of class, Jason's teacher had decided her new student was shy. She viewed Jason as an introvert who preferred being left alone. She attributed all of his behaviors to "shyness."

Many others in Jason's life see him the same way. The tendency to prefer simple explanations is universal; clinicians, educators, and family members can all form remarkably fast impressions without even realizing it. We think these impressions help us predict someone's future behavior. In some cases that's true, but drawing global conclusions is a disservice to children because it fails to predict more subtle or contradictory aspects of their personality.

Some of Jason's behaviors that his teacher attributed to shyness were: limited eye contact, restricted facial expressions, not joining in the loud laughter and chatter of his peers during recess, and standing unusually far away from the other kids while waiting in line for lunch.

Jason also exhibited behaviors that were not symptomatic of an introvert. Asch's studies predict the teacher would overlook or discount these behaviors, because they didn't match most of what she saw. For example: Jason made eye contact when his teacher talked about the weather, and he frowned when she used the word blizzard inaccurately. (He knew that snow does not even need to be falling for a blizzard to occur—that the exact requirements for a blizzard are sustained winds that last 3 hours or longer with frequent gusts to 35 mph or greater and either falling or blowing snow.)

Also, Jason's teacher probably missed his several attempts to socialize that first morning. Because his outreach to other children was awkward and subsequently rebuffed, Jason had quickly given up trying to interact with anyone. By afternoon, he had decided to keep to himself.

Jason also struggled with sensory overload. He stood apart from his peers to avoid being brushed up against, a sensation that caused him both physical and emotional discomfort. He created unusual interpersonal distance not because he was inherently shy; he simply needed more personal space than the average child.

If you were Jason's teacher (or clinician), how could you have avoided the trap of making global inferences?

Here are tips to help you appreciate a child's unique and varied nuances.

- Treat initial observations as unique data points. Do not rush to fit them into a pattern.
- Realize humans are wired to create patterns even where they do not exist. (Think of the times you've

seen images in clouds—and how others may see something entirely different.) Consciously resist this default tendency.

- When you observe a behavior, find out what happened before and after it. Understanding triggers and aftereffects can drastically change your interpretation of an act. For example, when Jason stood apart from his peers, his trigger was being jostled by a classmate, and the aftereffect was a startled response: a grimace and fearful, wide eyes. If his teacher had noted these reactions, she might have suspected sensory sensitivity rather than a personality trait.

- Actively look for atypical behaviors in a child. If his teacher had noticed that Jason's usual indirect and fleeting eye contact changed to direct, sustained eye contact when weather was being discussed, she might have realized his eye contact was situation and interest dependent.

- Be curious. If you notice inconsistencies in behavior, ask yourself what might have caused the change. Was something different in Jason's environment? Did you do something different?

- When you observe contradictory behaviors, view them as important clues to better understanding a child. When a child behaves out of character, you have hit an information gold mine. Don't discard the behavior as an irrelevant outlier; instead realize this specific behavior can illustrate vital nuances of a child. By studying these behaviors, you can better understand and help a child.

TENDENCY #2:   We tend to assume what we observe
                   happens all the time, in all situations.

> A psychologist evaluated Sarah, an
> 11-year-old sixth grader. The evaluation took place at a
> university clinic and consisted of cognitive testing as
> well as a clinical interview. It lasted about 4 hours, with
> two short breaks.
>
> The psychologist's report concluded Sarah
> appeared to meet criteria for an autism spectrum
> diagnosis and also stated Sarah had personality traits
> that, if she were an adult, could be seen as consistent
> with avoidant personality disorder. Recommendations
> were made to set up an Individualized Education Plan
> (IEP) and to begin individual psychotherapy.

The day of her evaluation, Sarah had woken up feeling anxious and irritable. She refused breakfast, eating only a slice of leftover pie from the previous night's dinner. She was worried about missing school and didn't understand the purpose of her appointment. She had no idea what a psychologist did, what to expect, or how long she would be there. Also, she had never been to the university campus before, which was large and bustling with students. The psychology clinic was not next to the parking lot; to get there, she and her parents had to navigate past and around several other nondescript, identical-looking buildings. There were no signs leading to the clinic. Her anxiety had increased by the time they found the correct building.

The psychologist's room had florescent lighting, something that often gave Sarah a headache. The afternoon sun glared through tilted mini-blinds, causing her to constantly squint. By the second hour of the evaluation, Sarah could feel a dull pain at both temples, plus uncomfortably tightness in her forehead. Her discomfort increased when she talked, so she kept her answers and responses short.

Sarah's favorite hobby was drawing. Her mother had enrolled her in a Saturday art class for children, and it was the highlight of her daughter's past week. Sarah had even made a friend there—someone who shared her interest in working with colored pencils to create sketches of animals, particularly horses.

She wished the psychologist had asked her to draw an animal, but she'd specifically been told to draw a house, a person, and a tree. Sarah had no enthusiasm for any of these, so she offered up minimal likenesses that did not reflect her abilities.

Sarah couldn't relax at all during the evaluation and felt on the brink of panic at several points. She didn't even remember to tell the psychologist about Emma, her art friend. When she felt panic, Sarah couldn't think or verbalize her thoughts very well.

In addition to her acute anxiety related to the evaluation, Sarah's stress had been heightened for months. Many things in this 11-year-old's life were changing. The girls in her class were different now—starting to giggle about boys (something she thought was really stupid) and always wanting to compare clothes (she preferred the same baggy jeans and soft sweater most days). Even Sarah's body was changing. She had begun to develop breasts at the beginning of the year, and now she was noticing traces of pubic hair.

You probably recognize that Sarah's lack of enthusiasm, minimal engagement, and nervousness can all be tied to external conditions, not necessarily to her personality. If you weren't thinking of Asch's research and this tendency, you might think Sarah's actions the day of her evaluation were typical behaviors.

The psychologist probably wasn't aware of crucial factors related to Sarah's presentation. He didn't know Sarah was in a biologically dysregulated state the morning of her evaluation. Her blood sugars were low, and the lighting had assaulted her senses and produced physical pain.

Sarah was also in an unfamiliar environment, she didn't have adequate information to make sense of her experience, and she was intimidated by her surroundings and the evaluator. (Even the kindest, friendliest evaluator may not be able to alleviate the confusion or fear of a child, especially one with autism.)

Sarah was feeling increasingly estranged from her peers. Many of them, like Sarah herself, had entered puberty. Hormones were in flux. Hormones and anxiety are often directly linked, and puberty can induce panic attacks in some children. The evaluator may not have taken this into consideration.

> *Puberty was one of the worst parts of my life. When puberty started, my panic attacks started. When estrogen levels rise, often anxiety rises, too."*
> TEMPLE

If you were evaluating Sarah, how could you have avoided the trap of attributing her behaviors to stable personality traits?

Here are tips to help you distinguish between temporary states and stable traits:

- Do not automatically assume a child's behavior during an evaluation represents their behavior in other settings or at other times. Keep in mind that a clinic setting is foreign, is often intimidating, and may elicit uncharacteristic behavior.

- Gather contextual information. What happened in the hours or days prior to the evaluation? What is the child's understanding of who you are and why you are meeting with them? Does the child want to be there? Reassure them it is okay to be honest in their answers. If they say they don't want to be there, ask them why and if there is anything you can do to make them more comfortable.

- Avoid introducing yourself as "Dr." unless you are conducting a medical exam. Children and teens don't distinguish between physicians and other professionals with doctorate degrees. If you use the term "doctor," they will probably assume you are a medical doctor. Younger children may even think you are going to give them a shot. If you're not doing a medical exam, but must use the term "Dr.," explain you are not that kind of doctor—tell them you are a doctor who finds out what is easy and what is hard for kids, so that grownups (or teachers or parents or therapists) can help them feel more confident and relaxed when they're learning new things. Your first name and this brief explanation are often all you need to explain to younger children. Kids don't care what your last name is or that you have a doctoral degree.

- Gather information ahead of time from parents and

teachers. Use questionnaires, phone calls, emails, or meetings. Review snippets of home videos if possible.

— Sometimes it is difficult for children and teens to qualitatively describe feelings and thoughts. Many kids will give sparse responses to open-ended questions like "How are you feeling?" Instead, use a rating scale. Ask "On a scale of 1 to 10, how nervous are you right now?" and then ask, "On the same scale of 1 to 10, how nervous are you usually [at home, at school, when you're alone in your room, when you meet a stranger, and so on]?" This helps you understand if the child's behavior that day is representative. It requires little effort from the child to respond. You can quickly insert this into any evaluation.

— Consider taking a few minutes for simple relaxation techniques if the child is open to it. Take a few breaths together, do a few stretches, or for more activated children, toss a pillow or easily caught large, soft ball back and forth a few times to help them relax and focus. You might need to use these techniques several times over the course of an evaluation. It will help bring out the highest potential of the child.

— Always assess and monitor sensory aspects of the evaluation room. Temperature, light, scent, sound, or movement can skew a child's behavior. Many children on the spectrum experience disruption of their emotional, cognitive, or physical equilibrium if they're overwhelmed by sensory input. In an initial evaluation, you want to assess a child's optimal functioning, not how they perform under sensory assault.

- Ask the child (and parent) about health, physical concerns, and current physical comfort. Is the child hungry? What did they eat before the evaluation? How did they sleep the night before? Do they have any pain? Are they too warm, or are they chilly?

- Let even verbal kids use nonverbal communication if it gives you more information. A simple strategy is to have a child use a tissue as a flag to let you know they are anxious or need a break. Demonstrate before beginning the evaluation by holding up the tissue and explaining its purpose. Use whatever you know about the child to personalize the demo. For example, if you know a child gets irritated easily, tell them to wave the flag if they feel mad.

- Sometimes clinicians forget the most obvious, simple strategy for learning about a child. When you have questions, ask the child directly, instead of wondering to yourself. This is not the time to be indirect or make guesses. For example, if you're wondering if a child is bored, ask them (and follow it up with having them rate on the 1 to 10 scale how bored they are).

- Always allow time to ask about and discuss the child's strengths and interests. For example, this evaluator could have used the standard person-house-tree test, but seeing Sarah's spare drawings, could have followed up by asking her if she liked to draw and, if so, what were her favorite subjects. Even when evaluations are slotted into fixed time slots, taking 5 or 10 minutes to let a child talk about or demonstrate a skill is well worth it.

- With children approaching puberty, always ask parents what changes are happening. Ask about mood changes and newly emerging differences from peers. (A child may be in puberty and you wouldn't guess it from their age. Puberty happens sooner than it used to—the age range in America is now 10 to 14 years for white girls, as early as 9 for some Black females, 12 to 16 for white boys, and 9 to 14 for some Black males.)

TENDENCY #3: We tend to artificially integrate divergent traits and behaviors into a unified narrative.

Liam, age 4 years, was given a diagnosis of autism by his pediatrician, who also noted delayed speech and recommended speech therapy. Liam is on a waiting list for a complete evaluation from a regional autism center, and his mother set up an appointment at a speech and language clinic in the meantime. The clinic director met with Liam's mother, who described her son as her "sweet one" —her youngest child who delighted in playing with his older sisters. She said he tended to be quiet, but sometimes could be a chatterbox at home. She noted that others rarely saw his more outgoing side, and his preschool teacher saw a different child than she experienced at home.

The director then assigned a staff member to work with Liam. This person wrote the following summary after their initial visit:

"Liam is a 4-year-old child whose behaviors displayed in this evaluation are explained by his autism. He showed difficulties in all areas consistent with the disorder; namely, problems with social interaction, communication, and stereotyped patterns of behavior. He showed marked deficits in both semantic and pragmatic language. He exhibited poverty of speech, with MLU (Mean Length of Utterance) one standard deviation below chronological age. Liam offered few spontaneous verbalizations and often responded to my questions with nonverbal gestures. He appeared particularly unable to recognize or produce emotion-laden vocabulary. Liam also showed impairment in tonality and cadence, exhibiting oddities in both. Impairment was also obvious in social functioning. Liam did not initiate two-way conversation, seemed in his own world, failed to respond to his name on one occasion, and made little eye contact. He evidenced no communicative intent with joint attention purposes. Liam didn't play with available toys, such as cars, blocks, balls, or crayons. He did not ask for help even when he struggled. He frequently engaged in repetitive, stereotyped movements of his hands."

Does this sound like the boy his mother described? Now let us tell you more about Liam . . .

Liam feels special when his big sisters and grandparents call him "Li-Li." At home, even his parents have picked up on the nickname. One time, when a new neighbor asked "And what is your name, young man?" Liam had responded "Li-Li" before his mother gave him a funny look and he remembered to say "Liam."

Liam doesn't like talking to strangers, but that's true for everyone in his family. His parents, who have recently adopted the American names Sue and John, are reserved, and there are few visitors to Liam's house. Six months after he was born, the family welcomed his "halmeoni" and his "hal-abeoji," doting grandparents who emigrated from Korea and now live in the converted basement apartment. Liam only understood a few of their Korean words, but they developed a system of gestures that worked well, and they played and drew pictures together in quiet familiarity.

Born 5 years before their baby brother, Liam's twin sisters Nari and Yumi had picked up their grandparents' Korean remarkably fast. They alternated between words and gestures, fluent in each. Liam's parents spoke both English and Korean to the children, but had no choice but to stick with Korean with the children's grandparents.

Because his grandparents never learned English, their ability to participate in the wider world was limited. Their perspective on America was based on the crime shows they liked (they could understand these from the actions of the characters) and the images on the local news. It's no surprise they came to see their new country as a dangerous place, and they developed the habit of locking and then rechecking all the doors in the house several times a day. They taught Liam and the girls to do the same. The twins were old enough not to take these lessons too seriously, but for Liam the lessons became rituals that he did automatically, and they later became anxious compulsions. When he couldn't actually get up and turn a lock (like at preschool or the speech clinic), he defaulted to mimicking the knob-twisting motion with his hands.

Liam's grandparents also taught him other lessons—how to respect his elders by never speaking unless spoken to, how to look down when spoken to by an adult, and how to sit quietly without touching what doesn't belong to him. They were traditional in those ways, and Liam's busy, overworked parents were happy to have them so involved.

If you were evaluating Liam, how could you have avoided the trap of creating a narrative that artificially integrated divergent traits and behaviors?

Here are tips to help you gather a more complete picture of a child.

- Clinicians conducting an evaluation should be thoroughly briefed by any other staff who gathered information or met or spoke to family or referral sources. Even routine admission screenings may elicit details that help put later observations into context.
- Evaluations are greatly enriched by the participation of extended family. Each family member has a unique perspective based on their relationship to the child and the types of activities and settings in which they observe the child participating.
- When family members are unable to attend an evaluation in person, consider sending them a questionnaire and following up with a phone call after you have reviewed their answers. The safety of distance can yield important details, especially those that cause discomfort or embarrassment.

- Parents may not understand or be receptive to the involvement of other relatives, especially if they feel judged by them. It is good to talk openly about this and to normalize how often parents endure unsolicited advice and even criticism of their parenting. Use this as an opportunity to support and let parents know you understand this part of their experience.

- Teachers, including preschool teachers, should be consulted whenever possible prior to evaluating a child. Having the educator's observations ahead of time is much more useful than after the evaluation is complete. Done in this order, observations will lead to the formulation of questions to be asked and perplexing or contradictory information to be carefully examined.

- Always seek information on the family's culture. Many people think of culture only in terms of race or nationality and ascribe generic stereotypes to members of those groups. Well-meaning professionals may pride themselves on taking culture into consideration, as they have been taught to do in their training. Yet they may not inquire (sometimes due to fear of being intrusive) into other aspects of a families' culture such as customs, rituals, beliefs, communication styles, idioms, trauma history, and values. It is useful to think of each family as having its unique culture that is in a way foreign to you and warrants exploration.

- When a child does not initiate an age-typical behavior (e. g., not reaching for toys that most children explore), go beyond noting it. Sometimes the child simply needs to be told it is permissible for them to engage in the activity. Initiate the activity yourself, without saying anything, and observe if the child joins in. If he does not, ask if he would like to, again reassuring him this is allowed.

- When a young child does not respond to their given name, ask what each member of the family calls them. Do not ask if they have a nickname, as they may not know that word. Just ask, "What does your Mommy call you?" (You may get some interesting answers to this one!)

- Sometimes children will give you valuable information if you ask them, "What are the rules at your house?" Another information question can be "What do you get in trouble for?"

- Always try to learn what interests each child. They are more likely to talk to you about things that truly engage them. What an adult examiner is interested in may not match the child's interest. Games, pets, siblings, and the child's room are good topics to try. These subjects may give you a more accurate sample of the child's verbal and interpersonal abilities.

TENDENCY #4:   We tend to explain away data that makes us uncomfortable or we can't make sense of.

It was August, and Chloe was turning 3 years old. She was a striking child, with curly brown hair and large, intense hazel eyes set in a delicate face.

Her parents had planned a real birthday party this year and invited other toddlers from her play group. The theme was princesses and purple—two things Chloe adored.

In fact, Chloe was rarely without her sparkly purple hair band and her favorite silky purple skirt. Her mother, Jenn, was amazed at how long Chloe could twirl in that skirt and not get dizzy. She called her "my little ballerina," both for the dressed-up spinning and for her funny way of daintily walking on her tippy toes. Jenn had taken dance classes as a young girl and it pleased her to picture Chloe in a real tutu and dance slippers.

Her mom also noticed that even though she was good at twirling, Chloe sometimes seemed remarkably clumsy, sometimes even falling over when she bent to reach a toy. She sustained more bumps and bruises than her older siblings ever had, but never sought out comfort for them, and Jenn usually only discovered the marks during bath time.

The day of the party, Chloe was excited, as always, to put on her purple skirt and hair band. She was happily twirling when the first little guests arrived. But when Jenn reached for her hand, to pull her over to the other toddlers, Chloe's happiness disappeared, replaced by shockingly strong protests and ear-splitting screams. Jenn was baffled and embarrassed, but told herself that Chloe was probably just revved up from the two cupcakes she'd let her have that morning as a special birthday treat. She made a note to limit

Chloe's sugar intake, reflecting that she should have
known better.

If you were Jenn, how could you have avoided discarding observations you didn't understand or found upsetting?

Here are tips to help you use all observations of a child for their benefit:

- Know you are likely to give disproportionate attention to what you want to see. You may ignore what causes you distress, especially if it threatens your idea of how things should be. Use your knowledge of this tendency to intentionally pay attention to what is confusing or uncomfortable.

- Realize you may be most likely to attribute false explanations for disturbing behaviors when those behaviors involve someone you love. Seeing your child in emotional or physical pain causes a primitive, visceral reaction in most parents. Defense mechanisms often kick in automatically.

- Realize there may be an evolutionary value in parents overidentifying with their child to the point of taking their child's behavior personally—as a reflection of their parenting or even their self-worth—when that child acts outside group norms. Sadly, a child who is different risks alienation, shaming, and bullying. Parents know this in their bones and hiding differentness can be seen as a loving (though misguided) act of protection. Resist this tendency.

- Realize humans are notoriously bad at living with uncertainty and create stories to connect otherwise confusing or contradictory pieces of information. Step back and simply list data before interpreting it. Put the brakes on premature conclusions.

- Pay attention when you have a visceral reaction to an observation. It's likely, for example, that when Jenn saw unexplained bruises on Chloe, and when she watched her stumble and fall over, she intuitively felt something was amiss. Yet she quickly dismissed the feelings—so fast that she virtually erased them from memory. Parents of children with autism routinely say that, following a diagnosis, they can look back and point to clues they had ignored. Listen to the clues, and get them checked out.

- Seek initial feedback by sharing observations with others who know a child but are not in a parental role. Sharing with a spouse, while important, can result in shared minimization of concerns. Share with a more distant relative, a neighbor, another parent of a similarly aged child (or one who has raised several children), a babysitter, or a teacher. Listen to what they say without defending.

- Don't dismiss unexplained behavior—these behaviors are your most valuable data. Usual behaviors, or ones we think we understand, may add little to our understanding of a child. The gold is found in those behaviors that do not fit. Reflect on them, write them down (to offset the tendency for our brain to forget them), and share them with others so the behaviors earn their rightful place as precious data sets.

While parents may sometimes want to explain away observations they can't make sense of, there's also a phenomenon known as *negativity bias* that comes into play once the observations are noted and accepted. This is the general human tendency to overfocus on and more easily recall any behaviors viewed as unusual, undesired, or objectionable. As noted above, the *DSM-5* focuses exclusively on deficits and impairments. Thus, once a child is given a diagnostic label, those involved in their care may unwittingly focus too much on those negatively viewed behaviors. Further, because children on the autism spectrum often exhibit unusual or uncommon behaviors, and we so often narrowly focused on modifying those behaviors, this tendency is magnified.

Diagnostic labels can also serve as cues that activate our stigma and stereotypes. Professionals, educators, and parents are not exempt from stigmatizing attitudes or behaviors, though they are generally unaware of their unconscious attitudes. Keeping the findings of Asch and other social psychologists in mind can both remind us that no one is immune from distortions in attitudes toward autism and also help prevent us from falling prey to the stereotypes.

The mindset of remembering that every child is more than autism helps us avoid overfocusing on deficits, falling into stigmatizing attitudes, and making global inferences that miss important aspects of a child.

How Pop Culture Has Influenced Our Views of Autism

How would you perceive autism if all you had to base it on was popular culture? Your viewpoint would partly depend on which movies, television shows, and books you'd been exposed to. The biggest influence on your perception would be your age.

The American film industry brought autism to the public via the hugely popular 1988 movie *Rain Man*. This comedy-drama mesmerized audiences, grossing more than any other film that year and winning four Oscars. It told the story of a successful businessman who discovers he has a brother named Raymond, who is in an institution and is the beneficiary of the family trust. Charlie decides to take care of Raymond so he can get the money earmarked for Raymond's institutional care.

Raymond is portrayed as a savant who has echolalia (the unsolicited repeating of noises or words), repetitive behaviors, impaired motor functioning, restricted facial expression, and meltdowns (emotional eruptions caused by sensory overload or other upsetting circumstances). His brother cannot understand or handle him, and the movie ends with Charlie returning Raymond to the institution.

The character of Raymond was actually based on a developmentally delayed man with severe brain malformations, but people who saw *Rain Man* now thought they knew what autism looked like.

Many of these indelible representations, while largely inaccurate, persist. Older clinicians, educators, and parents—if their introduction to autism was via the visceral experience of seeing *Rain Man*—may have lingering stereotypical opinions. Our first impressions lurk in the background even in the face of new data and can contaminate our thinking without conscious awareness. Movies aim to draw us in emotionally. They are especially potent in cementing images and opinions.

Rain Man included many inaccurate ideas about autism.

These included: all autistic people are savants, they can never function independently, their level of functioning is unchangeable, their life is controlled by rigid rituals, they cannot love, disruptive public meltdowns are inevitable, and they are best cared for in institutions.

Since *Rain Man*, many movies have either discussed autism or included characters who depicted autistic traits. The American Autism Institute website, founded by Bernard Rimland, lists 36 movies and television series that involve autism (American Autism Institute, 2020). The list reflects strides made in the diversity of portrayals: it divides movies into categories such as family friendly, young adult, adult, documentary, and series. From Julia, the first character on *Sesame Street* to have autism, to a series like *Atypical*, pop culture now includes neurodiversity.

HBO's 2010 biographical drama about Temple's life was the first big screen depiction of a real person with autism. *Temple Grandin*, with Claire Danes playing Temple, showed modern audiences that someone with severe autism in childhood could nevertheless find vocational success and independence in life. It was realistic, was not sugar-coated, and was well-received. The film received numerous awards, including five Emmys.

A milestone was reached in 2017 with the release of the film *Keep the Change*, in which the lead roles were played by actors on the spectrum. This adult comedy is also notable because the characters who have autism are more than their label. They each have individual personalities; their autism is part of their identity, but it does not define them.

Information about autism is now readily available on the internet. Many people who identify as autistic have started blogs or video channels. These can provide valuable and affirming support for people who live in isolated communities without local resources. However, because anyone can post on the internet, and there are no filters for quality or accuracy, it is critical that you use judgment and research any so-called treatments you find online.

A vetted site with dozens of free talks about autism, including personal stories, is ted.com, with the slogan "ideas worth spreading." TED employs curators as well as fact-checkers and topic-specific advisors. You can find Temple's 20-minute talk, *"The World Needs All Kinds of Minds"* there. It has been viewed over 5 million times.

Defining Autism

Autism has now been studied for more than six decades. Much funding and many hours have been devoted to figure out exactly what it is, what causes it, and how to best assist those impacted by it. There are many experts touting unproven origins and treatments, but the consensus of the scientific community is that we have not yet answered many basic questions. Particularly in the area of genetics, researchers seem to agree that autism is a very heterogeneous clinical disorder.

> *Each person with autism is unique. While there are shared behaviors, the heterogeneity is striking. The fact that kids who share the same diagnosis can be so different says the condition likely has multiple underlying causes and will present diverse developmental challenges."*
> TEMPLE

Many predict we will eventually delineate numerous subgroups of conditions. Most expect to find multiple causative factors—some that are powerful contributors by their very presence and others that become potent only when combined with other agents.

Human beings, whether authoring descriptions for an edition of the *DSM*, or simply trying to get their brain around an atypical set of behaviors, prefer simplicity. As discussed before, we build narratives to explain what we don't understand, and we create distortions or omissions in the process. We try hard to make disparate elements fit together.

The fact is, autism is too broad a term. What the current *DSM* (*DSM-5*) labels as a unitary condition existing on a spectrum of varying severity may in time be revised to specify at least multiple conditions.

Autism and Brain-Regulatory Functions

One useful way of thinking about autism is by considering differences in underlying brain operations. The constellation of diagnostic markers we term autism appears to be associated with multiple regulatory functions of the brain. Each person with autism struggles with at least one of these issues; some struggle with many. In understanding the unique experiences of a person on the spectrum, it is important to assess which regulatory functions are impaired. To maximize each person's potential, any impacted regulatory function must be addressed as part of a treatment plan.

If the brain's *electrical signaling system* has glitches, the results can range from interruptions or delays in information processing to full-blown seizures. The brain functions via chemical and electrical communication. Researchers are now able to view real time electrical activity. They've found autism is associated with abnormalities of information integration that can be caused both by a reduction in the connectivity between specialized neural networks in the brain or overconnectivity within individual neural assemblies. Both reduc-

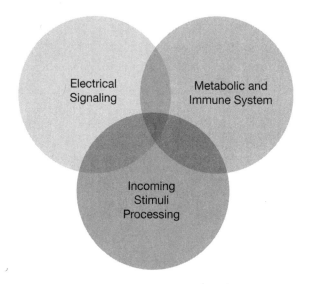

FIGURE 1.1 Autism and Brain-Regulatory Functions

tion in electrical communication or overactivity can manifest as disrupted functioning in any system: language, motor, or emotional/social. Imagine changes to the electrical functioning in your home. Sudden power surges can damage or render appliances inoperable. Too much voltage overheats the system and it seizes up. Loss of electrical connection, on the other hand, can cause spotty, inconsistent operations. One minute your printer works, and the next you get error messages or it stops completely. You wouldn't want to live in a house without consistent, appropriate levels of electrical connection. Your world would feel undependable, unpredictable, and unsafe. This is how it can feel for a person with autism.

Epilepsy it is the most visible disruption of electrical functioning. Epilepsy mostly develops during the first three years of life, but children with autism show a second spike in epilepsy in early adolescence. One study found up to 12.5% of autistic children aged 2 to 17 years have epilepsy. Children aged 13 to 17 have more than double that prevalence. Grand mal seizures are obvious to observers. Petit mal seizures, however, can happen and no one, including the child, realizes it. An undiagnosed seizure can be mistaken for inattention or poor memory. We'll discuss this medical condition associated with autism in more detail, with examples, in a later chapter.

Our *metabolic system* is the operation of chemical reactions involved in maintaining the life energy of our cells and our bodies. The way our bodies regulate and manage energy—our metabolism—and our body's ability to defend itself against pathogens—the *immune response*—are closely linked because a strong immune response relies on energy. Mitochondrial and metabolic dysfunction may partially underlie the complex pathophysiology of autism. Precise mechanisms remain elusive, and many questions remain unanswered.

Some of the immunological anomalies associated with autism involve cytokines, immunoglobulins, inflammation, and cellular activation. Some studies suggest that individuals with autism have different immune sensitivity to environmental toxins than neurotypical—typically developing—children. This may reflect differential genetic susceptibility or a breakdown of proper immune regulation. Many people with autism have problems with autoimmunity (Al-Ayadhi & Mostafa, 2012; Carissimi et al., 2019). Autoimmunity is when the immune system mistakenly targets the body's own tissues, resulting in various autoimmune disorders. Examples include lupus, rheumatoid arthritis, psoriasis, and inflammatory bowel disease.

A preponderance of data also supports the likelihood of a high prevalence of gastrointestinal symptoms and disorders in those with autism. Family members of individuals with autism also show various immune abnormalities. We'll talk more about these conditions in a later chapter, and we'll give you guidelines for detecting them in children with autism.

The brain's ability to process incoming stimuli depends on how well it can filter out unimportant incoming sensory information while at the same time intensifying what is important. When an infant or child brain cannot process incoming sensory information normally, their ability to self-regulate is diminished, and they may not be able to maintain an appropriate level of awareness to meet environmental demands.

There are three stages involved with processing incoming stimuli, and impairments can be present in one area but not another. First, the brain has to analyze and evaluate input to determine whether it is important. Then, the brain must be able to store the information for later use. It has to encode the data. Finally, the brain has to decide how to react to the stimuli. This may involve verbalization or gestures to communicate about or respond to the stimuli. It also involves applying the data to environmental challenges to solve problems—in essence, learning.

Much of this work is done by neuromodulators—chemical messengers released in response to signals from the limbic system, the group of brain structures largely responsible for innate seeking and avoidance behaviors and for emotional responses. These modulators adjust neural firing in ways that support our survival and well-being. When they work well, we notice important incoming information and can act on it, and we also tune out unnecessary or interfering stimuli. For example, we can hear, understand, and react to our name when it is called (because that is usually a necessary skill for survival), but we can direct our attention away from a passing siren that does not involve us.

The neuromodulators in a person with autism may work poorly or inconsistently. The ability to regulate incoming data may fluctuate with no apparent reason—one day, for example, the pain of a scraped knee is not noticed, while on a different day it registers as extreme agony. There are also timing issues—neuromodulation in a child with autism may be delayed, such that unexpected sensory input is registered as a potent assault that overwhelms them. For example, a child touched by someone they did not see approaching them from behind may experience terror, while that same child may tolerate or even enjoy touch if they can either see it coming or initiate it themselves.

Conceptualizing Autism Along a Social-Emotional Continuum

Another basic way of understanding a person with or without autism is to appreciate to what degree they process the world through a social-emotional versus a cognitive lens. Do they filter and make sense of incoming stimuli based on their emotional feelings and connections to others, or do they process it based on mental functions? Here's an example of two children who have different processing styles.

Social-Emotional   Cognitive

FIGURE 1.2 Conceptualizing Autism Along a Social-Emotional Continuum

Ethan was a sixth grader on his school's spring field trip. His class was visiting a nearby state park. Each child had been paired up with a partner for the day. (This was a help to the teacher and parent chaperones in keeping track of the kids.)

Part of the day was devoted to leading the students on a hike, and part of the day was spent inside the park museum, looking at exhibits and watching a film about the park's history. The children also had time on their own to relax or further explore the main headquarters housing the museum.

Ethan, who is moderately toward the cognitive end of the continuum, was intensely focused on the exhibits. He especially enjoyed the ones that illustrated and described the geological origins of the area around the park. He read each exhibit sign carefully and completely. He listened carefully when the park guide gave a short lecture about weather patterns in the park. When the man talked about how much rain and snow the mountain could get in just 24 hours, Ethan computed how much that meant per hour.

His partner, Cameron, who processed information more via social-emotional circuitry, was fidgety while he waited for Ethan to finish reading the exhibit labels. Cameron kept being drawn to a conversation the teacher was having with one of the parents—something that sounded like a secret because they were speaking very softly. This raised his curiosity. Cameron loved secrets and intrigue! He also wanted to get out of the stuffy museum and go sit in the sun. He thought he'd take some photos (his mom had let him bring his phone) of the sunshine on the profusion of blossoming flowers, bushes, and trees. Cameron wanted to show his photos to his mom, who loved flowers. He liked the park, but didn't really care about the museum except for the displays that showed how people used to live in the mountains years ago.

Within the autism spectrum, most people fall toward the cognitive end of the continuum, although there are both mild and significant variations. Recognizing where a person falls will help guide interactions and intervention. It's unhelpful to use social-emotional language with someone highly cognitive in their thought process. Educators will find that students learn more easily if lesson instructions and procedures match the orientation of the student. The same history module, for example, could be taught via an interactive role-playing, or by a timeline of important events and discoveries, perhaps supplemented by a visual catalogue of items used during the era in question. Neither approach is right nor wrong, but the more the particular approach matches a student's processing style, the more readily that student will engage, learn, and remember.

Clinicians are routinely taught that establishing rapport is the first and most vital ingredient in successful treatment. This may or may not hold true for those on the spectrum. Some clients on the spectrum—those more social-emotional—will appreciate typical behaviors therapists use to build trust and bonds. Examples include asking questions about how the client feels, empathizing with the client's feelings by sharing a similar experience, or reassuring a client that many people feel a certain way in response to certain situations.

For a heavily cognitive-leaning client, however, these well-intended comments may backfire. The cognitively oriented client may at best dismiss these words and at worst believe they are an irrelevant waste of time. Some clients may actually perceive such statements as indicative of the therapist's not understanding or of not being very bright.

For a cognitively oriented client, a therapist would do well to stick to data and logic. The client can take this in and respect the information. It is advisable, if you don't yet know how a client on the spectrum thinks, to assume a cognitive interaction style at the onset of therapy.

Other Variables That Make Each Person With Autism Unique

There are many diagnosable conditions that occur along with autism at rates higher than in the non-autistic person. These will be discussed in detail in Mindsets 4 and 5 and include other mental health, information processing, neurological, and general medical syndromes. They must always be included in an evaluation. If they are interfering with a person's functioning, they must be addressed and treated.

There are also other less obvious factors that make each person on the spectrum unique. These can be easily overlooked if a clinician or educator is focusing only on the broad umbrella of autism. Yet they may significantly influence a person—their self-perception, their way of navigating the world, and even the way the world reacts to and interacts with them.

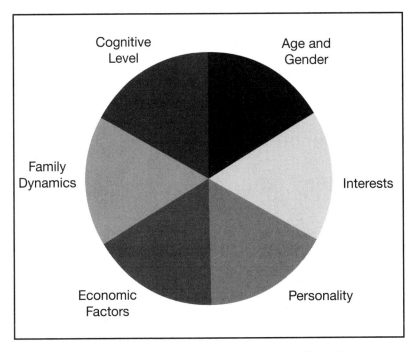

FIGURE 1.3 Additional Factors Impacting How Autism Manifests

The pie chart (Figure 1.3) shows each factor taking up equal space, but these factors don't necessarily create uniform influence on individuals. It is up to the clinician or educator to assess how important each ingredient is for the person with whom they are working. Since these variables are not a part of making a diagnosis, their influence—which may be significant—is often overlooked during assessments.

Without consideration of these other factors, any two children with the same diagnosis and rating of severity could be perceived as very similar. Recommendations for which resources and intervention each child needs might sound nearly identical. Feedback to each set of parents might be generic, instead of taking each family's unique situation into consideration. Here's an example of two children with the same diagnosis and functioning range who have different needs and whose interventions will not be the same.

Julie and Jeremy were each referred to a university autism clinic for evaluation. They were each found to meet diagnostic criteria for autism spectrum disorder, and each were rated in the moderately severe functioning range.

Julie was an easily startled, anxious 8-year-old who was an only child. Her parents were both architects. They owned a successful architectural firm and led busy, hectic lives. They traveled frequently, often being gone from home overnight. Julie was cared for by a live-in nanny who transported her to and from her private school. There was no extended family nearby; her father had moved the family in order to accept his current position. Julie didn't really have friends, and while the other students in her class accepted her, they didn't go out of their way to include her in activities or invite her to social activities outside of school. She was perceived by adults as sweet but uninteresting.

Julie had an IQ of 95, with verbal skills about one standard deviation below normal and visual-spatial skills about one standard deviation above normal. Her academic performance was unremarkable; reading was a bit difficult for her, and her teacher believed she didn't always comprehend what she read. She misused pronouns at times. Sometimes, she seemed to space out in class, and her teacher frequently had to repeat instructions to her. Julie didn't like group activities and she never volunteered answers or asked questions.

She loved to draw, though, and this was her main way of entertaining and soothing herself. Her drawings were highly detailed and elicitied praise from her parents and her teachers. Her parents paid for a local artist to give Julie lessons, to which she always looked forward. Her instructor believed her already remarkable skills were growing as she learned new techniques.

Jeremy was a 12-year-old who coincidentally also tested at an IQ of 95. His performance on the verbal and visual-spatial tasks, however, was basically the opposite of Julie's. His verbal skills were a standard deviation above normal and his visual-spatial performance were a standard deviation below. Jeremy was a nonstop talker. His teachers had to constantly remind him both to use his inside voice and to not interrupt classmates. His favorite topics were astronomy and weather and he could talk about them ad nauseam.

Jeremy's father was a pharmaceutical salesman who was known as the rep the medical office staff looked forward to seeing. He always had a joke to tell and had an uncanny memory for the names and birthdays of each doctor and nurse. Jeremy's mother didn't work outside the home. She had her hands full with four children including Jeremy, his 10-year-old brother Gavin, and a set of twins who had just turned 2 years old.

Jeremy and his brother shared a room, and it drove Jeremy crazy. Gavin loved playing video games, especially car and bike races. He also loved riding his Huffy bike, with streamers flying, often with "no hands." Jeremy's bike sat unused in the garage. He didn't enjoy riding and wasn't good at it, anyway. Jeremy preferred reading and then telling Gavin about what he'd learned. Gavin wasn't interested.

Jeremy seemed to have no sense of danger and unfortunately, he wasn't very coordinated, so he had more accidents than the average child. He had already broken his arm after falling from his upper bunk bed during a multilevel pillow fight with Gavin. When his father tried to teach him to ride his bike, Jeremy had several bad falls. He got hit in the face once when he missed a ball that Gavin had tossed his way.

Others viewed Jeremy as smart, but odd. They could tell he meant no harm, but when he used his stilted and rather loud "little professor" voice, most people found it off-putting. Other kids also avoided Jeremy when he launched an astronomy lecture, but they kept their distance for another reason as well. Jeremy was always bumping into them and didn't even seem to realize it.

Clearly, when their differences are pointed out, Julie and Jeremy emerge as distinctly different children with different strengths and challenges. Their clinical and academic needs are distinct and contrasting. Both interactions with them and planned interventions must reflect their unique selves. They have very different personalities and interests. A good educator or clinician will build on what each child cares about. Their families also have different resources, dynamics, and lifestyles. Professionals will get the most involvement and support if they recognize and work with these variables. Interventions will need to be considered vis-a-vis financial states as well.

Each child and their environment is clearly unique. They may both have the same diagnosis and, in this case, even the same IQ, but their needs are different. What works with one will not necessarily work with the another. Likewise, the families are different and will play unique roles in intervention teams. Julie, Jeremy, and their parents are much more than a diagnosis of autism.

Summary

Mindset 1 embraces the idea that every child is more than autism. This mindset recognizes that while diagnostic labels serve purposes, they can also lead to errors in perception. There are predictable ways that humans try to make sense of each other, especially when behaviors are outside the norm. Parents, educators, and clinicians working with autistic children are not immune from these false narratives. Recognizing and fighting against them, as well as battling unconscious images we may have gleaned from media, leads to more accurate understanding of each child and to more successful interventions.

To fully appreciate each child and adhere to our first mind-

set, we must bring conscious *When did geeks and*
awareness, an appreciation of *nerds become autism?*
each child's environment, and *That's a gray area.*
assessment of specific brain *Half the people in Silicon*
regulatory functions and ways *Valley probably have autism."*
of processing information into TEMPLE
our field of perception. By
replacing automatic assumptions and cultural influences with observations and questions based on these functions and cognitive styles,
we can be more successful in helping each child.

Autism has always been with us. Our understanding of it and
our diagnostic criteria have changed—and will continue to change.
It's clear that throughout history many people have experienced the
world in a way consistent with our modern label of autism. So-called
geeks have always existed and have advanced civilization in ways
that the average human did not. Many artists, tradespeople, and
scientists have been on the spectrum. While we didn't have labels
or diagnostic criteria in the past, we did have individuals who processed life in ways outside the statistical norm.

Today, we can use the advantages of labels (e.g., formal diagnoses allowing access to resources), yet still appreciate that each child
is more than that label. Instead of being overly focused on diagnostic criteria, we can balance those convenient groupings of behavior
with other criteria: individual characteristics, interests, and actions
viewed in context. This will help parents and professionals fulfill the
purpose of Mindset 1: to help each person—no matter what the diagnosis—to flourish, and reach their unique and full potential.

HOW PROFESSIONAL TRAINING
MIGHT LIMIT YOUR PERSPECTIVE

Psychiatrists

- May pay disproportionally more attention to behaviors known to respond to medications.
- May see more pathology than other clinicians.
- May identify other medical conditions more readily.
- May focus on diminishing or eliminating behaviors versus replacing them with healthier ones.
- May not be familiar with what other specialists offer. (Most aren't.)

Psychologists, social workers, and
other mental health clinicians

- May pay disproportionally more attention on outward behavior and miss the emotional or environmental components driving the behavior (especially if they are trained solely in cognitive behavioral therapy).
- May base treatment on insight to the detriment of behavior change (if solely trained in a psychoanalytic approach).
- May not be familiar with, and thus may miss, related conditions such as auditory processing disorder and pragmatic language disorder.
- May persevere in treating mood problems with talk therapy when medication would be more efficient and effective.
- May undervalue the role of siblings and parents if not trained in family systems.

- May not be used to working with school systems, and may avoid attending IEPs due to their personal discomfort.
- May not see the child in a natural environment due to insurance company restraints against treating outside the office.
- May rely too heavily on questionnaires and tests over observations.
- May undervalue the role of sensory sensitivity in behavior because it is not emphasized in the *DSM-5.*
- May not be used to coordinating with psychiatrists and psychologists.
- May miss the role of emotional dysregulation.
- May not involve family to see functioning in different settings.

Educators

- May never see the child outside the school setting.
- May not understand the language of neuropsychological evaluations and may be hesitant to ask for clarification.
- May be overwhelmed with regulation tasks (e.g., keeping the classroom quiet, keeping on time, completing mandated lessons) and unable to focus on nuances of the child.
- May artificially group children with very different needs for the sake of efficiency, especially when resources are limited.
- May overemphasize verbal skills as indicators of intellectual ability.
- May not understand the styles of thinking in autism and therefore they can't teach to those unique styles.

- May find the questioning of a verbal, bright child irritating or disruptive or threatening to their position of authority.
- May resent the extra attention the autistic child may need.
- May insist on arriving at answers in a standard way when some autistic children, especially visual thinkers, cannot process the information in that manner.
- May speak too fast or get irritated with the extra time an autistic child needs to respond and may incorrectly correlate it with cognitive impairment.
- May find the parent of an autistic child intrusive or demanding.

2

Whole Child Evaluations Are Vital

Mindset 1—that every child is more than a label—should naturally lead to *whole child* evaluations. Keeping all aspects of each unique child in mind, a substantive evaluation goes well beyond a search to confirm or rule out a diagnosis. A valuable assessment substantially expands upon labels. It reveals additional, detailed information about each child. This added data is vital to help both professionals and parents better understand and design successful interventions for a child.

Comprehensive whole child evaluations always include descriptions of the child's strengths as well as deficits. While reporting areas in which a child is developmentally delayed, they emphasize equally areas in which the child performs at or above the level expected for their age. These strengths are what treating therapists will build upon to help each child reach their full potential.

Evaluations are most useful when the person conducting them is interested in all aspects of a child, not only those associated with autism. A wise, experienced evaluator knows assessments can be customized. Testing materials can be carefully selected based on what is so far known about each child and what specific questions this assessment seeks to answer. Some evaluators give every child an identical assessment—using the same instruments and asking the same questions each time. This model of evaluation may miss data.

In this chapter, we will elaborate on what goes into a whole child evaluation. We will describe the difference between obtaining *content* and *process* data and why both are necessary. We'll give examples that show how observant evaluators can maximize the use of process data. We'll also discuss the importance of considering how a child and their family view the evaluation and how to establish a setting most conducive to obtaining an accurate view of a child's potential.

We'll also discuss screenings, their advantages and disadvantages, and how they compare to actual evaluations. We'll talk about when they should be used and how to maximize their effectiveness.

Often, during evaluations, signs of other associated concerns and conditions appear. These may be outside the expertise of the assessor and cannot be immediately addressed. We'll provide clues to these potential conditions and list the most common concerns that may warrant referrals for additional testing. We will steer you to the appropriate professionals in each case.

We'll share five concerns about the uniform, rigid application of standardized testing. To help you form a more comprehensive assessment of the whole child, we'll provide a checklist of questions all evaluators can consider when they design an evaluation.

Evaluations are only as useful as the reports they generate. We'll give you 10 tips on writing whole child reports, and we'll discuss how to share evaluation results with families and other professionals. We'll give you examples of ways evaluation results can be effectively translated into coordinated teamwork by parents and multiple professionals.

Finally, we'll address the potential problem of specialists overemphasizing certain aspects of a child simply because those behaviors or concerns fall within their area of expertise. We'll describe Michael, a hypothetical 9-year-old, and how different professions could interpret and diagnose him.

The last section of this chapter is directed at parents. We discuss the importance of obtaining copies of their child's records, having them readily accessible, and knowing how to best format and share these materials.

How to Add Process Data Into Evaluations

Experienced evaluators are extremely interested in a child's mannerisms and attitudes during an evaluation. They seek to describe how a child answers questions and completes tasks, not just the actual content of answers. They look beyond raw scores, standard scores, and percentile ranks. Two children with identical scores can be very different, yet undoubtedly, there can be significant differences between the two. In order to fully appreciate the nuances beyond a score, someone reading an evaluation report needs to know how a child went about responding to test questions and material. The details of how a child reacts during an evaluation give readers a richer sense of that child and of how they navigate their world.

To obtain these crucial details, a proficient evaluator must be familiar enough with their tools that they are able to maintain joint attention—to the child and, at the same time, to procedural steps of each testing instrument. A well-trained, experienced assessor is able to accurately record the child's responses to a question or task and simultaneously note other behaviors and reactions of the child. While adhering to accurate administration of the test, they're also picking up information about the process of the evaluation.

An evaluation's process is everything in addition to the concrete answers or actions of a child while completing an evaluation task. A skillful evaluator notices (and includes in their report) the child's nuances: the way they approach a task, how they interact with the assessor, and how they respond to knowing or not knowing an answer or to being able or unable to perform a task.

Process also includes what happens before and after the structured part of an evaluation. Important information comes from the little details observed while a child and their family are waiting for an evaluation to start, or during breaks, or even as they are leaving. People sometimes reveal the most useful information when they are unguarded. A vigilant assessor always notes any discrepancies in behavior between the structured part of an evaluation and more casual interactions.

Jay and his parents had arrived for his testing early, and the evaluator could hear their conversation through his open door. He overheard Jay's father saying that he thought the testing was unnecessary. He mentioned that Jay was "just like me," and "Nobody ever said I needed to see a psychologist." In response, Jay's mother replied it was important they cooperate with the examiner, and that times had changed, adding "Maybe if you were a child today, you would have been tested, and school wouldn't have been so hard for you."

When Jay's parents sat down with the psychologist, however, the child's father was mostly silent and seemed to agree with his wife about wanting his son tested. When the examiner took a family history, neither parent initially mentioned the father's academic struggles. Because he had listened to their waiting room conversation, however, the examiner knew to gently ask more specific questions, which eventually led to important information. He learned that not only did the father struggle in the past, but also that he continued to experience problems at work and that he blamed himself for his son's "condition." This added information would later prove very useful in coordinating efforts with the family and the treatment team. With these insights, everyone could better anticipate and understand the discomfort Jay's dad sometimes showed.

It's also important for test administrators to remember that although evaluations are routine for them, they are usually novel—and often anxiety provoking—for families and children. When people are fearful, they may not behave in their usual ways.

Paula, and her daughter, Rebecca, had a positive, close relationship. Even when Rebecca had a meltdown (which happened most days), Paula remained calm and comforting. She almost never lost her temper. Rebecca regularly went to her mom for support.

Paula was very anxious, though, the day of Rebecca's evaluation. Rebecca's pediatrician had referred them to Dr. Shah, a neurologist, and while Paula trusted their doctor, she had no idea what to expect. She was rather taken aback by the large, modern building that housed Dr. Shah's practice, and she wished she had dressed less casually.

Her nerves and lack of familiarity with the neighborhood were probably what caused Paula to get lost on the way to the appointment. She was generally a punctual woman, but this time they arrived 20 minutes late. She was embarrassed, and her heart was racing. She felt the beginnings of a headache.

Rebecca was anxious, too, and her mom's nervousness further heightened her own. She had a meltdown in the car, but Paula was able to distract and calm her down by the time they reached the office. Then they had to take an elevator, something that Rebecca hated. By the time they sat down in the waiting area, both were close to tears. When Rebecca had a second meltdown within 5 minutes of sitting down, Paula roughly grabbed her daughter's wrists, put her face close to Rebecca's, and angrily told her to "Stop it! Right now!" Her voice was as harsh as her movements.

The secretary noticed, and she walked back to the neurologist to pass on the information. She thought

Paula had acted inappropriately and abusively. It never occurred to her that this was behavior born of intense anxiety. Paula was terrified that if Rebecca had a meltdown before the evaluation, it might be called off. They had waited months for this day, and Paula was desperate to get her daughter help.

Fortunately, the neurologist was a kind, thoughtful evaluator, and while he always welcomed feedback from his secretary, he also appreciated the role of stress and novelty on the behavior of parents and knew to reserve judgment until he had much more information. He took additional time to calm both Paula and Rebecca prior to beginning his evaluation.

Many professionals are reluctant to note observations unless they feel qualified to interpret and explain their meaning. This reticence may come partly from not wanting to appear unknowledgeable, but it can also come from a common, ingrained aspect of their training. Most specialists were repeatedly admonished by their professors to never practice or offer advice outside their scope of expertise. However, this wise advice, meant to prevent ill-informed treatment decisions, should not stop an evaluator from consistently noting all observations, even ones they cannot explain.

The best professionals are the ones who get all the details about a child and then put those details into context. What does the child's behavior mean? Well, it depends. You have to know what happened before the behavior for one thing."
TEMPLE

Noting observations is not the same as interpreting data or proposing interventions. Useful reports simply mention all perceptions that raise questions begging further exploration. Quality reports often recommend additional investigation by appropriate, allied professionals. A thorough evaluator not only dares to include data they don't know how to interpret; they also recognize it as one of their critical responsibilities. While focused primarily within their specialty, a seasoned evaluator also gathers data that technically does fall outside their field. For example, educational evaluators observe a child's social interactions, psychologists note motor responses, and occupational therapists sense a child's mood.

Even narrow evaluations (such as hearing tests) often yield pieces of data that would be useful to another professional. The person who administers a hearing test should pay attention to the whole child, not just their ears.

During a cognitive assessment, a school psychologist noticed that 8-year-old Ryan seemed to zone out twice, for brief periods of about 10 seconds each. She also observed what she thought was a slight mouth twitch during the second occurrence of this behavior. She had no idea what to make of the behavior. Her first thought was that perhaps Ryan had an attention deficit, but neither his testing nor his teachers had indicated any problems in this area. She wrote it off to boredom typical of a third grade boy. She made no note of it in her report.

It was only when reviewing the evaluation with

her supervisor that she mentioned it. Her supervisor had asked her to describe Ryan in more detail, so while she wasn't convinced it mattered, she relayed the observations at that time. Her supervisor advised her to include this data in her report and to ask Ryan's parents if there was any history of epilepsy in the family. The supervisor wondered if these moments of staring into space could perhaps indicate petit mal seizures.

The school psychologist discovered that Ryan's uncle had mild epilepsy, and his father vaguely remembered his family talking about his grandfather's "spells." She wrote this additional history in the familial background section of her report and added a referral to a neurologist in her list of recommendations. Her observations—while uncertain and puzzling to her— would prove important. Ryan's parents took him to a neurologist who did diagnose epilepsy and who provided educational information about the condition to the family. Ryan's teachers were also informed.

Screenings Precede Full Assessments

Screenings are questionnaires that ask about broad manifestations of a condition. Full assessments are a more in-depth combination of clinical interviews, history taking, collection of data from allied professionals, review of any previous assessments, and administration of numerous questionnaires and tests. The exact content of an assessment depends on the questions it is designed to answer. These questions guide the selection of whom to interview, what history to focus on, and which instruments to administer. A full assessment is expected to generate both diagnoses and recommendations.

Screenings, being more limited, are not meant to provide diagnoses. They are simply a first step in determining if further investigation—generally in the form of a full assessment—is warranted. Screenings have several advantages: they can be done quickly, they are widely available online or in general pediatric practices and community health settings, and they are free or inexpensive. They do not require a trained professional to administer or score.

Screenings also have disadvantages. They cast a very wide net (by design), so they are subject to several errors. They will miss many children with less than severe manifestations of autism. Screenings may alternately indicate autism when a child actually is not on the spectrum, but has characteristics similar to or sometimes also found in autism. Other diagnoses, such as attention deficit disorder, social anxiety, and obsessive-compulsive disorder may be misattributed to autism spectrum disorder.

Screenings should be routinely conducted as part of a child's regular well-child pediatrician visits. The American Academy of Pediatrics recommends all children be screened for developmental delays and impairments beginning at 9 months (Council on Children with Disabilities, 2006). Subsequent evaluations should take place at 18 and 30 months. Additional screening is advised if a child is at high risk for developmental problems due to low birth weight or preterm birth, or if they have a sibling or parent with autism, or if symptoms are present.

A systemic review and meta-analysis of autism spectrum

disorder (ASD) screening tools for toddlers found that these measures detect autism with high specificity and sensitivity (Sánchez-García, 2019). Children younger than 3 years of age were evaluated in pediatric primary care settings. Given that children who begin autism interventions prior to age 3 years show better outcomes than those who go untreated prior to preschool, it is vital to identify these children as young as possible. The sooner a diagnosis is made and a comprehensive evaluation identifies their strengths and impairments, the sooner effective, targeted treatment can begin.

However, despite recommendations, most children in the United States are not diagnosed until 4 years of age, and there are disparities in diagnosis related to geographic area, ethnicity, and socioeconomic factors. Among 4-year-old children, girls and white children were more likely to receive their first comprehensive, developmental evaluation by age 3 years compared with boys and Black children.

Given the tremendous growth and organization happening in the child's brain during the first 3 years of life, behavioral interventions in toddlers during this time frame make critical differences. Treatments initiated during this limited window result in a range of positive changes including increases in social attention, language ability, and overall IQ scores. Absent screening, many children miss out on this time-restricted opportunity to benefit from interventions during this critical period of neuroplasticity.

Screenings must consist of parent-report and other quantitative instruments. Relying only on the pediatrician's observations is insufficient. In multiple studies, researchers have shown that developmental disorders are detected at low rates when physicians rely on judgment alone (Shipman, 2011). This is likely because, as the majority of studies found, primary care physicians have inadequate knowledge of autism and its treatment. This is especially true if they do not have personal experience with autism or have not taken continuing education classes on autism (McCormack et al., 2020).

Within the primary care setting, other factors contribute to lack of effective screening. The physician may not be familiar with available questionnaires. They may think there is not enough time to use the tools even if they have them. They may not know where to refer families when children screen positive for autism. Even if they know about resources, they might not have a regular system for effective and timely ways of connecting families to them.

This means that nonmedical providers, such as educators and clinicians, are the front line in assuring children are screened and referred for treatment. School districts, community clinics, and private practitioners can proactively educate physicians. They can provide screening instruments to pediatric practices. They can also give doctors a list of resources, as well as business cards or contact information to pass on to parents. Optimally, educators and clinicians regularly communicate with pediatricians and pediatric neurologists, but while medical providers are used to establishing regular referral circles, allied professionals usually aren't, and they may be hesitant to initiate contact. In a physician's world, though, this is normal procedure. Many physi-

> *The earlier a child is assessed, the better. Every professional working with a child should make sure others are putting eyes on the kid as well. They might catch something the first professional doesn't see, because there are so many functions impacted by autism."*
> TEMPLE

cians have told us that they wished providers would let them know about their services, because they are at a loss for referrals.

Table 2.1 shows a list of concerns and medical complaints that may warrant additional screening. We have listed the appropriate specialist who would generally be consulted for each concern. Additional details about medical and psychologist conditions associated with autism are discussed in Mindset 4 and 5.

Mood

Other issues noted during evaluations indicate the need for referral to nonmedical professionals. These specialists are ideally brought on early and are included as central members of a child's treatment team. Unfortunately, many families do not have access to these services due to financial constraints or lack of resources in their communities. In these cases educators and clinicians can help a child by steering parents to library books and online videos. While not a substitute for individualized private care, these options can give parents basic tools that make a difference.

The most common nonmedical concerns uncovered in evaluations are emotional issues, problems performing daily activities, language impairment or absence, and learning disorders or cognitive impairment. The professionals that an evaluation report should recommend in these cases include mental health clinicians, occupational or physical therapists, speech-language therapists or school psychologists, special education teachers, and educational psychologists.

Some children with autism appear severely limited in their ability to learn. If they are nonverbal, the impact of being unable to process speech must be assessed. There are some children who

TABLE 2.1 When To Consider Additional Screening: Medical And Other Concerns

Concerns	Possible Issues	Specialists to Consider
Pain after eating Abnormal bowel movements Chronic tummy pain Frequent belching or gas	Gastric inflammation Absorption issues	Gastroenterologist Nutritionist
Obesity, especially fat at waist Chronic fatigue/weakness Very early puberty onset	Metabolic issues Blood sugar issues	Endocrinologist Metabolic blood panel
Unusual/unexplained symptoms Unusual body structure Family history of genetic conditions	Genetic condition	Genetic counselor
Lag in developmental milestones Lagging behind a younger sibling Significantly shorter stature or weight than peers	Numerous developmental disorders	Developmental pediatrician Child psychologist
Unresponsive to name Does not startle to loud noise	Hearing issue	Audiologist
Poor judgment of distance Viewing writing or objects from side Constant squinting Frequent spilling of things or stumbling	Vision issue	Ophthalmologist
Severe headaches Brief periods of nonresponsiveness Motor/movement abnormalities	Seizure disorder Other nerve disorders Vascular disorders	Pediatric neurologist*

* Autism impacts a broad range of neurological functions. Some of these functions result in differences in the way information is processed but do not cause significant impairment. Other neurological differences can result in major limitations across numerous domains, including the intellectual, emotional, and motor arenas. Most autistic children with language impairment or obvious motor challenges will benefit from a neurology screening.

appear intellectually impaired but when given assistive technology are able to express themselves at a significantly higher cognitive level than exhibited prior to its use. Children with autism often show marked variability between components of intellect. It is vital to know more than one IQ score. Memory, processing speed, spatial abilities, and verbal comprehension are parts of intellect that need individual assessment.

Timing Matters

A child's assessments should be conducted in a logical order. The child's most basic and impactful impairments should be examined first because these may cause or add to other impairments. For example, if there are two concerns about a child—whether they can hear, and also if they understand the content of what is said—the first step is to get their hearing tested. The results of that consultation will be necessary for a subsequent speech and language evaluation.

Another example is a child who has abnormal bowel movements and frequently rubs their tummy. This child may also have issues with speech production, information processing, and focusing. All of these issues need assessing, but this child should first get a thorough medical evaluation before examinations by other evaluating professionals such as psychologists, occupational, or physical therapists are con-

> *I was a different person after my anxiety was treated. Until that was diagnosed and treated, I could not think or behave as well as I do now. If I had been evaluated at the height of my anxiety, the results would not have represented my real capacity for thought or work."*
> TEMPLE

ducted. A child can't be expected to perform at their full potential if conditions such as gastric discomfort are interfering. An examination conducted under these conditions will likely produce skewed or even grossly inaccurate results.

A Word of Caution About Standardized Testing

Each profession has their unique set of tools to make diagnoses. Here are some cautions when using any of these structured tests.

First, stay aware of the "If all you have is a hammer, everything looks like a nail" phenomenon. If a clinician only works with autism they might filter all their observations through the lens of autism. Social awkwardness, for example, might always be viewed as a sign of an inability to read social cues. Yet it could also be a sign of anxiety, depression, or a personality disorder.

Another example would be always interpreting repeated hand movements as repetitive behaviors common in autism, even though they also could be related to obsessive-compulsive disorder, a neurological condition, or anxiety. Abnormal vocal patterns could be related to autism but could also be indicators of a auditory problem or a malformation of any part of the body used to produce speech. All clinicians must think outside the box of their own profession and intentionally rule out other conditions that could mimic aspects of autism. Evaluators should always have a list of experienced professionals in other disciplines to refer to as necessary.

Second, evaluators must always search out and understand the motivation behind a child's behavior. For example, a professional with true expertise can tell the difference between a child who is not making eye contact because they're shy or anxious and a child who doesn't understand how to use eye contact to deepen social communication. Another example is recognizing the difference between a young child who has been traumatized and is no longer speaking because they have shut down and a child who is unable to produce speech due to neural impairment.

Third, clinicians and educators must not put children into categories based only on test scores. Even the best tests are there to assist in making a diagnosis—not in automatically assigning a child to a category. A wise assessor relies on their observations first and tests second. If a child shows signs of autism but does not meet strict diagnostic criteria, more questions must be asked. Sometimes other tests can be used, but often it's better to just ask more questions or even get a second opinion. Access to resources often depends on a child meeting a list of strict criteria or even simply getting a score cutoff. Many children have been denied needed and appropriate services because of rigid examiners who did not take the extra steps necessary to flush out subtle signs of autism.

Fourth, information obtained from screening questionnaires and other diagnostic tests must always be considered in the context of other information about the child. This other information should come from both the evaluator and also adults who know the child well. Teachers, parents, grandparents, older siblings, and any treating therapists can provide invaluable details about a child's current behaviors. Interviewers must be skilled at making these adults comfortable enough to share all the child's behaviors. Interviewing parents separately can often yield more accurate information than seeing them together, because one parent may be reluctant to disagree with the other.

Children with autism also often show marked variability between different cognitive skills. An overall IQ score doesn't tell you enough. Memory, processing speed, spatial abilities, and verbal comprehension are parts of intellect that need individual assessment.

Finally, getting a good developmental history is vital. As children grow older, their behavior may become more subtle because they learn to compensate. Parents may have grown used to behaviors that once stood out to them. If you ask a parent about current impairments only, you can miss useful details. Asking about developmental milestones and what concerns they had during their child's infancy and early childhood will give you important data. It sometimes helps jog the memories of parents if you ask about specific occasions such as holidays, vacations, or birthdays. Reviewing home videos form a child's earlier years can also be a helpful addition to a evaluation.

A CHECKLIST FOR EVALUATORS: QUESTIONS YOU SHOULD ALWAYS ASK

General Presentation

- What do you notice about the child's hygiene and dress?
- What do you notice about the child's body structure?
- Are there any unusual features or asymmetries?
- What do you notice about the child's mood?
- Who brought the child and how would you describe the interaction between the child and anyone accompanying them?
- How does the child respond to you?

Motor and Expressive Language Skills

- How is the child's balance? If deficits are noted, does the child seem aware of them?
- What is noticeable about the child's mobility?
- Are any movements restricted, awkward, or choppy?
- Which movements are fluid or even graceful?
- How does the child get from one position to another, such as moving across a room and then sitting down?
- Do they bump into things or drop things?
- Can any observations be made about the child's physical strength?
- Are there particular activities that showcase deficits or abilities?
- Let the child try some things in order to get information. For instance, let them open a door, hand you something, or pick up something from the floor.
- Is the child coordinated? Are they able to move large muscle groups smoothly?
- Are they able to perform fine motor movements adequately?
- Are there oddities to how they move or use their hands or any parts of their body?
- How is the child's dexterity? Can they manipulate objects successfully?
- Does the child exhibit any motor tics?

Language and Information Processing

- Does the child seem to understand what you say to them?

- Do they miss parts of what you say?
- Is the child able to follow a sequence of commands, or do you have to give them one step at a time?
- Does the child remember what you have said?
- Can the child organize and communicate their thoughts?
- Is the child is verbal, how would you characterize their response time?
- Can you easily understand the child's speech? Do you notice oddities in their speech?
- Does the child exhibit any verbal tics?
- Does the child exhibit echolalia (the unsolicited repeating of noises or speech)?
- Does the child understand humor? Are there types of humor they do not understand?
- Does the child understand idioms?

Social Interaction and Reactions to the Environment

- Does the child understand your gestures?
- Does the child respond to them appropriately?
- Does the child initiate communication or only respond when asked to?
- Do the facial expressions of the child match what is happening or being talked about?
- What happens if something unexpected occurs during the evaluation? How does the child react?
- If a problem arises, how does the child react? Do they try to solve it?
- How do they approach problems? Are they able to modify their behavior to work around a problem?

- Does the child initiate communication or only respond when asked to?
- Does the child exhibit any verbal or motor or behavioral tics?
- Does the child do anything that is dangerous?

Attention, Motivation, and Self-Awareness

- Does the child seem to care about their performance? About pleasing the examiner?
- Does the child notice their mistakes? If so, what is their reaction? Do they take any actions after mistakes (e.g., want to try again, give up, ask questions, change their approach to the next task)?
- How is the child's endurance? Does their functioning change over the course of the evaluation? This applies to all aspects of their performance: physical, emotional, social, and cognitive.
- How well can the child attend? Can they sustain their attention?
- What distracts them? If distracted, what is it like to get them refocused? Can they shift their attention?
- Does the child seem able to accurately perceive their environment and the objects in it?
- Does the child change over the course of the evaluation? Note changes in: energy level, mood, communication, concentration, motor skills, and cognitive skills.

Emotional State

- How would you describe the child's emotional state?
- Does the child show outward signs of emotional distress?

- How would you describe the child's anxiety, if present? How do they exhibit it? What triggers it?
- Does the child seem frightened?
- Does the child seem angry? How can you tell?
- Does the child take delight in anything? How is it expressed?
- Does the child have any emotional outbursts of any kind?
- Is the child aggressive toward themselves or you?
- Does the child damage any objects?
- Is the child able to verbalize their emotions?
- If nonverbal, is the child able to correctly identify emotions?

Sensory Reactions

- How does the child react to the environment?
- Do they show any signs of discomfort?
- Do you notice any aversion to light, sound, odors, touch, or other sensory input?
- Does the child respond as expected to anything that would reasonably expect to cause discomfort or pain?

Strengths and Interests

- Which activities is the child able to complete with ease?
- Do these activities tend to be physical, emotional, motivational, social, or cognitive?
- What tasks does the child find interesting?
- Which tasks do they enjoy? Do they enjoy talking about these tasks?
- Which activities relax them?

Challenges and Dislikes

- What activities is the child unable to complete?
- Can you tell if the problem is due to physical, emotional, motivational, social, or cognitive challenges?
- What tasks does the child find boring?
- Which activities do they avoid?
- Which activities make them anxious?

How to Write a Whole Child Report

- Always explicitly state the reasons for the evaluation and who requested it. What questions are you seeking to answer?
- Describe the context of your evaluation. What was the environment? What was the child's mood and physical health the day of the exam? Were there any disruptions or abnormalities in the test administration?
- Always include a summary. Clearly state your conclusions and succinctly review the data that led to them.
- Always include recommendations for interventions and additional referrals.
- If your evaluation did not yield answers to some of your questions, explain why, and say how and where more information might be obtained.
- Avoid jargon. Other professionals and parents will read your report, and they may not be familiar with the specialized terminology used in your field. Write so they can interpret your findings.
- Consider a summary specifically for parents. We believe parents are entitled to all reports in full, but a summary

can be a useful way for parents to share the main points with others such as caretakers, aides, and extended family. Assessments should show parents where their child is developmentally and help them better understand and guide them. Every child has a parent. Every evaluator should communicate their findings to parents.

- Include a list of resources when appropriate. This can include books, articles, websites, or activities. You may have a separate list of resources for parents and for professionals.

- Always explicitly state the need for retesting in the future. Children's abilities and challenges often change. There are four main reasons for these changes: the child gets older, interventions produce progress, trauma or ineffective interventions create regression, and developmental tasks become more complex over time. Retesting should not result from a crisis: it should be a standard, anticipated part of a child's treatment plan.

- Always provide hope. No one has a crystal ball, and countless children have surpassed an evaluator's expectations. Be straightforward about impairments, but never assume they will stop a child from progressing beyond current challenges.

Sharing Assessment Results and Coordinating Interventions

A child's records are protected by professional, state, and federal guidelines. Parents and professionals should discuss expectations of record sharing at the outset of treatment or evaluation. If you are a parent, you should sign a form that details specifically to whom and under what conditions you authorize the release of specific records of your child and for what purposes. (If you are working with a healthcare professional who is bound by the Health Insurance Portability and Accountability Act (HIPAA), you may need to sign a formal HIPAA authorization. You should ask the professional with whom you are working whether this is necessary.) Again, this should be done from the start of a working relationship with any professional, not midstream.

Professionals should never share routine information about a child with another professional unless they have written permission from that child's parents. Professionals should know their state guidelines regulating release of records to parents who are noncustodial.

When asking for permission to share information, professionals should explain what and why they want to discuss a child's data. This helps create the respect and trust necessary for an effective team that is on the same page regarding a child's treatment.

It is not only helpful, but also imperative, that all the specialists involved in helping a child understand what the other specialists have as their goals for the child. Further, while differing professions are not expected to be knowledgeable about the details of other experts' intervention tools, they should know what specific behaviors, both strengths and challenges, those experts are addressing.

Having this information allows team members to coordinate efforts. For example, for a child who needs to learn turn taking, the psychologist can be doing role-playing, the occupational therapist (OT) can reinforce the skill during motor training, and the speech therapist can build turn taking into language exercises. With each professional reinforcing the other, the child is more likely to progress faster and to generalize the skill.

It is typical for specialists to value their particular role in a child's life. Some professionals, especially if they are not familiar with the work and value of another specialty, may fail to fully appreciate the input from other team members. Having ongoing communication—either via exchanged records, phone calls, or meetings—helps avoid this.

Here are two examples of how different specialists and parents can work well together:

EXAMPLE #1

Dr. Johnston, a psychiatrist, prescribes antianxiety medication for 17-year-old Caroline. He sees her once every 2 months. Two other professionals also work with Caroline: a psychologist who sees her weekly and a counselor who leads a twice-monthly social skills group for teens. Each specialist has a signed consent to release and receive records from each other. Since Caroline has not reached the age of majority, her parents have signed these forms. However, because she is an older teen, and both able to understand and sensitive to confidentiality, all team members have discussed their guidelines for sharing information with Caroline.

Caroline's group counselor emails the psychologist a brief summary after each meeting (in protected email format). She bullet points what the group worked on, any other subjects that came up, and Caroline's contribution to the group and her progress.

The psychologist leaves a voice mail for the group counselor anytime she is aware of specific social challenges that are happening or coming up for Caroline. The counselor acknowledges receipt in a quick email and asks questions if she needs more information. Otherwise, the psychologist checks in with the group counselor on an as-needed basis, but once every 2 months at a minimum.

The psychiatrist notifies the psychologist any time a dosage adjustment or change is made in Caroline's medications. The psychologist and psychiatrist have an understanding that each will alert the other of any significant changes in Caroline's anxiety or mood.

EXAMPLE #2

Hassan, age 8 years, has the following team members: a speech and language pathologist (SLP), a classroom aide, an occupational therapist (OT), a school psychologist, his regular teacher, and a special education teacher for reading.

Hassan's yearly IEPs are vital, but much more frequent communication between team members is necessary to ensure he progresses academically and socially. While there are no other regularly scheduled meetings, each professional feels free to reach out to another at any time, and they do. They also send out treatment and progress summaries to each other without being asked.

With the exception of his OT, Hassan's team members work together in the same school building at least 1 day per week. The school psychologist circulates among several schools within the district and is there only on Mondays. The SLP is there 3 days per week. Each team member knows the others' schedules.

Hassan's classroom aide and regular teacher casually touch base for a few minutes each day. They schedule an actual meeting anytime Hassan has a major, disruptive meltdown or begins to develop any pattern of agitation or distress. His SLP is always aware of what the classroom teacher is working on, so that she can tailor interventions to enhance Hassan's learning. The special education (reading) teacher is likewise up to date on classroom topics and also on Hassan's moods and behaviors.

The school psychologist conducted Hassan's initial evaluation and detailed his strengths and weaknesses. She presented the report in detail at his IEP and provided a copy to each team member (with parental permission) and a parent summary to each parent (Hassan's parents are divorced; they each received their own copy). Her report contained specific recommendations for each team member. When any team member observes Hassan having major struggles, they are comfortable requesting the psychologist schedule a meeting with him.

Hassan's parents have met with each team member. They have received occasional phone calls from most of them and have successfully requested additional face-to-face meetings in between scheduled IEP reviews.

Failure to See the Whole Child

Working as a team helps ensure each child benefits from divergent perspectives. Regular communication between team members prevents any one specialist from putting too much emphasis on their interpretation of the child's behavior.

Imagine the various professionals listed below coming into contact with 9-year-old Michael. In our hypothetical example, Michael acts exactly the same in the presence of each specialist. He did not reach all his developmental milestones on time; he struggles academically and is below grade level in reading; his social skills are poor; he is poor at regulating his emotions; he is prone to anxiety, irritability, and moodiness; his focus and concentration wander; his handwriting is poor; he mispronounces words and speech sounds; he is clumsy; his dental and bathing hygiene is poor; he hates seeing doctors and dentists; he refuses to eat certain foods; and he insists on rigid routines.

If the professionals view Michael only through the lens of conditions and diagnoses within their specialties, they may each interpret his behaviors very differently. They may or may not suspect autism in addition to these interpretations.

TABLE 2.2 Possible Differential Interpretations of Michael's Behavior By Profession

Profession	Possible Interpretation
Pediatrician	Normal development lag found in boys
Teacher	Low intellect ability, lack of discipline, ADHD
Mental health professional	Trauma, lack of effective parenting skills, mood disorder, oppositional disorder, conduct disorder, obsessive-compulsive disorder
Educational psychologist	Dyslexia, ADHD, learning disorder
Speech-Language pathologist	Auditory processing disorder, childhood apraxia of speech, speech sound disorder
Physical therapist	Hypotonia (low muscle tone), traumatic brain injury, dyspraxia
Occupational therapist	Lack of skill training
Dentist	Fear, lack of discipline

A Note For Parents

Parents should have copies of all information about their child. Whether data is kept as hard copies or in digital files, the most important facet of having this information is that it is organized and therefore easily accessible. Over the course of a childhood, and with a team of professionals involved, the amount of data can be overwhelming. Parents want to be able to go back and find previous reports quickly, so that they can be sent or given to new team members fast enough to be integrated into current interventions plans.

Without knowing what has been tried (and either was or wasn't effective) with a child before, a new team member can waste valuable time pursuing dead ends or duplicating efforts. Without these insights into a child, they may also misinterpret behaviors or miss nuances of your child's challenges and strengths.

Keep digital data in folders organized by date and profession. Keep hard copies in binders with similar organization. Print out or send data to new team members ahead of appointments. This saves valuable time in meetings. You only want to summarize your child's past interventions, not go over all the details every time you start with a new provider.

Professionals are not always able to provide copies of records in a timely manner, especially if they work for a large institution that has a separate records department. Having a copy on hand lets a parent get new information to a provider as soon as they have it themselves.

Parents should give each provider a written request for all records at the first appointment. An exception to this is the older child being seen by a mental health specialist. In this case, it is usually not a good idea to share each chart note with parents. Older children and teens need to know that their sessions are confidential, with the exception of any information indicating they may be a danger to themselves or others. Periodic summaries, however, are an excellent idea.

Summary

If we regard each child as a unique being who is much more than any label they've been given, then it naturally follows that we carry that perspective into evaluations. Each child with autism deserves assessments that are customized and designed to bring out their highest potential. When a child benefits from assistive devices, the devices need to be used during evaluations.

Skilled evaluators recognize the need to help a child be as comfortable as possible before beginning testing. They also know the value of supplementing standardized tests with thorough developmental and family histories. They have awareness of and empathy for the significant anxiety both children and families may have about being evaluated.

The most discerning evaluators glean data from many sources. They appreciate the process of an evaluation and note and value observations of how a child responds, not only what their response is. Numerical and percentile test scores are regarded as broad indicators of functioning and are interpreted in the context of environment, testing conditions, and process observations.

Evaluations are as good as their design and the communication of their findings. Reports are useful to the degree that they answer questions specific to the issues of each child and to the extent that they guide the family to appropriate resources. Reports include unanswered questions and areas that need further investigation.

Once a evaluation is complete and a report is written, the results are most useful when shared openly with parents and all team members. To avoid confusion in interpreting results or recommendations, everyone working with a child needs to share their understanding of the findings and coordinate their plans for implementing them.

The following chapter will detail steps team members can take so that these plans and interventions have the best chance of succeeding.

3

Take These Steps Before Beginning Any Intervention

Operating from a whole child approach, the next mindset of helping a child navigate autism is to begin planning interventions that take their unique strengths and challenges into consideration. This mindset customizes interventions to each child and formulates them with the help and input of a team of professionals who each take a whole child approach.

While general protocols exist for addressing the diagnostic markers of autism, following this third mindset means moving beyond automatically applying standard protocols. Operating from this framework, professionals first design a personalized foundation and overall plan for treatment before they begin to implement interventions. They review all assessments that are available and carefully choose which specialists a child should work with in order to reach their full potential.

The step of selecting the most appropriate specialists for a child's treatment team is ideally done thoughtfully and deliberately. We recognize that some parents and communities have few options in this step due to financial or resource constraints. In part because the prevalence rate of autism has risen significantly in the past decade, it has been difficult for many locations to meet increasing demand. Yet even when choices are limited, each should be weighed carefully.

For example, if a child goes to a school with two classrooms for each grade, which class and teacher that child has will make a difference. It's advisable for parents and clinicians to seek data and ask questions when there are any options at all. Does either teacher have experience with autism? What is their classroom environment like? One teacher may paper most of the classroom wall space with bright posters of every color imaginable. Perhaps there are also a couple of mobiles hanging in the room. If the second teacher has created a unified, simple space with soft beanbags for children who need a few minutes of self-regulation, this is critical information for the parents to have. This classroom is a very different environment from the first. An autistic child who gets overwhelmed by too much visual input or by movement, or children who need their own space to calm down, will react much better to the second classroom.

Here's another example of the importance of taking time to evaluate options. Let's imagine a family or referring professional wants to select between two occupational therapy (OT) clinics. First, they may want to visit each facility. A clinic that cares about their clients and the quality of service they provide will welcome a parent or allied professional to visit and observe. Professionals who work with autistic children routinely refer to each other, and this should not be done blindly. While the recommendations of colleagues are often relied on, the most diligent professionals find the time to meet the people and the clinic staff to whom they send referrals. If autism is your expertise, you could make hundreds of referrals over the course of your career. Isn't it worth investing the time to have personal knowledge of where you are sending children?

Because there is no one symptom or behavior that defines children with autism, there is no one provider or single treatment that will work for each child on the spectrum. Taking the time to build a team that best fits a child will increase the likelihood of that child reaching their potential. It will also decrease the likelihood that disruptive changes will need to be made mid-treatment due to poor fit between a child and a teacher or provider.

A Unified Team Approach

Too often, individuals working with an autistic child begin their activities and interventions in isolation, without knowing what others involved with the child have planned. It is rare that a child has the luxury of receiving multiple types of help all in one place. Children usually have several therapists at different clinics, in addition to their educational team. This can create a number of negative scenarios. There may be discrepancy at the most basic level; different professionals may have applied different diagnostic labels to the child. For example, if the child was assessed by three evaluators of different specialties—one a mental health clinician, one an educator, and one a speech and language pathologist— the nomenclature each used may be different. Before enacting interventions, these providers need to see if they have a common understanding of the child's core issues.

It is also important that separate providers are aware of each other's plan of intervention. Otherwise, clinicians may spend precious time duplicating activities. Even worse, they may be using interventions that will not be effective because they don't realize that child has not yet learned the foundational skills necessary to complete those tasks.

An ideal situation for a family is to have a central specialist who is designated as the hub of the wheel of interventionists. This person should be someone experienced, in frequent contact with the child, and an effective communicator with allied professionals. These qualities are more important than which specialty they belong to.

The resulting team needs to meet each other so they can put faces to names and develop a closer working relationship. For most situations, this is impractical to do in a live setting. However, an initial 1-hour virtual meeting is not a luxury, but a doable step that should be standard. (Note, though, that some platforms are not HIPAA-compliant, which may be an issue if any of the participants is bound by HIPAA.) If a particular team member cannot attend for the entire hour, they can at least check in, introduce themselves, and see who else is helping the child. Physicians (pediatricians and neurologists) often argue they do not have time for this. Their schedules are often overbooked, but if scheduled during a lunch break and with the expectation of only giving minutes of their time, they are often willing to try. They should always be invited.

Virtual meetings should happen frequently between the educators and therapists who work with the child on a daily or weekly basis. Monthly is ideal; quarterly is minimal. These meetings might include the child's regular teacher, special education teacher, speech and language pathologist, physical therapist, occupational therapist, dietician, applied behavioral analysis (ABA) or other treatment provider, and mental health provider. Including parents in the meetings is often helpful. Often teams who are feeling frustrated with a parent (for whatever reason) will avoid including the family. These circumstances, however, may be the most important time to include them so that straightforward discussion can address the perceived obstacles and solutions can be proposed.

The purposes of this initial meeting are to:

- Ensure each team member knows who is working with the child.
- Increase familiarity among team members to enhance their communication.
- Assure that each team member has read and understood the child's evaluation.
- Inform the team of each member's skills and treatment focus.
- Find out how each team member quantifies progress in their specialty.
- Find out how each professional documents and shares data.
- Set agreed upon priorities for the child.
- Set initial agreed upon short- and long-term goals for the child.
- Set a flexible sequence of skills the child will learn.
- Define critical times requiring communication among the team.

All of these discussion points surround the basic premise of getting all team members to view the child as a unique, multifaceted person who is more than their autism. Treatments must be based on each child's unique needs, strengths, and challenges. Making sure everyone is fully informed about the child and is on board with common goals is the main point of the virtual meeting. Most families impacted by autism are financially strained from the multitude of interventions and out-of-pocket costs. They deserve a team that communicates enough to maximize how far their funds go as well as maximizing the child's benefits from those specialists.

We realize this is a high bar to set. Parents and professionals have been presented with an array of conflicting messages about which treatment options work best for children with autism. The fact is, each child responds to treatment differently. Each family should be given information about the gold standard options and choose what they feel is in the best interest of their child and family, based on their knowledge of that child and what resources are available.

If a comprehensive evaluation was done appropriately, it will be the basis for these decisions. A thorough assessment has laid out the child's strengths and weaknesses, and this data informs the selection and ordering of interventions. The interventions selected should be ones that match the level of the child's current functioning and are paired with information about the child's likely highest potential. How much the child can achieve, however, should always be a tentative assumption, revisited at regular intervals based on treatment outcome along the way.

Parents Are Equal Team Members

The most effective teams include informed, involved parents. Parents will be your co-therapists—there when you can't be and during crises you may not witness. They need to be fully informed so that they can assist their child in a manner consistent with the team's goals and framework.

If a child spends significant time with other family members (e.g., perhaps grandparents live in the home or regularly babysit) these people should also be on board. Regular babysitters who are not family members also need to understand autism and how it affects the child under their care. All of these individuals need these basics: what the particular challenges and strengths are of the child they care for, what triggers this child to become upset or have a meltdown, what comforts this child, what motivates this child (e.g., what their interests are and what they regard as rewards), and what self-regulation skills the child is able to use. They also need to understand what the child is capable of cognitively: Can they understand two-step commands, do they need extra time to process incoming information (whether written or verbal), do they need extra time to respond to requests or questions, are they capable of abstract thought, what basic daily skills have they mastered and which do they need help with, what frightens them the most, what are their particular sensory sensitivities, and are there ways they are prone to self-harm (e.g., running, head banging, eating non-food items, falling, being unaware of danger, not feeling pain)?

Repeated studies (Crane, Batty, et al., 2018: Crane, Chester, et al., 2016: Mulligan et al., 2012; Siklos & Kerns, 2007) have found that parents are largely dissatisfied with the information and support they receive from professionals. They reported feeling directionless after getting their child diagnosed, complaining that they did not get the follow-up appointments they needed or a person to support and direct them (Crane, Chester, et al., 2018).

Fathers, in particular, may feel neglected by team members. One of the few researchers who interviewed dads found that most of the 184 she contacted felt unsupported by professionals involved with their child (Potter, 2017). The fathers said they experienced immediate anxieties upon their child's diagnosis, anger in response to what they viewed as insensitive delivery of diagnostic results, and frustration with the paucity of initial information and ongoing support they were given.

A common source of disappointment and frustration for parents is the letdown that happens soon after diagnosis. Parents seek diagnostic evaluations both to better understand their child and also to have that child be eligible for services. Many, if not most, parents are not aware that it can take months to find and secure these resources and to get an actual appointment. Additionally, the cost of these services is often far greater than anticipated.

One parent, who participated in in-depth interviews by researchers interested in the partnership between parents and providers, had this to say. "It felt like you're being taken to the edge of a cliff. You've been given the diagnosis, you got shoved off the end, and then it was, 'Oh, by the way, we haven't got the parachute. You'll need to get that for yourself.' You feel like you finally got there and you're quite happy, you're ready to fly, but then all of a sudden, you don't have the rest of the equipment you need to fly with."

> *The doctor made a big mistake when he assumed he could tell my mother what to do. Parents deserve respect and they need to be listened to."*
> TEMPLE

How Educators, Clinicians, and Other Professionals Can Support Parents

- Recognize and acknowledge the wide mix of emotions parents may experience after their child is diagnosed.

Some parents will feel relief at finding reasons for their child's behaviors. Others will need to process grief and loss. Many feel helpless and afraid. They need to know you understand and accept this.

- You can maintain professional ethics of appropriate boundaries and still show genuine caring and concern for families. Parents appreciate authenticity and transparency.

- Do not use jargon in speaking with parents. Communicate plainly and fully. Talk to them the way you would want another professional to talk to you.

- Most parents are hungry for information, but there is a range of how quickly they want it and how much they can process at once. Ask them what they need. Be direct. Empower parents with as much knowledge as they are ready for. For those who want more information, direct them to resources: books, websites, movies, online videos, and support groups. Support groups are often where parents find resources that professionals don't know about. Examples include organizations that provide financial aid, therapists who provide sliding fees, university clinics who provide interns at reduced cost, churches who provide respite care, local special interest groups for children, or high school or college students who will provide peer socialization.

- Always let parents know what interventions you plan before you begin them. Instead of simply telling the parents a name of an intervention (which may not mean anything to them), explain why you are choosing the intervention, what goals you are striving for, and how both you and the parents will recognize progress. Ask if they have any questions. All interventions have theories behind them. Hearing the theory behind your chosen treatment plan will help parents understand better what it is you are trying to do.

- When you convey information, deliver it in an honest yet hopeful manner. Be sure the team communicates these fundamental truths to all parents: each child with autism is unique; they each have strengths alongside their challenges; the child's ability can change (and probably will) over time because development of all children is irregular, bumpy at times, and unpredictable; it is the parent's right to find professionals they and their child like and trust; it is a parent's right and responsibility to ask questions; and there are many unproven, so-called cures or treatments being touted, and parents must do their homework.

- Of all the basic information a parent needs, most sorely need to hear this: your child is capable of loving you. If they do not show affection the way other children do, it is not personal. Parents will learn over time to recognize how their child expresses their connection to the parent.

- Some professionals are blind to their own insecurity around very informed parents. It is not only acceptable, but great news, if a parent is more informed than you are. No one will care about a child as much as the average parent, and for those with the time and ability to become informed, they may delve deeper into some aspects of autism than you have. Respect, appreciate, and acknowledge this.

Many parents will not be able to afford all the therapies recommended for their child. They need to know that important therapy takes place in the home as well and that the child's team will teach them how to personally help their child. They also need to know that nonprofessionals such as extended family and friends can play critical roles in their child's development. For example, an hour a week practicing turn taking with a grandparent counts as a genuinely therapeutic interaction.

Team Planning for Children Depends on Their Age

Families with children younger than school age have different team needs than those with older children. First, it is crucial that the parents of newly diagnosed children are actively included in their child's plan. Working alongside involved parents is recognized as a best practice during early intervention. A parent is a crucial part of a team, and in addition to proven benefits to the child's progress, family involvement empowers parents. Families who have been involved in treatment from the start show more resiliency and ability to manage their child's care (Taylor et al., 2014). Parents benefit from information about autism, as well as parent training (PT) in how to respond to disruptive behavior. While parents report benefit from each, their satisfaction level is higher when they receive specific PT, and these programs were also superior for reducing problematic behaviors (Bearss et al., 2015).

Postdiagnosis psycho-educational workshops and family support can be offered in group settings for increased efficiency and to build connections between families. An ideal situation is for affiliated professionals to rotate leading monthly or quarterly workshops. Professionals who do not formally work together can still join efforts to offer infrequent but regular, free, or low-cost introductory sessions.

Family-focused intervention soon after diagnosis has been found to have the largest impact on multiple domains. Positive effects include improvements in social communication between the child and their caregiver, better social functioning in general, and longer term impact on autism symptoms as the child develops (Green & Garg, 2018). One group of researchers trained parents to mediate social communication of children aged 2–4 years and then followed up after 5 years. They found that benefits in the form of an increase in child-to-parent communication continued to be significant (Pickles et al., 2016).

When the newly diagnosed child is of elementary school age, the team has other considerations. This is a time of increasing stress and complexity for both child and parents. A new, often overwhelming environment has been introduced. It's important for the team to address the frequent challenges that arise among the child, their family, and members of the educational setting. Parents need help understanding the reasoning behind the strategies used by their child's teachers. Educational goals need to be spelled out in detail and revisited frequently in formalized meetings.

Classroom and special education teachers also need to understand the family's priorities and goals. This transactional approach acknowledges that difficulties for the child and parents in understanding the school environment are often matched by those of the environment understanding the child and their family. Proactive communication and the mindset of all parties being empowered as team members create a working relationship more likely to withstand inevitable crises.

The team should address the child's educational environment to see if it needs adjustment to accommodate differences in information or sensory processing and subsequent learning capacity. Poorly adapted physical environments can derail a child with autism. A mindset of seeing the whole child always includes observing their surroundings in order to maximize the child's well-being and potential.

The elementary school years are also a key period to notice comorbid conditions (signs to look for will be discussed in depth in the following chapter). Team meetings should routinely include time to ask members if anyone has noticed psychiatric or medical symptoms in a child. Without including this as a regular item on the meeting's agenda, these concerns can easily be overlooked. While symptoms will often need to be assessed by specialists outside the central team, these meetings can be very helpful in distinguishing core autism impairments from co-occurring problems. It is imperative that all team members have information about these conditions and how they impact children with autism.

When children enter puberty and adolescence, additional issues emerge for the team. Whether a team has worked long term with a child, or whether they are just beginning to work with a teen, there are new interventions at this point. Typical areas that warrant specific intervention planning include hygiene, body changes, mood fluctuations, shifts in peer relationships, and increased academic demands. It is a time of intense change, and the risk for crises increases. A good team works to stay on top of the teen's stress level, partly by frequently sharing observations with each other and the parents.

A core concept of a successful team is that helping a child or teen with autism is a dynamic process. Multiple sets of eyes making multiple observations provide enough data points to reveal a child's patterns as well as evolving shifts in their patterns. The presumption of a whole child team is that part of the uniqueness of each child is the individuality of their developmental trajectory. In contrast to providers who try to fit each child into standard protocols, effective teams fit interventions to the child in a continually shape-shifting dance.

Whole child planning continues to provide support to parents and siblings throughout a child's journey, with the goal of optimized self-care and resiliency. Rather than waiting for a crisis, or reacting only when a situation becomes urgent, a strong team views treatment planning for children or teens with autism as an ongoing, constantly adapting process. Tracking changes and quantifying progress is an integral part of the team's work.

As children grow older, many will increasingly voice their own priorities and goals. These will not always align with what parents or professionals desire. Teams that have included parents and the child all along will be in a much stronger position to have successful communication during this stage of a young person's move toward increased independence.

> *My needs changed as I grew. Good therapists are constantly adapting to the child.*
> *They don't expect the child to adapt to them."*
> TEMPLE

How to Apply Mindset 3 to Educational Planning

When educational staff members fail to carefully plan prior to working with autistic children, all stakeholders can suffer. One group of researchers conducted focus groups that included parents, classroom teachers, and school administrators. Their participants had the following complaints about educational planning: unreliable implementation, inappropriate goals, ineffective communication, and inadequate involvement of all decision makers in the initial planning process (Snell-Rood et al., 2020).

Classroom, special education, and resource teachers, along with school psychologists and school administration, are often overwhelmed with the growing number of their students with autism. Some feel unprepared to meet the needs of these children, with whom these professionals may not have been specifically trained to work. Unless they graduated in the past decade or so, they may have been told they would encounter few students with autism. It was assumed children with severe impairments would be in residential care or workshops; less impaired children were generally undiagnosed.

Even newly trained classroom teachers feel unprepared. One study interviewed teacher candidates in three university programs (Blackwell et al., 2017). The candidates were asked to identify all sources of their knowledge about autism. The most frequently cited sources were a friend or family member who knew about autism (66.7%) or mass media, most often television (65.5%). This was followed by personal experience with someone with autism (50.6%). About a third of the teachers in training cited autism awareness activities such as walks, telethons, or class presentations as their source of knowledge. Only 23% had obtained knowledge from actual coursework or workshops, and 3.4% said they had no knowledge of autism.

The study participants were then asked to answer true or false questions that assessed their knowledge of autism. Questions were divided into categories of basic characteristics, early signs, prevalence, causes, diagnosis, and intervention. They received six scores—one for each group of questions—and an overall total score. Their overall knowledge of autism was no more accurate than would be expected by chance (53%). Their highest scores were in recognizing basic characteristics (70.1%) and early signs (57.1%). Scores in the categories of prevalence, causes, diagnosis, and intervention all clustered in an approximate 10% spread (37.3% to 49.4%). Almost 75% of respondents said they "did not know" in response to questions about interventions.

These students were dangerously unaware of their lack of knowledge. The majority thought they knew "quite a bit" about autism (79.3%). This self-assessment did not vary significantly by university, school year, or gender. The students who had more personal and direct experiences with autism—either by knowing someone autistic, personal communication, or autism awareness activities—had more accurate knowledge.

How much classroom teachers know about autism has real world consequences. Previous studies have shown that general classroom teachers who know more about autism view the inclusion of autistic children more favorably (Busby et al., 2012, Segall & Campbell, 2012). Other research has shown that children perform more strongly with teachers holding positive views of the academic potential of children with disabilities than do students of teachers with low expectations of them (Klehm, 2014).

It is no surprise then that studies have identified multiple needs of classroom teachers that could be met if Mindset 3 were standard practice. Elementary and secondary general education teachers lack confidence teaching in an inclusive classroom and believe they are not very effective working with special education students (McCray & McHatton, 2011). Many voiced concerns that any academic preparation they had was more focused on dis-abilities in general and was a broad overview, with little practical information about autism. They were struck by the diversity of their autistic students. The teachers seemed to recognize the need for interacting with each child according to that child's specific needs, but had no foundation of knowledge to help them meet this goal. As one teacher in this study remarked, "I don't have any kind of special education background, so some training on how to work with these students is really needed."

Focus groups of teachers across all grade levels also reported they wanted more social support for their autistic students, along with assistance in transitioning and teaching the children how to self-advocate and ask for help. They observed changes in non-autistic peers' developmental expectations and degree of accep-tance of their autistic classmates according to grade level. While the teachers wanted all non-autistic students to be more informed about ASD, they observed more bullying in higher grades. They thought students in junior and senior high in particular needed to be involved with programs emphasizing acceptance and tolerance (Able et al., 2014).

Teachers want the support of multidisciplinary teams, but they report that even in schools that intend to have collaborative practices, they are not always implemented. In one study, while 92% of the teachers believed their schools planned collaborative approaches for students, only 57% of them said these practices were actually put in place (Damore & Murray, 2009). The edu-cators had specific suggestions for ways collaboration could be used. They felt IEPs were not designed in a way that gave them good understanding of a student's individual characteristics and accommodation needs. They wanted advance information instead of having to rely on their own "three to four week learning curve" to figure a child out. They also stated systematic information sharing from previous teachers would help them avoid reinventing the wheel for each student.

These teachers recognized the need to have teams composed of various professionals as well as the student's parents. They believed collaboration with the special education teachers, the school counselors, and the school psychologist was essential.

The best educational teams help develop each member's knowledge base and proficiency. Transparency in each member's efforts, sharing of information (both about autism in general and about the children the team works with), and regularly soliciting feedback so that improvements and modifications can be made are all ways for teams to improve. The most effective teams are in almost daily contact—chatting informally at lunch or in the hallway—because they find their work and the kids they apply it to genuinely interesting. These teams care and are excited about how to help a child grow and they love to see a child's world get bigger.

As one special education teacher told us, "Most professionals who enter and remain in the field of special education or autism find the work exciting and great. We see the kids as people who contribute and who *we* can learn from. We don't feel sorry for the kids. We've seen enough to know that in addition to contributing, these kids have a combination of skills that make them see things in a different way, especially in terms of how their hearts view the world. Many maintain the best qualities of younger children— they celebrate things younger children care about, and they have an innocence the world needs more of. They want to please us, and they want to be helpful. The best mindset educators—or anyone— can have is that these kids are valuable and have a lot to offer. If you work closely with them, you will know that quickly" (D. Mini, personal communication, May 16, 2020).

A Research-Based Model for Educators of Autistic Children

In Great Britain, the Autism Education Trust (AET), a government-funded group of 10 researchers, was tasked with exploring how well the school system was preparing children and young people with autism for good adult outcomes. From their findings, they developed standards for delivering best practices within education when working with children with autism. They echo the special education teacher quoted above, as their first marker of quality is that the team have high levels of ambition and aspiration for the students, both at school and also in their future adult lives. They also echo the importance of highly trained, unified teams that routinely share data and enhance each member's work with a child.

The researchers found effective systems for monitoring and recording learning progress was vital. They suggest using a range of outcome measures, some geared specifically to social-emotional curricula. In addition to using standard written records, they creatively propose the use of photographs and videos of the children (although you should not photograph or video a child for this purpose without their parents' express written consent). A short video of a child speaking or completing a task can be compared to the same performance in a video from a previous date.

A great deal of data across multiple domains can be captured this way. While many progress reports emphasize one domain, for example language, a video captures language plus many other variables such as motor skills, emotional tone, mood, expressiveness, and energy level. Video samples submitted by parents have a uniquely valuable role. They will help educators see how well skills are generalizing outside the classroom.

The AET model that resulted from the research advocates delivering curriculum to children in a variety of ways. The AET advises using both adapted forms of standard curriculum, along with autism-specific programs targeting social communication and other delayed skills. Flexibility is key, with the recommended use of individualized learning packages to meet a child's unique learning styles and needs, along with adjustment of expectations of learning outcomes as needed.

A *quality-first* approach to educating autistic children is defined as a combination of inclusive practice and personalized learning. The Autism Education Trust emphasizes that the best schools regard staff training in autism as a vital component of this type of service delivery. These personnel ideally work jointly and have close and consistent contact. They observe each other's work. Each specialist must be able to communicate effectively not only with each other, but also with students and parents. The specialists must be good listeners.

Scheduled meetings were found to benefit children in ways beyond educational progress. They also supported the students' and the families' emotional well-being, and provided a place to discuss daily living issues that occur outside the classroom (AETTrainingHubs, 2016).

Adjusting Interventions to Fit a Child: Two Examples of Team Brainstorming and Flexibility

Detailed knowledge of each child is necessary to design effective interventions for any setting. Even if you are applying a standardized protocol, the best results are obtained when it is flexible and adapted to the needs of the child. The parts of an intervention that can be changed without contaminating its integrity include the setting, the pacing, the motivators used, and the rewards given. These variables may often need to be adjusted due to the child's age, intellectual capacity, emotional state, sensory issues, language impairment, or motivation level.

The *sensory setting* of an intervention can determine whether a child can successfully attend and learn. Often, changing what appear to a provider or parent as negligible factors results in a child suddenly starting to focus and enjoy a task. Making adjustments to a classroom, therapy office, clinic, or the child's home may have to be done on a regular basis, as sensory sensitivities change over time. With more than half of autistic children thought to have sensory irregularities (Jussila et al., 2020; Wiggins et al., 2009), this variable deserves continual attention. Those with sensory sensitivity are more likely to have repetitive behaviors (Chen et al., 2009).

EXAMPLE #1: A Team of Four Uncover the Cause of a Student's Distress

John started working with a reading specialist in second grade. The special education teacher, Mrs. Alvarez, pulled John out of his regular classroom three times a week. She met with him at the end of the day in a room a few doors down the hall. John was usually an even-tempered child. He rarely had meltdowns and he had never been aggressive toward others.

Mrs. Alvarez, however, had a very different experience with John. He willingly came to their lessons but frequently became irritable within minutes. By mid-lesson, he was crying and refusing to cooperate. He started to chew on his fingers and twist in his seat. He once bolted from the room and hid in the boy's room. He could not explain to Mrs. Alvarez what was wrong, and she initially assumed the change in environment, or the work itself, was overwhelming him.

After exhausting all her strategies to connect with John, Mrs. Alvarez called a team meeting. She hoped by brainstorming together a solution could be found. John's mother attended their meeting, along with his classroom teacher, Mrs. Alvarez, and John's school counselor.

The two teachers discussed how different John was in each of their classrooms. The counselor's sense of John was similar to that of his general classroom teacher. John's mother echoed them all, saying that her son usually liked school and came home in a good mood. But on the days he was pulled out of the classroom for resource reading with Mrs. Alvarez, she (in retrospect) noticed he complained of tiredness and occasionally of headaches.

The four adults began to think about what was different during John's reading session. It was the child's mother who suddenly had a hunch. She had noticed—but thought nothing of it—that Mrs. Alvarez was wearing a mild, sweet-smelling perfume. It was barely noticeable. Now that they were chatting, and she got another whiff of the scent, she realized her son could be reacting to it. She knew how sensitive John was to olfactory input, particularly chemicals, something that the school personnel didn't seem aware of.

She brought it up and the others looked knowingly at each other. Not only did Mrs. Alvarez wear a bit of perfume, but also more importantly, her classroom was next to the janitor's room, where cleaning supplies were kept. The janitor often left a bucket of water containing Clorox in the closet. The chemical probably seeped through both the ventilation system and the small opening under the doors.

> *Sensory sensitivity is a huge issue for kids. Too many kids are being overwhelmed by too much data coming in at once. Teachers love active, involved students, but autistic children need time for quiet and space."*
> TEMPLE

When Mrs. Alvarez stopped wearing perfume and she and John met in a room in another wing of the school building, he was fine. His repetitive behaviors and his crying stopped. He was able to enjoy Mrs. Alvarez and took pride in his reading progress.

EXAMPLE #2: Adapting Occupational Therapy in the Age of COVID

Mr. Berman was an experienced occupational therapist (OT) with his own clinic where he supervised other OTs. They all regularly used standard exercises to help their young clients with motor planning and sensory challenges. His clinic was outfitted with typical equipment such as balls, cushions, swings, hammocks, and an array of items with various textures.

When the COVID-19 pandemic hit, Mr. Berman's clinic shuttered its doors. The mother of Kevin, one of his clients, wanted to continue her son's therapy and asked Mr. Berman if he could come up with an alternative to the clinic. Kevin was 4 years old; in pre-K special education; and struggling with significant anxiety, impaired visual motor skills and motor planning, and poor coordination.

Mr. Berman's team met to discuss how they could best continue to provide services to their clients. It was obvious that they would need to be more creative and flexible than ever. Initially, it was difficult to see how they could proceed, but as they threw out ideas, the options grew and their excitement rose.

At this point, public spaces were still open, and Mr. Berman scoped out a nearby park as an alternative site to conduct treatment. There was a small, curved slide there, but no other vestibular equipment. There was grass and an area of mulch around the playground equipment.

Kevin and his mother met Mr. Berman at the park. Kevin's mom sat nearby, enjoying some respite. Kevin was clearly not thrilled to be there. He did not like his routine of the clinic changed and he had never been to this unfamiliar park. He was anxious and unmotivated, even though he and Mr. Berman usually had a positive, playful relationship. Mr. Berman, unsure how or if this was going to work, was a bit anxious, too.

Mr. Berman suggested Kevin try going down the small slide, and Kevin refused. He got the distinct impression that Kevin was going to reject anything that was suggested. Mr. Berman shifted, and asked Kevin what he usually likes to do when he and his Mom go outside. Kevin said he liked going for ice cream. Mr. Berman ran with it, "I love ice cream! We should make some ice cream right now!" He turned to Kevin's mom and asked her if it would be okay for them to go get ice cream after their session if they first made some right now. She said yes.

Kevin seemed interested, so Mr. Berman led him over to where the grass met the mulch and they sat down. They proceeded to "make ice cream" by using the mulch to form mounds, which they then pretended to sell. Kevin was getting a ton of tactile play. Mr. Berman made sure he positioned the ice cream so that Kevin would get in lots of bending and moving and crossing his midline. He gave Kevin tasks like creating piles of ice cream, so he was required to use both hands together. He continually engaged in interactive, turn-taking tasks and talk.

During this time, Kevin had transitioned from reluctance to engagement and excitement. After they finished making ice cream, Mr. Berman used this enthusiasm to again suggest going down the slide. This time, Kevin was willing. He went down sitting up, and then went down backwards on his tummy! Mr. Berman was pleased—their park session had resulted in a variety of tactile and sensory experiences, and now Kevin was getting even more new tactile experiences, as well as body awareness feedback. As important, the hour had progressed from rigidity to flexibility and risk taking. Kevin had practiced motor planning and was laying new neuronal tracks.

Then Kevin wanted Mr. Berman to go down the curvy slide, and the OT used this to create an opportunity for reciprocal play. First, Mr. Berman went down the small slide—a tight fit that he overemphasized with animated movements and sounds. At one snug curve, his body naturally slowed, so he went with it and pretended to be completely stuck. Kevin found that hilarious.

The OT then added another piece so that Kevin's limbic system could get a workout. He had Kevin stand at the bottom of the slide and guess when Mr. Berman would come down. Kevin had to stay on alert—to wait and watch. He asked Kevin to "catch" him—but only at the very end—not to anticipate his arrival too quickly and not to let his feet touch the ground before catching him.

By this time, Kevin was fully engaged, but his arousal had reached a level that precluded effective motor planning. He had started to run aimlessly and sloppily. Mr. Berman knew he had to help Kevin increase his awareness of his movements and make intentional changes to them. He decided to invite Kevin on a "leprechaun hunt." The two of them slowly jogged together over to some trees. They began a search for twigs to build "leprechaun huts." Kevin got more tactile experience and the equivalent of several sets of bending over and balance exercises. He didn't mind the repetition, which Mr. Berman let him do enough of to build skill carryover.

What could have been a cancelled OT appointment turned into a rich session. Kevin worked on many skills, including transitioning, increasing tactile awareness and desensitization, reciprocal play, motor planning and execution, and hand-eye coordination. To an outside observer, it would have looked like Kevin and Mr. Berman were simply playing. Because he took his OT knowledge and purposefully adapted it to the setting and Kevin's needs, the play was as valuable as any in-clinic session.

Summary

Mindset 3 for successful navigation of autism is to take all of the unique strengths and challenges of a child and form a collaborative team of providers that approaches intervention planning with a whole child perspective. Clear intentions and goals and agreed upon markers of progress prevent professionals from working at cross-purposes or duplicating efforts. This approach also increases parent satisfaction.

Taking the time to customize a child's treatment plan replaces reliance on standard protocols with carefully chosen tools and strategies adapted to each individual. Flexibility is an inherent component of good interventions, and modifications needed to help interventions succeed benefit from team brainstorming.

Allocating space for this step in the process respects not only the child and their family, but also the specialists caring for the child.

SELECTING YOUR CHILD'S TEAM: A GUIDELINE FOR PARENTS

You may not have an initial choice in who works with your child. However, as you observe your child with team members, you have a right and a responsibility to let your opinions be known. If you believe a specific team member is a poor fit for your child, it is always appropriate to speak to the team to see if adjustments can be made. If adjustments do not solve the problem, or if the problem involves your child's safety or well-being, speaking with a supervisor (or clinical director, principal, or school district administrator) is a recommended step.

If you are able to make selections of team members yourself, these are questions that you may want to ask:

- Is the professional credentialed in their field? Is the credential in good standing? Are there any legal actions, current or past, against promoters, consumers, or practitioners of the intervention? Parents can go online and find the professional association for each provider and check the state regulating organization for any actions taken against their license. Lawsuits also often show up online.
- How long have they been working with children with needs similar to yours?
- If the professional or clinic works with diverse populations, what percentage are children with autism? How many are similar to my child (e.g., age group or verbal or nonverbal)?
- What approach do they use and what is the purpose of that approach?
- How will I know if their approach is working? What will I observe in my child?
- Is this approach verified as effective for children like mine? Where can I read more about the proven benefits?
- How effective has this intervention been with other children similar to mine?
- How long will my child need to be involved in this intervention for it to be beneficial?
- Are there any known physical or psychological side effects

or harm that has happened to other children using this approach?

- If my child is not mainstreamed, does this intervention increase the likelihood that they could be in the future? What has the rate of transition to mainstream with other children?

- What other interventions are available that we forego in choosing this provider's orientation?

- What are the expected costs in terms of both time and money associated with this treatment? Will my insurance or any other source cover these expenses? (It is wise to make a few phone calls to compare costs of the same intervention by different providers. Cost is not the only consideration for selection, but providers should be able to provide reasonable explanations for significant differences in cost.)

- Can the provider, after obtaining appropriate permission, supply a short list of other families with whom they have worked?

- Does the provider's approach fit with my child's other treatment interventions?

- How are the interventions scheduled?

- How are the interventions delivered? Will someone work one-on-one with my child? Who will that person be and what is their background?

- How is progress measured? In what way and how often will my child's behaviors be observed and recorded?

- Will the provider integrate my child's individual interests into activities to motivate them?

- How will the provider use my child's strengths to build skills?
- In what environment will the intervention take place? Will distractions and sensory stimuli be monitored? How?
- How are meltdowns handled? Can the professional walk me through what steps they will take to calm my child?
- How will the provider prepare me as a parent to continue and build on this approach at home?
- How will the provider communicate with me? How frequently will they communicate, and in what form?

4

Know These Medical Conditions Associated With Autism

Now that a team has been solidified and each member has a deep understanding of the child, there is one more step prior to implementation of targeted interventions. There are numerous medical, psychological, and sensory conditions that, if unrecognized or unmitigated, usually interfere with successful treatment. Because the majority of autistic children have difficulty communicating, they seldom directly report these issues. It is up to providers, educators, and parents to assess their presence. If these conditions are missed or untreated, a child's progress and quality of life will suffer. This chapter will review the most common medical conditions associated with autism and give you a list of behaviors that may indicate their hidden presence in a child. The following chapter will review the most common psychological and psychiatric conditions.

Assessing Conditions Associated With Autism: The Impact of Language, Sensory, and Perceptual Differences

Despite the high prevalence of medical and psychiatric issues in autistic children, many of these conditions are not routinely looked for (Buie et al., 2010; Malow et al., 2012). Both parents and professionals are often uninformed about behavioral symptoms that may reflect an underlying, undiagnosed medical or psychiatric condition.

In order to recognize these problems, there must be reliable ways to gather the information. Within the population of children with ASD, there are common barriers to that must be taken into consideration.

One reason the rate of untreated medical and psychiatric conditions is higher for children with autism than for neurotypical children is because behavior, not spoken communication, is the most common way this population expresses itself. For those with no or limited language capacity, actions are often the sole medium. In addition to language impairments, social and executive function limitations play a role. A child who does not know how to ask for help is unlikely to directly reach out to a caregiver or provider for assistance with a physical ailment. A child who cannot plan, initiate, or follow through on a sequence of actions may be ineffective in recognizing or remembering to tell someone about their symptoms.

Sensory issues can also interfere with a child getting appropriate help for medical or psychiatric problems. Most children with autism have some impairment of sensory processing. The most commonly discussed condition is one of dysregulation. The child either underreacts to stimuli, or they process the incoming stimuli as heightened. For example, one child may not hear someone calling them, yet another child may be able to hear and be distressed by sounds others do not notice.

Atypical sensory experiences are estimated to occur in as many as 90% of autistic individuals. They impact every sensory modality, including taste, touch, hearing, smell, vision, proprioception, and balance.

A review of the properties of sensory processing in autism (Robertson & Baron-Cohen, 2017) suggests that the autistic cortex is affected by distinct, low-level changes in neural circuitry that is dedicated to perceptual processing (including primary sensory areas). Perceptual irregularities in individuals with autism are evident early in development, account for independent variance in diagnostic criteria of the condition, and show a persistent relationship to clinical measures of higher order social cognition and behavior. The authors suggest that an understanding of the perceptual symptoms in autism may provide insight into signature differences in neural circuitry that might underpin multiple levels of autistic features and may thus help to elucidate autistic neurobiology.

There are numerous other sensory differences that can also contribute to a failure of recognizing and treating comorbid conditions. Some children with autism, for instance, cannot distinguish between foreground and background information. Pain or distress may just blend into a chaotic mix of sensations. If this is a child's experience, they may not report even severe pain.

Other autistic children may experience fragmented perception—the inability to take in multiple pieces of information at once. Instead, they experience the world in bits that do not fit together into recognizable patterns they can conceptualize or verbalize. A child living this way would not be expected to report medical or emotional distress.

Other children may have what is called *sensory agnosia.* These individuals fail to recognize incoming sensory data, yet their primary sensory functions are intact and they have no general mental impairment. If their agnosia is specific to pain, serious medical conditions may go undetected until manifestations other than pain become obvious.

In some children, the ability to accurately recognize, process, and report incoming sensory stimuli can vary dramatically from day to day. Imagine a child whose pain perception is inconsistent in this way and has a urinary tract infection. Over the course of a week, he may one day not feel any sensation, while another day he has mild distress, and yet another day he is wailing from pain. These fluctuations of experience and reporting can delay diagnoses or even result in a parent or provider dismissing the child's complaints.

These children may also experience *sensory synesthesia,* which is a cross channeling of incoming data. This is when sensory input—such as sound—gets processed as, or alongside, another sense—such as color. The child may, for example, see the color red whenever they hear a certain musical tone. This is not well researched in the area of pain, but it is possible some children with autism experience a similar cross channeling when they feel pain.

It is easy to envision the diminished diagnostic accuracy of conditions associated with autism when we remember how many factors impact pain perception and reporting. Many children with autism will not be able to successfully convey their experience. They are unlikely to have or use the typical language to which physicians or other providers are accustomed.

Accurate determination of pain or emotional distress encounters another issue when providers rely on their usual questionnaires to gather data. Studies have shown that on these types of assessment measures, as compared to typically developing (neurotypical) children, some autistic children tend to self-enhance, fail to complete the measure, lack self-awareness, or interpret items in an overly literal manner. There is research indicating this may correlate with the level of impairment in a child—the less impairment present, the more self-awareness is comparable to that of neurotypical (typically developing) youth (Schriber et al., 2014).

Another impediment to accurate assessment and access to care is that children with autism may have their symptoms ignored or minimized, even if reported. Their symptoms may overlap with behaviors or complaints inherent to autism, resulting in misdiagnosis. What may look like classic repetitive behavior, for example, may actually be a sign of obsessive-compulsive disorder. The distinction is vital to successful intervention, as etiology and intervention differ for the two conditions.

Assessment of these co-occurring medical problems is critically important in the initial evaluation procedures for individuals with ASD, as well as in ongoing treatment management. As part of a multidisciplinary approach, systematic and evidence-based screening for the most common conditions should be recommended as part of both the original diagnostic evaluation as well as throughout a child's development and during regular, ongoing health monitoring. In order to maximize general well-being, the treatment team must be vigilant for signs of physical, sensory, and emotional upset that the child does not reveal themself. Because of how easily medical conditions are missed, some professionals believe nonroutine and noninvasive procedures, as long as they do not put children at unnecessary risk, should be a standard part of a thorough evaluation (Isaksen et al., 2013). Examples include genetic testing for other hidden conditions, and electroencephalograms (EEGs) for undetected epilepsy.

When children with autism do receive medical assessment or intervention, it is important that whenever possible they are treated by medical and psychiatric providers familiar and experienced with this population. Communication problems will be amplified if interacting with inexperienced personnel or those made uncomfortable by children with autism (Mason et al., 2019).

> *Teachers, parents, and therapists have to directly ask kids about how they're feeling. The kids aren't necessarily going to volunteer the information."*
> TEMPLE

The Most Common Medical Conditions Associated With Autism

Professionals and parents need to know which conditions are most commonly present alongside autism so they can recognize behaviors and signs that may signal their presence. If suspected, some of these disorders will require medical tests, others will lead to further psychiatric exams, and a few may call for genetic testing.

The remainder of this chapter will primarily discuss the most prevalent associated medical conditions. The most common medical issues are pain, gastrointestinal problems, sleep disruption, and seizures. Less prevalent medical and genetic conditions will be briefly described.

The Prevalence and Impact of
Associated Medical Conditions

Epidemiological evidence indicates that medical disorders are more prevalent in children with autism compared to children in the general population and that at least 10% of individuals on the spectrum have at least one physiological symptom requiring medical evaluation (Kohane, 2012). As would be expected in a condition marked by wide variability in severity and presentation, prevalence estimates cover a large range as well. Estimates for some conditions are likely higher. Kohane's research (2012) was a large study that examined hospital records of American children and teens with a diagnosis of autism. They found that gastrointestinal and seizure disorders stood out—occurring at much higher levels in the autistic population compared to the general hospital population.

Other studies have affirmed that children with autism have elevated rates of specific clusters of medical conditions (Cummings et al., 2016; Doshi-Velez et al., 2014). Significantly higher rates of gastrointestinal (GI) symptoms are found in autistic children than in typically developing children (Valicenti-McDermott et al., 2006).

The mortality ratio in the autistic population has been estimated as high as 2.4 times that of the general population (Gillberg et al., 2010; Mouridsen, Brønnum-Hansen, et al., 2008). This markedly heightened rate of early death is not thought to be due to autism itself, but to be primarily caused by complications specific to co-occurring health issues (Hirvikoski et al., 2016). If these conditions were more widely recognized and treated early in a child's life perhaps this rate could lower significantly.

These conditions and the disabilities they cause can influence development beyond a child's physical state. They impact how a child navigates their social world, how they learn, and how well positioned they are to transition into employment or higher education. Treatment plans and prognosis are altered by a child's medical status.

Pain

Pain impacts mood, motivation, and behavior. When a child is in pain, they can't be expected to focus, comply, or connect. It is vital that providers and parents learn to recognize and try to relieve the child's pain. Children with autism are especially vulnerable to the negative impacts of pain for three main reasons: they may not be able to verbalize or otherwise communicate they are in pain; the way their brains process pain may be different (either not registering pain or diminishing or amplifying it); and because numerous medical conditions occur more frequently than in the general population, they experience pain more often.

Practitioners and parents can use the Non-Communicating Children's Pain Checklist–Revised (NCCPC-R) in identifying pain in children and teens with autism. It has been shown to be a valid and reliable tool (Palese, 2020) and is available free online. Questions on the checklist fall into six categories: vocal, social, facial, activity, body and limbs, and physiological. Examples of vocal behavior that may indicate pain include soft whimpering, a specific sound (which they note can even sound like a laugh) or word, or crying. Social indicators include withdrawal or seeking physical closeness. Facial cues include wide-open eyes or puckered lips. Activity signs may include jumping around or not moving. Body and limb indicators could be gesturing to a part of the body or guarding a part of the body. Physiological changes may be seen as sharp intakes of breath or changes in sleep. There are many other items for raters to consider in each of the six categories.

Dental pain can be particularly difficult to identify in nonverbal or noncommunicative children. Those with autism have higher rates of cavities and gingivitis, yet lower rates of dental treatment (Jaber, 2011). The overall rate of cavities for children with autism in one study was 77%, and the average for controls was 46%. All of the autistic children studied needed a dental cleaning; 41% of controls did. Good dental hygiene was assessed in 59% of the children in the control group. Only 3.3% of the children with autism were assessed to have good dental hygiene. A striking 97% of the autistic children had gingivitis. In 79% of instances the gum disease was generalized, while in the remaining 22% of children, the inflammation was localized. This is probably due to a combination of factors, including lack of access to treatment due to either paucity of providers who work with autistic children and/or the child's aversion to treatment. Children with autism also tend to have certain conditions and behaviors that increase risk of dental problems: generalized increase in inflammation in the body, tendency to pouch food inside the mouth instead of swallowing due to poor tongue coordination, difficulty brushing or flossing due to poor fine motor control, lack of motivation for personal hygiene in general, or sensory discomfort or actual pain when their mouths are touched. For some children, dietary restrictions, with high levels of sugar or food items that tend to adhere to teeth or gums (e.g., peanut butter) may also contribute to increased risk of dental problems.

The Dental Discomfort Questionnaire (DDQ) is an observational instrument intended to measure dental discomfort and/or pain in children less than 5 years of age. It can be found free online. Questions include items such as biting with molars instead of front teeth, crying while eating, reaching for the cheek while eating, and chewing on one side (Penmetsa et al., 2019).

Lots of pediatricians aren't trained to work with autistic children. When you combine that with kids not being able to tell the doctor about their symptoms, you have a big problem. Too many kids with autism have untreated pain."

TEMPLE

Parent education, often by an occupational or physical therapist, can increase beneficial dental habits and lower rates of cavities and gum disease. Social stories about brushing and flossing and visiting the dentist are recommended. For children afraid of the dentist, an initial visit to simply see the offices, meet the staff, and sit in the dental chair and touch some instruments can lower anxiety enough for them to tolerate actual treatment at the next visit.

Don't Miss These Possible Signs of Pain

- Negative change in behavior: more crying, acting out, or withdrawal.
- Change in body movements: writhing, contorting, jerking, or favoring one side or body part.
- Obsession with a body part: frequent rubbing, biting, smacking, pointing to, or guarding.
- Change in facial expressions or movements near the mouth: wide-open or scrunched eyes, grimacing, grinding teeth, putting fingers in the mouth, and holding the jaw or face.

- Changes in or during eating patterns: refusing hard or chewy foods, increased distress at mealtime.
- Changes in hygiene routines: increased resistance to brushing teeth, having parts of body washed, or hair shampooed.
- Changes in vocalization: new sounds, crying out, moaning, whimpering, and a repeated word.
- Changes in social behaviors: aggression, withdrawal, increased sensitivity to touch, or clinging behavior.
- Changes in activity level: increased self-injury; increased aggression; increased, decreased, or absence of movement.
- Physiological changes: sharp intakes of breath, changes in breathing pattern, changes in perspiration, or changes in sleep.

Epilepsy

Epilepsy and autism often co-occur. Underlying factors in both diagnoses likely predispose children to experiencing both conditions. These may include genetic and chromosomal variables, metabolic conditions, and environmental factors such as in uteri influences and neonatal status. Epilepsy occurs in 1–2% of the general population. The Centers for Disease Control (CDC) cited a 1.2% prevalence rate in the United States in 2015 (Zach & Kobau, 2017). In the autism population, the median overall prevalence of epilepsy is 12.1%, with a range of 1.8–60% (Lukmanji et al., 2019). Some researchers have found the type of seizure most prevalent in ASD is complex partial seizures (Matsuo et al., 2010). Knowing this is critical so that manifestations of these less obvious seizures are not mistakenly attributed to a child's autism. For example, a child with undiagnosed partial seizures may exhibit repetitive movements during a seizure. If caretakers or providers are not informed about epilepsy, they would probably assume the movements were inherent to the child's autism.

Another example is a child who does not respond to his name. This could be an information processing or sensory issue related to autism, but it could also be the result of a partial seizure. Petit mal seizures are also referred to as *absence* seizures because most observers cannot detect these brief disturbances, which generally last less than 15 seconds.

Other studies have found the highest rate of epilepsy occurred in autistic adults with severe intellectual disability (60%). Citing an examination of the US National Survey of Children's Health (2011–2012), Thomas et al. found that epilepsy was reported to co-occur in 8.6% of children on the spectrum. Higher rates of epilepsy were associated with increasing child age, female gender, intellectual disability, speech problems, and lower socioeconomic status (2017).

Evaluation of epilepsy should occur early in life. There is evidence that onset is often at a young age, that prompt treatment helps, and that the consequences of neglecting this condition can be deadly. In examining medical files of hospitalized children, researchers found most children experienced their first recognized episode of epilepsy prior to the age of 7 years (Pacheva et al., 2019). Some researchers have found that almost 20% of infants with infantile spasms will develop autism (Strasser et al., 2018). With early diagnosis and treatment, response to seizures was good: 58% of the children became seizure-free, and 27% had greater than a 50% reduction in seizures. Pacheva and colleagues (2019) noted that autistic behaviors did not change with treatment.

The morbidity rate of those with both autism and epilepsy is up to twice that of the general population, especially for females. (Gillberg et al., 2010; Hirvikoshi et al., 2016; Mouridsen, Rich et al., 2011; Shavelle et al., 2001). These studies also report that sudden, unexpected death due to epilepsy is more common in individuals with both autism and epilepsy, compared to individuals with only epilepsy. These children, they advise, are likely to require increased medical monitoring to prevent avoidable death over their lifespan.

Untreated epilepsy may also be correlated with behavioral, intellectual, and emotional conditions. Some researchers have found that children with both autism and epilepsy have higher rates of self-injury, compulsions, intellectual disability, and impaired face recognition (Richard et al., 2017), along with greater challenges in social interactions and eye contact (Turk et al., 2009). Epilepsy and sleep disorders are also highly correlated. Having either disorder increases the odds of the other being present. Unfortunately, medication for epilepsy can also negatively impact sleep (Eriksson, 2011).

The added challenges showed up in statistically significant differences on behavioral assessments of children with both autism and epilepsy. Children who later developed seizures had lower baseline scores on all domains of the Vineland Adaptive Behavior Scales, rated more hyperactive on the Aberrant Behavior Checklist, and obtained scores indicating lower physical quality of life on the Pediatric Quality of Life Inventory (Capal et al., 2020).

In addition to controlling seizure activity, treatment of epilepsy would reasonably be expected to have secondary positive impacts on a child. These benefits may include improved mood, increased focus and attention, and more consistent sleep. Appropriate detection of epilepsy is a clear and urgent part of effective treatment of the whole child.

Don't Miss These Possible Signs of Seizures

- Sudden stop in motion without falling.
- Being very still.
- Suddenly stopping talking.
- Lip smacking.
- Eyelid flutters.
- Chewing or mouth motions.
- Finger rubbing.
- Small movements of both hands.
- Brief loss of attention.
- Inability to recall what you just said.
- Not being able to answer a question you know they know the answer to.
- An unfocused gaze.
- Looking through you.
- Appearing unable to hear you.
- Suddenly returning to prior activity when the seizure ends.
- Hyperventilation prior to any of these signs.

Gastrointestinal (GI) Disorders

Gastrointestinal complaints are common in children on the spectrum. The cause of GI distress and abnormalities has been a subject of debate, with genetics, diet, generalized inflammation, endocrine and neurotransmitter dysregulation, and anxiety and impaired parasympathetic activity posited as possible contributors.

There is a wide range of prevalence rates cited in the literature. This may reflect different assessment measures in evaluating GI symptoms in children with autism. Clinical reports and questionnaires rely on parent observations, which are subject to subjective interpretation. In a review examining studies dating back to 1980, the prevalence range of GI symptoms was cited as low as 9% and as high as 91%, with almost half of the children

> *I've had plenty of GI problems and lots of kids on the spectrum do, too. Sometimes there are easy solutions, but you have to identify the problem. For me, over-the-counter antacids really helped."*
> TEMPLE

having at least one GI problem. The median prevalence of constipation was 22.2%, and diarrhea had a median prevalence rate of 13.0% (Holingue et al., 2018).

In one review of journal articles from 2005 to 2017, the most common GI symptoms reported in children with autism were constipation, abdominal pain, diarrhea, acid reflux, and food selectivity. Of these, constipation was found to be the most common, occurring in 80% of the studies. Diarrhea was the second most common complaint, with 53% of the studies reporting this symptom (Lefter et al., 2020).

A study of 340 children and teens with a diagnosis of autism also found constipation to be the most common GI issue (65%) and also found stomachache or stomach pain in about half of the children (47.9%). Additionally, they found nausea (23.2%) and diarrhea (29.7%) occurring at rates higher than in typically developing children (Ferguson et al., 2019).

A study specifically focused on preschoolers found a higher percentage of autistic children having GI symptoms compared to typically developing children. Fulceri and colleagues (2016) found rates of 37.4% of preschoolers with a diagnosis of autism complained of gastrointestinal problems as compared to 14.8% of the controls. Constipation and "not eating" were the most common problem for both groups of children, but were rated as more severe in the ASD group (Fulceri et al., 2016).

Other GI symptoms in the autistic population (in addition to constipation and diarrhea), found using data from the UK General Practice Research Database, include bloating, acid reflux, painful bowel movement, abdominal pain, and vomiting. Chronic constipation was again the most prevalent problem, found in 22% of this group of children (Black et al., 2002).

Immune dysfunction is often hypothesized as the cause of many GI diseases. Autistic children with gastrointestinal symptoms may have higher rates of immune irregularities. Numerous studies have reported immune abnormalities and inflammatory profiles in the majority of individuals with ASD. Decreased rates of specific subsets of T cells (which help regulate the gut) have been found in children on the spectrum, while increased rates of specific T cells (which are associated with inflammation) have been observed (Rose et al., 2020).

GI symptoms often coincide with both behavior problems and internalizing symptoms (Mannion & Leader, 2016). Correlations have been found between gastrointestinal problems and social withdrawal and stereotyped, repetitive, and ritualistic behavior (Lefter et al., 2019). Further, these investigators found that clusters of GI problems, anxiety, and autonomic dysfunction likely suggest and characterize subsets of the ASD population. A strong relationship between stress reactivity and GI problems was also found in another sample of 120 children with autism (Ferguson et al., 2019). Alvares et al. reported GI problems and sleep are also highly correlated in children with autism (Alvares et al., 2018) These researchers found that in a child with ASD, the presence of GI issues predicts sleep problems and vice versa, with an approximately twofold odds ratio in each direction.

A study of children at the University of Missouri Thompson Center for Autism and Neurodevelopmental Disorders found that young children with aggressive problem behaviors were 11.2% more likely to have co-occurring nausea. In older children, there were complex associations between GI symptoms and internalizing symptoms. Older children with higher anxiety were 11% more likely to experience constipation, but 9% less likely to experience stomachaches. Older children who exhibited more withdrawal were 10.9% more likely to experience stomachaches, but 8.7% less likely to experience constipation. Older children reporting more somatic complaints in general were 11.4% more likely to experience nausea and 11.5% more likely to experience stomachaches (Lefter et al., 2020).

This data points to the need for parents and professionals to realize the age of a child may partially determine how they express physiological pain or discomfort. In addition to variance in an individual child's temperament, there is an additional possible explanation for the difference in correlations between physiological and behavioral or emotional states of younger versus older children. The most direct way for young children to express invisible medical issues is to act out either in aggression toward others or in self-injurious behavior. This is especially true for preverbal children or those unable to express their pain with language. If their GI (or other) symptoms are not recognized or treated, over time these children may realize that externalized behaviors do not provide relief. At that point, they may keep their distress inside and begin to experience secondary anxiety, which feeds social withdrawal.

Underlying, undiagnosed GI problems in children of any age will likely present in outward manifestations (Mannion & Leader, 2014). Other studies have found a strong and significant relationship between GI symptoms and more episodes of irritability and hyperactivity along with social withdrawal (Chaidez et al., 2014), as well as anxiety and heightened sensory sensitivity (Mazurek et al., 2013).

In typically developing children, common lore suggests children may complain of stomachaches as a way to avoid school or other responsibilities. These complaints tend to be mild and they cease once the aversive situation is eliminated. Professionals and parents would be wise to assume autistic children are more likely to have genuine underlying medical issues when they complain of stomach issues.

A number of studies suggest a range of abnormal inflammatory responses that correlate with GI symptoms in children with autism (Tye et al., 2019). Increased or more severe restricted and repetitive behaviors have been correlated with measurably altered gut bacteria profiles in autistic children (Lefter et al., 2020). Additionally, there appear to be significant underlying differences in the gut and fecal metabolites of children with autism compared to typically developing children. In the latter group, gut microbes become more diverse as a child gets older. This does not happen in autistic children. The microbial environment within the gut can cause downstream effects throughout a child's body. Some possible impacts include differences in levels or regulation of neurotransmitters including serotonin and dopamine (Dan et al., 2020).

Other secondary problems, both behavioral and medical, can arise from GI abnormalities. Children who experience gastric distress while eating or digesting their food may begin to adjust their eating patterns. They may spit up or refuse all or certain kinds of food, even ones they used to like. They may gag, cough, or choke during or after swallowing. They may eat abnormally slowly. They may show unusual body postures while eating, such as arching their back or tilting their head. They may hold or push in their stomach while eating or put their fist into their mouth or bite their hands or wrists. Behavior problems may escalate at mealtime.

Some children may develop associated bowel and elimination problems. Bowel movements may look or smell unusual, be of unusual size, or be accompanied by mucus, phlegm, or blood. Constipation may cause a child to have pain with bowel movements. This pain may result in refusal to use the bathroom or to develop fear about having a bowel movement. In turn, this fear and avoidance can lead to holding their bowels until they soil themselves. They may stiffen or squeeze their buttocks or legs together when they feel the urge to defecate. Or they may rush to the bathroom to have a bowel movement. If they experience shame or frustration as a result of soiling after age 4 years, they may then engage in other behavior problems.

Medically, GI abnormalities can result in nutritional deficiencies. These insufficiencies can cascade into other medical problems. Possible signs of nutritional problems include loss of weight, tooth problems, delayed growth, decreased energy, and pale skin color.

There can be a reciprocal relationship between sensory sensitivity and GI problems. A child's eating behavior can be greatly influenced by their reaction to the taste or odor of food. What is a mild spice to a typically developing child may be overwhelming for an autistic child. The temperature that a meal is served at may be fine for one child and perceived as unbearably hot for another. What smells good to one child may make another with heightened or unusual smell perception nauseated. In addition to the basics of taste and odor, even the size, shape, color, or arrangement of food on a child's plate can cause strong reactions. For autistic children with a strong need for sameness, these variables may cause much more distress than parents or professionals realize. If a child is having problems with GI distress or problems associated with eating, the adults must experiment with both the actual food and with its presentation.

Assessing hidden GI problems is similar to assessing hidden pain. Professionals must rely on knowledge of the common ways children with autism might express their distress. Adults should recognize that many autistic children are not able to make sense of or verbalize internal discomfort. Its presence will often be signaled only by changes in behavior or emotional state. Underlying medical issues are more common in children on the spectrum than in their typically developing peers. Professionals working with them need to consistently watch for indirect signs of these conditions and alert both parents and appropriate allied professionals so that an evaluation can take place.

Margolis et al. described the development of a parent-report screen for common gastrointestinal disorders present in children with autism. The questionnaire was designed in 2005 by the Autism Speaks–Autism Treatment Network to assess signs and symptoms of three common GI problems. It specifically screened for constipation, diarrhea, and acid reflux disease. More recently, a brief 17-item screening tool was developed based on the original instrument. It examines the same three conditions and relies minimally on the child's ability to verbalize or localize GI pain. In a clinical sample of children with autism, this questionnaire identified those having one or more of these disorders with a sensitivity rate of 84%, a specificity rate of 43%, and a positive predictive value of 67% (Margolis et al., 2019).

To summarize, children with autism have significantly higher rates of gastrointestinal problems than typically developing children, and these issues in turn often result in secondary behavioral or emotional manifestations. Especially to those with autism, GI pain is often difficult for children to localize and describe, so recognition of these symptoms frequently falls to parents or professionals working with the child. When adults keep this common comorbid condition in mind when a child's behavior changes, it will increase that child's opportunity for appropriate treatment and improved quality of life.

Don't Miss These Possible Signs of GI Distress

- Stomach clutching, tilting head, or arching the back.
- Grimacing or moaning.
- Squeezing or stiffening of legs or buttocks.
- Unusual bowel movement size, frequency, or odor.
- Soiling of underwear.
- Rushing to the bathroom.
- Fear, delay, or avoidance of bowel movements.
- Diarrhea or constipation.
- Increased anxiety or acting out at mealtime.
- Gagging, coughing, or choking after swallowing.
- Putting fist in mouth or biting hands.

- Any increased self-injury.
- Unusual body movements at mealtime, snack time, or bathroom time.
- Increased repetitive or restrictive behavior.

Sleep

Sleep problems are a common complaint in children with autism. Cortese et al. conducted a systematic search of available studies on the epidemiology, diagnosis, and management of sleep problems in children and teens with autism (Cortese et al., 2020). Using a pooled prevalence rate, they found 13% of autistic children and teens experienced sleep disorders, compared to 3.7% of children and teens in the general population (Cortese et al., 2020). Other studies have found a wide range in prevalence rates (40–86%) of severe disorders of the sleep-wake cycle (Humphreys et al., 2014; Liu et al., 2006; Maski & Kothare, 2013; Richdale & Schreck, 2009). One study found insomnia was present in two-thirds of autistic children (Souders et al., 2017).

Up to 50% of caregivers and parents of children with autism frequently cite insomnia as a significant issue for their children (Miano & Ferri, 2010). Insomnia can include a variety of symptoms, including difficulty getting or staying asleep, waking during sleep, and not being able to get back to sleep once awake.

Numerous other factors can impede a child's sleep. Some are behavioral, with emotional triggers. These include resistance to going to bed, frequently getting up from bed, or refusal to sleep alone or in their own room. Other medical conditions such as teeth grinding, chronic congestion, or other disorders related to airway obstruction can also be unrecognized contributors. These problems can cause sleep apnea or snoring, each resulting in the child waking up. Lack of bladder control wakes some children from sleep.

Parasomnias impact some children on the spectrum. These disorders include nightmares, waking up screaming, making complex and disruptive movements during sleep, and dreams that cause the child to awaken. Some children with autism experience restless leg syndrome. All of these conditions interfere with duration and quality of sleep (Miano & Ferri, 2010).

Unrecognized sleep disorders can have a cascade effect. Sleep has a vital role in child development and serves multiple functions, including energy conservation, brain growth, memory consolidation, and cognition (Neumeyer et al., 2019). Sleep disorders impact daytime functioning in all realms. Children with inadequate good-quality sleep find it harder to learn: they experience impaired attention, focus, and recall. They are also impacted emotionally, frequently feeling anxious, depressed, or irritable. Clinicians working in behavior-analytic programs for children with ASD are often faced with problematic daytime behaviors that may be indicative of poor sleep (Abel et al., 2017).

Poor sleep makes it more difficult for children with autism to engage in successful social interactions, as they're more likely to get easily frustrated or discouraged. Poor sleep may heighten sensory sensitivity, and the child with poor sleep has fewer resources to cope with overwhelming incoming stimuli. With fewer resources, a child is

If I don't get my sleep, I'm in trouble.

I need to do regular exercise every single night before I go to bed. That helps me expend energy so I can sleep."

TEMPLE

more likely to have meltdowns and to exhibit repetitive, stereo-typed behaviors.

The impact of sleep problems extends past the child to their entire family. Caregivers awakened during the night will experience many of the same negative effects. A vicious cycle can be established—a sleep-deprived child and a sleep-deprived parent may trigger each other more quickly. Stress levels of mothers of autistic children with unresolved sleep issues are higher than those whose autistic children have no sleep impairment (Hoffman et al., 2008).

Whether transient or chronic, sleep disorders left unidentified wreak havoc with the autistic child. Cognitive and neurological functioning is negatively impacted (O'Brien & Gozal, 2004). Professionals working with an autistic child should regularly inquire about the child's sleep patterns. Any change in behavior or treatment progress calls for assessing current sleep patterns. The Pediatric Sleep Questionnaire can be used to assess sleep-disordered breathing, snoring, daytime sleepiness, and related behavioral problems (Chervin et al., 2000). The Children's Sleep Habits Questionnaire can be used specifically for school-aged children (Owens et al., 2000).

Autism and sleep disorders have a bidirectional relationship. They can each trigger or exacerbate elements of the other condition. Symptoms of autism, such as reduced sensitivity to the sleep-wake circadian system, perseverative thoughts or behaviors, anxiety, and environmental hypersensitivity can all make sleep problems more likely. Sensory discomforts such as being aversive to the texture of a sheet, hearing traffic that others don't notice, or being bothered by a streetlight, can be particularly interfering for a child with autism. These simple environmental factors should be the first place to look for clues to sleep problems.

Other physical or psychiatric distress can also lead to sleep disturbance. A child with unrecognized pain or gastric distress is unlikely to sleep well. A child having nocturnal seizures will generally wake up. A hyperactive or anxious child may find it difficult to get to sleep. A depressed child who is experiencing ruminative thoughts will likely have delayed sleep onset as well.

Remembering how sleep disorders can cause a cascade of effects and how they have a bidirectional relationship with other comorbid conditions is critical to the mindset of viewing the whole child. Professionals and parents who keep this in mind will be more likely to spot signs that a child is not sleeping well and will also be more apt to gather data on the possible consequences of that disturbance.

Don't Miss These Possible Signs of Sleep Disorder

- *Changes in mood:* increased irritability, apathy or anxiety.
- *Changes in social behavior:* increased aggression or withdrawal.
- *Changes in academic behavior or responses:* decreased attention, focus, retention, or compliance.
- *Sleepiness during the daytime:* yawning, rubbing eyes, closing eyes, putting head in hands or on desk, wanting to be on the floor, excess clinginess.
- *Changes in activity level:* hyperarousal or lethargy.
- *Changes in general behavior:* more meltdowns, increased self-injury or perseverate behaviors, lower frustration tolerance.

— *Changes in bedtime behaviors:* resistance to bedtime, anxiety about going to bed (possibly related to nightmares or bed-wetting due to sleep disturbance).

Summary

Children with autism usually contend with at least one of the medical conditions commonly associated with being on the spectrum. Because autistic children struggle to identify and verbalize (whether they are fully verbal, partially verbal, or nonverbal) bodily symptoms, it's easy to miss these conditions. When this happens, parents and professionals can mistake behaviors as central parts of a child's autism when those behaviors are actually signs of medical distress.

Recognizing and treating medical conditions in autistic children is also more complicated than for their typically developing peers because many children suffer from multiple problems. These issues often occur at the same time, and they are associated with greater impairment when occurring in children on the spectrum (Aldinger et al., 2015).

Thus, it's generally up to providers, educators, and parents to assess the presence of these conditions. Nonmedical providers play a vital role in questioning whether behaviors they observe could indicate pain or distress in a child. Professionals who are familiar with common signs of the most prevalent medical conditions associated with autism provide a significant benefit to the children with whom they work. If missed or left untreated, any of these issues can halt a child's progress and diminish their quality of life.

5

Know These Psychiatric Conditions Associated With Autism

Numerous studies have found that the majority of children on the spectrum qualify for a secondary psychiatric diagnosis. Prevalence rates are striking—estimates were as high as 90.5% in one study of 101 children aged 4.5–9.8 years (Salazar et al., 2015). Another found that 83% of the children assessed qualified for a psychiatric referral (Joshi et al., 2014). In epidemiological surveys or community clinic studies, the prevalence rates generally fall in the 70–75% range (De Bruin et al., 2007: Simonoff et al., 2008). Rates may be even higher, though, due to psychiatric symptoms being missed or viewed as a component of the child's autism instead of a separate condition (Marin et al., 2018; Meera et al., 2013). Across childhood and adolescence an estimated 40% of autistic children have two or more psychiatric conditions (Houghton, 2017).

In this mindset we will detail the most common psychiatric conditions associated with autism. As we did in the previous mindset, we will provide a list of warning signs you don't want to miss or ignore. Autistic children struggling with emotional and psychiatric symptoms are unlikely to disclose them to adults. It's up to adults to recognize signs of the most common psychological and psychiatric obstacles a child might face. We'll focus in this mindset on the most frequently occurring problems, which include attention deficit disorders, anxiety disorders, obsessive-compulsive disorder, depression, and post-traumatic disorder.

Attention Deficit Disorders

Rates of co-occurring autism and attention deficit disorder are high. Attention deficit hyperactivity disorder (ADHD) is the most frequently diagnosed co-occurring disorder in children with autism (Belardinelli & Raza, 2016). Four reviews reported the prevalence of co-occurring attention deficit hyperactivity disorder (ADHD) among children with autism and found rates ranging from 25.7% to 65% (Hedley & Uljarević, 2018; Lai et al., 2019; Lugo-Marín et al., 2019; Salazar et al., 2015). Twin studies show up to 72% of the co-variance of ADHD and autism symptoms can be explained by shared genetic factors (May, 2018).

New research using brain scans suggests there are underlying neurological similarities between autism and attention deficit hyperactivity disorder. The brain's cortical regions responsible for social communication show significantly similar behavior when either condition is present. One study found more similarities than differences between ASD and ADHD, even on an ASD-specific outcome measure. They concluded this supported a common underlying biology and that diagnostic boundaries between these two disorders are indistinct (Baribeau et al., 2019).

This fits with what has become known as the *generalist genes hypothesis*—the idea that the same set of genetic risk factors will influence symptoms across disorders (Plomin & Kovas, 2005). In one study of 1312 children who were twins, researchers found a set of generalist genes that influenced inattention, hyperactivity-impulsivity and autistic-like social-communication traits (Pinto et al., 2016).

With so many overlapping symptoms, teasing apart diagnostic markers can be difficult. For professionals who mostly confine their work to those with autism, a secondary diagnosis of attention deficit disorder can be missed because they attribute attentional symptoms – whether they are primarily characterized by impulsive or hyperactive behaviors, inattention, or a combination of the two - to the child's autism. This deprives the child of targeted interventions for their attention disorder.

Similarly, professionals who specialize in ADD/ADHD may miss the signs of a spectrum disorder. There is some evidence that children with less than severe autism symptoms may receive a diagnosis of ADHD prior to their autism being recognized (Shattuck et al., 2009). About half of the children who received a late ASD diagnosis had either been previously diagnosed with another neurodevelopmental disorder or had shown ADHD symptoms during their initial evaluation (Davidovitch et al., 2015; Jónsdóttir et al., 2011). These children's ASD diagnoses were delayed by approximately 1 to 3 years (Frenette et al., 2013; Miodovnik et al., 2015). One study also found gender differences, with boys with a preexisting ADHD diagnosis having an average 1.5-year delay in being diagnosed with autism, while girls experienced a 2.6-year delay (Kentrou et al., 2018).

Prior to starting treatment interventions, it is necessary for providers to recognize any impairments of attention that may impact a child's ability to learn, socialize, and regulate their emotions. Children diagnosed with both ASD and an attention disorder are likely to have greater treatment needs, as well as additional co-occurring conditions. In one study, dually diagnosed autistic children were most likely to have a combined hyperactive/impulsive and inattentive ADHD subtype (Zablotsky et al., 2017). This complex combination requires fine-tuned assessment and intervention.

Don't Miss These Possible Signs of an Attention Disorder

- Forgetfulness.
- Distractibility.
- Frequent daydreaming.
- Trouble following directions.
- Difficulty multitasking.
- Tantrums or meltdowns triggered by impatience or having made a mistake.
- Problems arising from lack of impulse control.
- Impaired ability to organize schoolwork or other things.
- Problems finishing a task unless it is very enjoyable.
- Social struggles due to impulsive or intrusive interactions or not being able to follow the rules of a game or activity.
- Academic reprimands due to excessive talking or motor activity or classroom interruptions.
- Learning problems caused by failure to focus, rather than intellectual deficits.
- Difficulty sitting still when required (at mealtime, during quiet activities, while doing independent classroom work).
- Problems waiting in line or waiting for a turn.
- Frequent nonproductive movements such as foot or hand jiggling, or squirming in one's seat.

- Needing to pick up objects and fiddle with them.
- Missing nonverbal cues due to overly focusing on one thing.
- Not being able to find things due to impairment in honing focus.
- Not understanding why one is in trouble, or not understanding the consequences of impulsivity.
- Tendency to play roughly and to take physical risks without awareness of the danger.

> *There's lots of crossover between autism and ADHD. I've talked to many parents whose child's diagnosis has been switched back and forth between the two. Over half of the kids with autism will have attention problems."*
> TEMPLE

Other Psychiatric Disorders

Autistic children commonly struggle with several other psychiatric conditions as well. As with attention deficit disorders, when symptoms of these problems go unrecognized and untreated, a child's daily quality of life is greatly impacted. Depression, anxiety, trauma, and other emotional challenges make it more difficult for a child to succeed either academically or socially. Understanding the patterns of psychiatric conditions associated with autism is a prerequisite for tailoring effective treatment plans that address the whole child.

While mood disorders and trauma-related symptoms cause suffering in many children on the spectrum, several studies have found these conditions are more common in autistic females. Symptoms may show up as early as ages 2–4 years (Kreiser & White, 2015; Nordahl et al., 2020; Solomon et al., 2012). These syndromes are also found more frequently in children with an enlarged amygdala, the brain structure responsible for emotional perception and regulation (Nordahl et al., 2020). Like attention disorders, it appears that trauma and mood disorders measurably correlate with a specific brain area.

A 2019 study used the Mini International Neuropsychiatric Interview (MINI) to assess autistic children, teens, and young adults for associated psychiatric disorders. In this research, 91% of autistic children and teens and 31% of young adults qualified for a diagnosis of one or more co-occuring DSM-IV diagnoses (Mosner et al., 2019). This test has shown to be valid and reliable and takes little time to administer (Sheehan et al., 2010).

Mood and Anxiety Disorders

Prevalence rates of mood disorders alongside autism seem to cluster around 10–15%. One study of over 21,000 adults on the spectrum found 18.8% of them also had a mood disorder (Lugo-Marín et al., 2019). Hudson et al., who reviewed 66 studies of autism and depressive disorders, found an average prevalence rate of 12.3% for current depressive symptoms, and 14.4% for lifetime prevalence. These studies either asked for ratings from observers, ratings from individuals with autism, or responses to standardized questionnaires. In the studies that used standardized assessments, rates for depression were 28.5% over a lifetime, and 15.3% for a current episode. Studies relying on self-report found a much higher prevalence: 48.6% lifetime, and 25.9% for a current episode (Hudson et al., 2019). These are striking differences and indicate the need for further study to determine the accuracy of self-report. In the meantime, it seems wise to use a combination of structured questionnaires plus self-report in screening for depression and other mood disorders. If discrepancies in reported symptoms occur between the two, discussing these differences with the autistic person is advisable.

Depression is even higher in autistic children with anxiety. One study looked at children with normal cognitive functioning who had a diagnosis of autism accompanied by elevated anxiety. More than 35% of these children reported clinical levels of depression, with girls reporting significantly higher levels of symptoms than boys. When the parents of these children were surveyed, the rates were higher yet. Over 75% of them thought their child showed signs of depression (Jussila et al., 2020). Even more disturbing, about one-third of these children reported having suicidal thoughts in the past, and 2.2% of them had current ideation. No gender differences were found in rates of suicidal ideation (Jussila et al., 2020). Clinical samples suggest that suicide occurs more frequently in high-functioning autism. Physical and sexual abuse, bullying, and changes in routine are precipitating events associated with suicide risk (Richa et al., 2014).

Children with autism also have elevated prevalence rates of other conditions within the diagnostic group collectively referred to as anxiety disorders. With the exception of panic disorder, rates of specific anxiety disorders on average occurred twice as often in children with autism (Costello et al., 2005). A meta-analysis of 31 studies of autistic children under the age of 18 years found almost 40% had at least one associated anxiety disorder. Nearly 30% of them qualified for a diagnosis of social phobia, and 16.6% met criteria for social anxiety disorder. The older the child, the more likely they received a diagnosis of generalized anxiety disorder (van Steensel, 2011) or agoraphobia (Salazar et al., 2015). These studies and others also found a correlation between higher intelligence and anxiety (Costello et al., 2005; Salazar et al., 2015).

Two researchers (Russell & Sofronoff, 2005) examined two groups of children: typically developing children with clinical signs of anxiety and children diagnosed with Asperger's disorder who had not been diagnosed with anxiety. The researchers found that even though the children with ASD had not come to the attention of professionals, they still showed similar scores on overall anxiety levels, as well as on six anxiety subscales. The parents of the autistic children reported higher ratings of overall anxiety, more obsessive-compulsive symptoms, and also more physical injury fears than the typically developing children with actual anxiety diagnoses.

Several other psychiatric or neuropsychiatric conditions may tend to occur in children with autism. Obsessive-compulsive disorder (OCD) is a specific anxiety disorder associated with autism at rates above that found those in the general population. A 2019 study found that 22% of autistic children (as compared to just over 2% of the general population) are likely to experience OCD at some point in their life (Hollocks et al., 2019). Tourette's syndrome and other tic disorders are also conditions associated with autism, and they require targeted intervention separate from those for the child's autism (Kalyva et al., 2016). Eating disorders can also be associated with autism, but much more research is needed. So far, it appears that eating disorders can evolve either from symptoms of autism or other psychiatric issues linked to autism (Nickel et al., 2019).

> *An anxious kid can't learn. You have to figure out whether something in the environment is making the kid anxious, or if their nervous system is just overaroused. Sometimes a low dose of an antidepressant (which is used for anxiety, too) really helps. It did for me."*
> TEMPLE

Researchers have also explored the association between schizophrenia and ASD, but the findings are inconsistent. One systematic meta-analysis of epidemiological studies included

1,950,113 individuals with schizophrenia and 14,945 individuals with autism. A random effects model was chosen to synthesize the effect sizes of individual studies. Results indicated that the prevalence rate of schizophrenia was significantly higher in individuals with autism than in controls (Zheng et al., 2018).

When both autism and anxiety are present in a child, either condition may exacerbate symptoms of the other diagnosis. An anxious child, whether autistic or neurotypical, is likely to have a lower trigger point for both frustration and overstimulation. Depending on each child's unique coping style, challenges may result in externalizing behaviors, such as aggression or meltdowns, or internalizing behaviors, such as withdrawal or rumination.

To formulate help for a child, it's important to differentiate between behaviors arising from aspects of autism versus from a separate anxiety disorder. Consider that many autistic children lack the insight or language needed to accurately report their internal experiences. Moreover, some questions on standard testing instruments can equally apply to a child's anxiety or autism. For example, asking, "Do you have problems speaking in front of others?" doesn't discriminate between an anxiety disorder and a social communication impairment. In-depth analysis of triggers, and more specific questions that highlight conditions under which symptoms occur, help discern the origin of symptoms and guide subsequent interventions.

A major key to discerning a mood disorder from inherent manifestations of autism is noticing changes in a particular child. For example, lack of facial expression may be the norm for one child and have no relationship to depression. For another child, who typically shows a range of facial expressions, an absence of these usual repertoire of expressions requires further assessment.

Don't Miss These Possible Signs of a Mood Disorder

- Withdrawal from or lack of interest in usual activities.
- Decreased use of language or refusal to talk in front of others or at school.
- Language marked by negative, pessimistic content.
- Statements about death or dying.
- Increased clinginess or problems being apart from a parent or home.
- Resistance or refusal to go to school or participate in therapeutic activities.
- Changes in sleep patterns, including sleeping more or nightmares.
- Changes in eating habits.
- Complaints of headaches, stomachaches, or other vague aches and pains.
- Changes in bowel habits.
- Voiced worries about the future or asking repeated questions about the future.
- Fear of being alone.
- Frequent sadness, tearfulness, or crying.
- Voiced hopelessness or helplessness.
- Statements indicating a pervasive sense of guilt.
- Decreased self-confidence or willingness to try new things.
- Increased perfectionism or self-criticism.
- New complaints of being picked on (by a parent or professional who has not changed their behavior).
- Decreased energy or complaints of tiredness or boredom.
- Increased desire to be alone or increased time behind closed doors.

- Decreased willingness to spend time with other children.
- Negative changes in school performance or attendance.
- Decreased concentration, attention, or memory.
- Statements about wanting to run away or efforts to run away.
- Self-harm or statements about wanting to hurt oneself.
- Increased risk-taking or seeming to be oblivious to danger.
- Repetitive or new body movements, such as picking at skin or fingernails, tugging on hair or a body part, grinding teeth, cracking joints, or foot or hand tapping or jiggling.
- Increased irritability or grumpiness, meltdowns, or anger outbursts.
- Decreased patience.
- Increased indecisiveness.
- Increased or decreased appetite or weight.
- Inability to relax.
- Absence of emotional expression including flatness of voice tone or lack of facial expressions.
- Increased stereotypic behaviors, such as pacing, snapping fingers, rocking, hand flapping, spinning, head banging, or clapping.
- Increased unsolicited repetition of sounds or words (echolalia).
- Increased facial tics, such as eye blinking, eye scrunching, grimacing, or tongue movements.
- Heightened startle response.

Oppositional and Conduct Disorders

Oppositional and conduct disorders are also diagnosed in many children with autism. These diagnostic categories are problematic. They can be default diagnoses for children whose defiance and aggression have not responded to interventions. Labeling a child with either disorder is descriptive at best and provides no guidance for professionals or parents. The cause of the problematic behavior needs careful evaluation. It could be neurological, could stem from trauma, or could be the result of learned and reinforced maladaptive patterns of behavior. For example, a child who experiences rage that he cannot inhibit may have an overreactive amygdala, may be acting out aggression they have endured against themselves, or may be repeating behaviors observed and learned in their family. The source of behavior is the best guide to intervention.

> *Oppositional and defiant disorder labels are what I call 'garbage labels.'*
> *Kids get these labels when adults don't understand their behaviors or know how to help them. Instead of finding out what the real problem is, they just toss these labels around."*
> TEMPLE

One simple intervention that often helps children who are argumentative or defiant is to give them choices instead of demanding they do something. This increases a sense of control, and builds decision-making skills. It also usually decreases a child's need to assert opposition, which may just be their way of claiming autonomy. All people, children included, need choices.

Post-Traumatic Stress Disorder (PTSD)

Post-traumatic stress disorder (PTSD) is just beginning to be studied in autistic children. Kids on the spectrum are frequently exposed to potentially traumatic and other frightening experiences (Hoover et al., 2019; Kerns et al., 2015). Researchers have so far found discrepancies in PTSD prevalence rates in this population. One systematic review of the literature showed that children and teens with autism had similar, or higher, prevalence rates of PTSD compared to the general population (Rumball, 2019). Another analysis of the literature, however, found that the caregivers of children with autism or other developmental disorders were significantly less likely to report the child had been exposed to trauma than parents of typically developing children. The same study found clinicians were less likely to diagnosis PTSD in children with autism (Hoch & Youssef, 2020).

> *Autistic kids are bullied all the time. Teachers can help by talking to the kids in the classroom and explaining how Johnny is different in some ways, but mainly just a regular kid."*
> TEMPLE

When autistic kids are traumatized, the most frequent source of that trauma is bullying. Children with autism are two to three times more likely to be victims than their typically developing siblings or other typically developing children. Notably, it appears that autism carries particular and specific risks for bullying. Children with other disabilities did not show tremendously heightened risk (Hoover & Kaufman, 2018; Maclean et al., 2017; Maïano et al., 2016; Zeedyk et al., 2014).

Berg and colleagues (2016) examined incidents of adverse conditions (which did not necessarily meet diagnostic criteria for PTSD) and found numerous categories of negative experiences more prevalent in autistic children than typically developing peers. These researchers used 2011–2012 surveys from the National Center for Health Statistics of the Centers for Disease Control and Prevention, tallying interview data from over 95,000 parents, about 1600 of them with autistic children. Significant disparities in exposure to adverse child experiences were found in four areas, even after controlling for poverty and household moves. These disparities were: neighborhood violence, parental divorce, mental illness, and substance abuse. The children also had higher cumulative adverse event scores and were twice as likely to experience four or more adverse childhood experiences than non-autistic children. The study also found that children with moderate to severe autism symptoms were at greater risk for adverse events than those with mild symptoms.

It is possible that parents and professionals are missing signs of trauma or adverse events in autistic children. Symptom overlap might also be contributing to lower reporting. For example, a hallmark trauma symptom is the presence of intrusive, recurring thoughts. In a child on the spectrum, a preoccupation with repetitive thoughts may be attributed to restricted or fixated interests inherent to autism.

Another common symptom after trauma or excessive stress is disturbed sleep. As already seen, this is a frequent problem for autistic children, so it may not be a change from their usual challenges and thus may not stand out to a parent or treatment provider. Even nightmares or night terrors may seem unremarkable in a child who routinely has disrupted and fraught sleep.

Another confounding factor may be the manner in which children with autism react to adversity or trauma. Typically developing children may be more likely to verbalize both their experiences and their distress. Children without language, or for whom language production is difficult, may instead act out or internalize their upset. They may also be less likely to seek emotional or social comforting.

Children with either social or communication impairments also may not be able to accurately recognize when they have been abused. If the perpetrator told them the behavior was acceptable, even older children with autism may not have the social or cognitive skills to see that it was not. If they were told to keep the behavior a secret, they may be even more likely than typically developing peers to take that as a literal command. This possibility is strengthened by the findings of one group of researchers who found that autistic youth had more difficulty identifying verbal inappropriateness (i.e., insults) in video scenes of social interactions, relative to typically developing peers (Loveland et al., 2001).

Many children with autism are accustomed to being bullied and victimized. The frequency and chronicity of these adverse experiences can have devastating impact. Some children never verbalize their experiences, or they even deny them out of fear or lack of social cognition. Enduring this type of ongoing stress affects the nervous system, leading to secondary somatic and emotional problems.

The neurological bases of autism may also contribute to risks of post-trauma disorders in children on the spectrum. Based on a review of the neuropsychobiological literature, one group of researchers suggest there may be a relationship between the structure of the amygdala and prefrontal cortex (areas important in the regulation of emotions), which in turn may impact how those with autism are impacted by trauma (Kerns et al., 2015).

Recognizing when children with autism have experienced adversity or trauma is particularly important because aspects of their autism can increase the subjective impact of these events. Children with less cognitive flexibility may be more prone to ruminate on past incidents, leading to greater levels of stress-related disorders. Danger of self-injury may increase for children who typically react to any stress with head banging, biting, or other harmful behaviors. Children who have a pattern of running away may default to this behavior after an experience of trauma.

Several studies have identified increased comorbid problems following trauma. Increased rates of anxiety, depression, and suicidality, along with regression in adaptive behavior, have all been found in traumatized autistic children (Bleil Walters et al., 2013; Copeland et al, 2007; Mayes et al., 2013; Mehtar & Mukaddes, 2011; Valenti et al., 2012). Increased levels of lethargy and irritability have also been found (Brenner et al., 2018), along with aggression, distractibility, and appetite disturbances in the autistic children who reported trauma compared to autistic children who did not (Mehtar & Mukkades, 2011).

Relying on autistic children, especially those with more severe language or cognitive impairment, to relate episodes of trauma or abuse may be unrealistic. Caregivers and professionals must recognize markers and follow up with interactions with the child, the family, and other professionals. Structured questionnaires and interviews are available to supplement in-depth interviews.

The Stress Survey Schedule for Persons with Autism and Other Developmental Disabilities was developed to assess for events that may be uniquely stressful to children with disabilities (Groden et al., 2001). Other tools, developed to measure trauma exposure and effects in children with intellectual disabilities, include the Lancaster and Northgate Trauma Scales (Wigham et al., 2014) and the Anxiety Disorders Interview Schedule-Children Intellectual Disabilities (Mevissen et al., 2016). These may be helpful with a subset of autistic children.

Researchers are also investigating the use of web-based touch screens to help autistic children report trauma exposure. One prototype for children able to respond to written and spoken English was piloted with 20 children diagnosed with autism and having a known trauma exposure. Seventy-five percent of these children had reported being teased, and 70% had reported being bullied. The measure was sensitive to the self-reports, and user satisfaction and reported ease of use was high.

> *Severe bullying is a real trauma.*
> *Kids with autism are really vulnerable, especially if they can't communicate verbally."*
> TEMPLE

Validity was assessed via comparisons with the UCLA Posttraumatic Stress Disorder Reaction Index for DSM-5 and analysis of participants' trauma exposures and symptoms (Hoover & Romero, 2019).

Don't Miss These Possible Signs of a Traumatized Child

- Regression in any area, including language, social communication, ability to attend and learn, or ability to regulate behavior.
- The sudden presence or increase in baseline of any negative emotion, including sadness, apathy, irritability, anger, anxiety, or fear.
- The sudden appearance or increase in baseline of any negative behavior, including acting out (e.g., aggression, meltdowns, self-injury) or internalizing behaviors (e.g., sulking, withdrawal, refusal to talk).

- A change in usual physical markers, including breathing rate, perspiration, skin temperature, somatic complaints.
- Aggression toward other children or animals.
- Destructive behaviors, including fire setting, property damage, or stealing.
- An increase in minor lying or lying about major things.
- Refusal to do usual activities, including attending school or therapy sessions.
- Refusal to go to any usual place, including others' homes, church, parks, doctor offices, certain rooms of the house, or specific areas of the school.
- Lack of interest in usual play activities, special interest topics, or friends.
- Presence or increase in weepiness or crying or any other sounds such as whimpering or moaning.
- Perseveration on a topic related to a specific person or place known to the child. This can also show up as repeated drawings.
- Perseveration on topics related to mistreatment or injustice.
- Perseveration on topics related to dangerous things (e.g., monsters, storms, floods, illness). Again, this can manifest as obsession with drawing any of these things.
- Acting out themes of violence, injury, or violation in play. Any playtime reenactments of abuse or trauma.
- Questions or comments about injury to the body or death.
- Changes in sleep behaviors, including bad dreams, resistance to bedtime, refusing to sleep with the light off, and refusal to sleep alone.

- Regression in toileting behavior, including bed-wetting, soiling, and resistance to using the bathroom.
- Changes in eating behaviors, including decreased or increased appetite or difficulty swallowing.
- Changes in response to touch, including increased resistance in the form of either aggression or withdrawal.
- Refusal to let you see any part of their body.
- Sudden refusal to undress in front of you.
- Changes in comfort-seeking behavior, including refusal to be comforted as usual (e.g., hugs, shoulder rubs) or increased need for comfort (e.g., clinging to you, repeatedly touching you).
- A marked startle response when surprised.
- Flinching, running away, or showing distress when approached.
- Resistance to having their back to you.
- Resistance to being alone or having you leave the room.
- Changes in hygiene, including resistance to bathing or dental care.
- Increase or sudden presence of motor or verbal tics.
- Increase or sudden presence of hair pulling, skin or nail picking, tugging at any body part.
- Increased stereotypic behaviors such as flapping, clapping, or spinning.
- Deterioration in school performance, including decreased attention, focus, or compliance or inability to follow instructions or work independently.
- A deterioration in memory.
- Sudden, abrupt changes in mood or behavior in the middle of an activity or quiet time.

- Seeming to be numb or unresponsive emotionally.
- Increase in impulsive or risk-taking behaviors.
- Engaging in clearly dangerous behaviors such as playing with fire, jumping from high places, or running full speed into objects.
- Not being able to remember, or refusal to talk about, a specific event or period of time.
- Presence or increase in self-critical statements, such as "I'm weak," or "I'm bad."
- Presence or increase in statements critical of others, such as "People are bad," "Nothing's fair."

Summary

A number of conditions in autistic children occur at rates significantly higher than in typically developing children. Assessment of these associated challenges is critically important both during the initial diagnostic procedures, as well as throughout a child's development. As part of a multidisciplinary approach to seeing and treating the whole child, parents and providers need to be mindful of the sometimes subtle or nuanced markers of these conditions. When it's available, evidence-based screening should be recommended for affected or vulnerable children.

Although the conditions may not be present in all individuals with autism, the overall increased risk of mortality in this population points to a need for heightened vigilance. Providers can inform family caregivers about how these conditions might affect their children and how to recognize changes in behaviors and emotions that may signal their presence.

The relationship between autism and associated conditions is complex and bidirectional. There can be a cascade effect, with the presence of one condition increasing the odds of a second emerging. In addition to the damage any condition can impart on its own, this cumulative process makes it even more vital that these children are identified.

For example, pain increases the odds of a child having disturbed sleep. If the pain is unrecognized and untreated, the child may develop an ongoing sleep disorder that is more difficult to remedy. In turn, sleep disorders themselves can increase the odds of medical or psychiatric conditions due to lowered immune health or daytime mood dysregulation.

Any of these associated conditions are likely to decrease functioning in multiple areas. A child with medical or psychological distress is less able to learn, socialize, or communicate. Impairment in any physical or emotional area can result in a cluster of symptoms and regression in other areas (Tye et al., 2019).

The high degree of interconnection between comorbid conditions necessitates that we assess children not only for an apparent condition, such as GI upset, but also for other conditions that may be contributing to the syndrome (Muskens et al., 2017). For example, instead of simply giving a child medicine for an upset stomach, their sleep and emotional state should also be assessed and addressed. It's possible their GI problems are better explained by these or other associated conditions that themselves require intervention. A child with diarrhea, for example, may also be a child with chronic anxiety or a child who has been traumatized.

The interconnection between conditions reflects interconnections between the body's regulatory systems. Alterations in one system often create changes in other systems. For example, it is possible that children with autism who have overreactive amygdalas will develop behavioral and emotional patterns that throw other systems out of a regulated state. If a child is in a frequent state of arousal, what began as a brain difference may then contribute to a metabolic or immune difference. Improvements in one system could potentially positively impact upon other regulatory systems (Irwin et al., 2016).

Providers and parents, not the child, will often be the first to notice a symptom of a comorbid condition. That symptom may be falsely attributed to an aspect of the child's autism, precluding a separate evaluation and appropriate treatment and alleviation. It takes informed and astute adult observers to override an autistic child's inability to sense and communicate their medical or psychiatric distress.

There is also a great need for pediatric providers who are fully informed both about the high prevalence rates of the discussed comorbidities, as well as how closely they are connected. Providers of medical and psychiatric services to children with autism need specialized knowledge and skill in order to be effective. As with educators and clinicians, they will serve children best if they embrace a whole child mindset and welcome information about all aspects of a child's life and experiences.

Autistic children grow into adults. If their comorbid conditions are not diagnosed and treated, their adult outcomes will be impacted. We know that adults with autism have significantly increased rates of all major psychiatric disorders including depression, anxiety, bipolar disorder, obsessive-compulsive disorder, schizophrenia, and suicide attempts (Vannucchi et al., 2014). In an analysis of over 1500 autistic adults insured by Kaiser Permanente Northern California between 2008 and 2012, it was found that nearly all medical conditions were significantly more common in adults with autism, including immune system disorders, gastrointestinal and sleep disorders, seizures, obesity, high cholesterol, hypertension, and diabetes. Less common conditions, such as stroke and Parkinson's disease, were also significantly more common among adults with autism (Croen et al., 2015). These rates could likely be lowered if childhood markers are recognized and symptoms are treated.

6

Prepare Kids for the Real World

The sixth mindset necessary to successfully navigate autism is to prepare children for the real world. The best interventions are designed to provide skills and information children can transfer and generalize for use in their daily lives. All children with autism, no matter how severely impacted, need and deserve tools that apply to ordinary life situations they may later encounter.

This mindset requires all professionals and parents to think ahead. Whether teaching, parenting, providing a specialized intervention, or offering counseling, adults helping an autistic child should always be mindful that the child eventually becomes an adult. When a child reaches that stage of life, they will have to interact in some capacity with others, and they will need meaningful daily activities. To prepare a child for that day, effective team members design treatments that provide a scaffold for stepping into situations likely to be encountered in adulthood.

Children on the spectrum often flounder once they leave school. A big reason for that is insufficient preparation for life after graduation. They're usually not ready to integrate into and find their own place in a less structured arena. Transition planning may not have been given priority in their IEP. It may have started too late, with not enough time for the teen to learn and retain skills. A pervasive lack of young adult transition resources is another big part of this poor outcome. When there are no programs for this age group, it's even more important that foundations for adulthood have been laid ahead of time.

Cognitive, motor, and emotional capabilities impact the degree to which a child can enter and immerse themselves in the wider world after school. The vast diversity across the spectrum dictates a wide range of interventions and goals. Nevertheless, most children will need certain basic competencies. Even if living in a residential facility, an individual who has been taught these skills will be more content and productive. Though some children may not enter the paid workplace or may never live on their own, they still benefit from direct instruction in simple tasks of daily living and simple emotional-regulation skills.

For a child who can't produce understandable speech, but has the cognitive capacity to communicate in other ways, preparation for the real world may mean learning to use adaptive technology. The earlier this starts, the more comfortable and proficient the person will be. There are still too many nonverbal children whose intelligence is unrecognized. They are unnecessarily trapped because no one has tried to find other ways they can express themselves. Lack of language does not have to mean a child cannot let someone know their needs.

We believe there are basic areas most children on the spectrum should master. Here are domains of daily living that deserve special attention.

Personal Hygiene and Self-Presentation

Self-care is not intrinsically a high priority for many children on the spectrum. These children need to be explicitly taught to recognize signs of inadequate or inappropriate self-care. For example, children need to know what bad breath and body odor are and how they impact others. They need to know how to recognize when their hair is dirty or when their clothes are soiled. Females need to be explicitly taught how to care for themselves during their menstrual cycles.

Hygiene activities can be easily incorporated into routines. Visual aids are helpful as reminders, and the child or teen can check off each item once it has been done. These visual tools must be posted at the site of the activity, not in some central location. Reminders for showering, washing hands and face, combing and shampooing hair, brushing teeth, and putting on deodorant go right on the bathroom mirror. The supplies necessary for each of these activities also have to be visible—not in a closet or drawer. Grouping items used together in one basket or container makes finding them and putting them away easier.

> *Don't assume a child, or even an adult, thinks about personal hygiene. Tell them directly if they have body odor.*
> *My boss had to tell me, and I'm glad he did."*
> TEMPLE

Another aspect of personal presentation is how we greet and physically interact with others. Children with autism may need to be explicitly taught some mannerisms that other children learn and internalize through observation. For example, by the time a child is past toddlerhood, most realize there are unspoken rules for how they can touch others. They know it's fine to run up and hug Grandma, but not the lady in the grocery store. They know they can't grab a stranger's hand. They realize they need to maintain some distance between themselves and the person to whom they are talking.

They also start to modulate their voices according to the situation. Most neurotypical children realize during their elementary school years (if not earlier) that voice volume has purpose and rules. They realize more volume is used when needed for others to hear them and is also allowable in celebratory situations such as cheering on a sports team. They learn that softer volume is the rule in places like churches, libraries, and museums. Children with autism often struggle with modulating the volume of their voice; they require guidance and practice in addition to knowing the rules.

Safety Skills

Children need to have a rudimentary understanding of what is dangerous. Some of these lessons, such as not running into the street or going off with a stranger, should start at a very early age. Children in elementary school are old enough to learn the meaning of basic visual safety signs such as stop signs, exit and entrance signs, toilet signs, streetlights, symbols for poison or electrical danger, and signs prohibiting entry. If children cannot read, they need to understand visuals such as signs with a hand's palm facing out to signal they must stop. Another example is a sign with a red circle with a slash across a picture. Kids needs to know this means they cannot do whatever the picture is, such as riding their bike where the sign is. These sorts of skills lend themselves instruction from social stories.

Children who are able to use the phone and know the rules for what is an emergency should be taught how and when to call 911 as soon as possible.

Professionals should not assume a child is incapable of learning a safety skill until they try to teach it. This instruction must be repeated and presented in multiple ways. One child might get it with a picture, another with repeated role-playing, and another with a bullet list of instructions. If a child cannot understand at one age, the instruction should be given again and again as they age. You never know when a child can suddenly comprehend a safety lesson.

Children who live independently and who get around on their own need many other safety skills. Examples include knowing to lock the door and closing windows each time they leave the house, how to use a door's peephole and rules for letting people in, and whom to call in urgent but not emergency situations. Knowing to call a parent when their toilet is stopped up or a window is broken are two practical examples. Having a backup person in addition to a parent (a neighbor is a great choice if they are the helpful sort) is advised, and their name and phone number should be prominently displayed.

Home Living Skills

Some autistic children perfectly capable of a variety of household chores are never given the opportunity to master them. Parents may be too focused on academic and social skills to take on the additional task of teaching a resistant child to do chores. Professionals should regard helping children learn practical living skills as a priority. When Debra Moore (the co-author of this text) counseled autistic children and teens, family sessions were integrated into the work so that everyone was clear on what roles each member, including the child, were responsible for. Weekly assignments were agreed upon, and the child and parent would report back on what went well and what needed adjustment. Moore found that parents seldom initiated chore allotment—if she had not introduced it as a crucial component of the child's growth, most of her clients would not have learned how to do basic household tasks.

Other specialists can easily integrate home chores into their work. Occupational and physical therapists can work on fine and gross motor skills by using real items from the child's home. Simple examples of using such items are folding clothes, learning to rake leaves, or mastering the ability to accurately measure a cup of water or safely lift a pan off the stove.

Children gain confidence by having responsibility equal to their ability. Younger children can learn to pick up and put away toys. Older children can set the table and later put the dishes in the dishwasher. As soon as they are able, children should learn to make their own bed and to clean up after themselves. Wiping down the area around the sink after brushing their teeth is one easy task that should become routine.

Be sure to rotate a child's regular chores so they learn a variety of tasks. One month they might be responsible for feeding the dog. Then, the next month, switch their job to brushing the dog, and then switch to walking the dog the month after that.

Don't get too caught up in basing chores on whether a child is likely to live independently. Often, that can't reliably be predicted when a child is young. If they are able to understand and physically carry out a household task, have them learn it. Even if they end up living in a group home or other facility that doesn't require they handle all the tasks they learned, they still benefit.

They learned not only the specific task, but also all the executive skills and cognitive steps needed to carry it out, such as initiating, sequencing, planning, and following through. Emotionally, they gained self-efficacy, pride in their accomplishment, and the feeling of being a valued member of their family.

Recreation, Leisure, and Hobby Skills

This category of skills is often overlooked, as though leisure activities are not important. Yet everyone needs interests that bring them pleasure and relaxation. Recreation also has a number of important secondary benefits: it's often an emotional regulator and helps improve mood; it may have built-in social benefits; and it can result in many health benefits such as weight control, cardiac health, and mobility. Being able to identify and engage in independent recreational and leisure activities also increases a person's independence and confidence.

Leisure skills can be built into standard interventions—they don't have to be introduced separately. For example, a speech and language pathologist can take a child outside and make a game of identifying, naming, and practicing the correct pronunciation of whatever is found in that environment (e.g., trees, birds, grass, sidewalk, sky, clouds). For some children, this will foster an appreciation of their neighborhood, and they may be more likely to take walks or to develop an interest in an aspect of their surroundings. This would be perfect, for example, for a child who is already interested in the weather.

Autistic children do not usually have the built-in wiring to successfully and spontaneously join others in a recreational activity. These skills need to be taught. The child needs to know how to approach others; how to take turns; how to handle mistakes and learning curves; and, if the activity is competitive, how to gracefully handle both winning and losing.

Whatever topic or activity a child is interested in can be channeled into a hobby (or a vocation in many cases). Say a child likes animated children's movies. That interest can be taken in a multitude of directions. A physical or occupational therapist can use the movements or action of a movie character to have the child practice motor skills. The motor skills can later be paired with lines from the movie. A creative speech and language pathologist can find ways to interlace the child's speech practice with the movie script. The child can be helped to put on a play for their parents or neighbors. Perhaps rudimentary costume accessories can be made, exposing the child to fabric and sewing or working with craft materials. The music of the movie score can be carefully listened to if the child is an auditory learner or has musical interest. Any of these explorations, woven into standard interventions, might lead to a hobby that becomes a beneficial part of that child's life.

Transportation Skills

Not all autistic individuals will have the cognitive skills to take public transportation on their own. Others can, with repeated exposure and explicit instruction, learn to ride the bus or subway. Once mastered, this often ends up being a regular routine that is no big deal. Still other individuals will learn to drive, opening a broad range of opportunities for self-sufficiency and employment.

Transportation can be daunting for several reasons. Public transportation spaces, such as bus stops or metro stations, can overwhelm the senses—they may be crowded, stinky, and full of surprises like sudden loud noises or last-minute changes in schedules.

There are also a host of other competencies someone learning to take public transportation may gain. They might have to learn how to buy a bus ticket or subway pass; how to navigate turnstiles, escalators, and automatic doors; and how to read schedules and signs. These are all great opportunities to gain confidence, as long as the person is not overwhelmed with too much at once.

Driving, in particular, can be extremely stressful, and instruction needs to progress very, very slowly. If hours of off-street practice are provided, though, many teens or young adults can master driving. They'll enjoy the freedom and benefit from the opportunities it brings. It's important that parents and providers be patient. They must realize there will need to be many carefully planned, graduated exposures for an autistic person. Anxiety, rather than cognitive or motor skill limitations, may be the most frequent barrier to driving.

> *If I hadn't learned to drive, I would never have been able to do the work I do. It took me longer than other kids to learn, but that's OK. I had to drive a long way to my aunt's mailbox every day and that got me the extensive practice I needed."*
> TEMPLE

Autistic teens or adults may say they don't want to learn to drive, but a wise adult has to determine if this is their anxiety talking. If it is, that can almost always be overcome with help from an experienced counselor or driving instructor familiar with autism.

Self-Advocacy and Communicating One's Needs

Every child, no matter how autism impacts them, needs to learn ways to express their needs and make their wishes known. Both verbal and nonverbal children need to know their basic rights. These rights need to be stated in specific language, pictures, or social stories, with concrete examples. Some of these rights include being fed, having appropriate clothing for the weather, not being intentionally physically hurt, and having the right to sleep undisturbed. These may seem like obvious rights, but they should be made explicit, because they may not occur to some children.

An example of teaching the right to wear appropriate clothes might be a social story with pictures of cold weather and a person wearing a heavy coat and rainy weather and the person wearing a raincoat and holding an umbrella. A picture of sunny weather could show sunglasses, a visor or light hat, and short sleeves. This social story could also be an opportunity to teach self-care in the form of asking for a cold glass of water on a hot day. These are simple, practical survival skills.

Many of a child's needs involve sensory overload. Children need to understand how to advocate for themselves when they are being overwhelmed. For example, they can be given scripts to follow that will help if they are subjected to overly loud noises. (We are assuming the child has also been taught through desensitization to cope with unavoidable stimuli.) Older children may not need a script; they can be taught ways to politely and appropriately request that others respect their sensory sensitivity. For example, individuals with autism who get nauseated around perfume need to know what to do when someone they have frequent contact with wears a heavy scent. Each situation a child might encounter cannot be predicted, of course, but general rules can be practiced. Children can learn phrases that come in handy in many situations. For example, they can be taught to say "Excuse me" to get someone's attention or to preface a request with "I'd like to ask if you could . . ."

Giving a child tools to let their needs be known gives them a sense of control over their environment. Without this, they are at risk for both physiological and emotional stress and dysregulation.

Money Skills

Children with the intellectual capacity to use money must be taught not only the arithmetic involved, but also a number of concepts and protocols. Recognizing coins and bills and counting change are only part of handling money. For those who are able to live independently, they must also know how to pay bills, to handle cashiers and banking, and to make wise choices in the supermarket. Children should be taught basics as soon as they are able to approach a cashier on their own to buy a simple item. The ability to handle money requires repeated practice. It can't wait until a young adult moves into his own place. How to handle money should be gradually taught over time.

Some individuals on the spectrum will also need to be explicitly taught how to literally handle money. Money is dirty—they need to know not to put it in their mouth. Money can be stolen—they need to know not to flash it in public, and they need to know where it's appropriate to keep extra money. They might also need help selecting a wallet or other type of holder for the money they carry with them.

College students on the spectrum may be living away from home but totally unprepared to manage their finances. Lack of experience combined with executive functioning deficits can result in disaster. Parents may learn their child has spent their entire monthly budget in the first week of the month or that they grossly overpaid for an item. On their own for the first time—and in a setting with little or no oversight—they may just go with the flow and purchase items others have, even if they don't particularly need or care about them. They may confuse owning things that others have with fitting in.

A final money-related skill that's often overlooked is knowing how to recognize and avoid financial scams. The autistic adult living on their own needs to know that offers will come in the mail that they should ignore. They need to know, for example, that they may get numerous offers of credit cards and that they do not have to respond to these offers. There was a young man Debra Moore worked with who thought that because his name appeared on the application, he had to complete it and send it back. Young adults can be helped to identify someone they can rely on to review any mail they don't understand. They also need to know that phone scams are common, and they must understand not to give out personal or financial information to strangers either in person or by phone or email.

Some scams can be anticipated, and pointed out to autistic teens (Cohen, 2013) These could include:

- If you get an email that looks like it is from your bank, and it asks for your account number, do not open any attachment, and do not answer the email.
- If you get an email from another country offering you

money if you help them transfer money from that country, delete the email.

- If someone asks you to keep their money, or deliver
  money to someone, or to cash a check from them,
  refuse to do it.
- If a salesperson or an email or an internet site says they
  have a great deal for you, but you must buy the item
  right away, do not buy that item.

All of these money-related skills can be integrated into other
interventions. Classes that teach financial skills are great, but
many autistic children will never get exposed to this sort of class.
Wise professionals and educators can instead integrate money lessons into other classes. If a child is introduced early and often to
these concepts, in age-appropriate ways, they will be at far less
risk down the road.

Community Awareness Skills

Whether a child eventually lives independently or in a group setting, they will belong to a community with norms, expectations,
and opportunities. It is necessary to make the rules and guidelines of that community explicit. Don't assume that someone on
the spectrum will pick up the unspoken rules simply by observing
others. For example, different communities may have very different customs and norms. Some of these are practical routines, such
as what day the trash is taken out and where it is put. There may
be rules saying if or for how long visitors can park in front of the
home. Many apartments specify whether and what kind of pets
are allowed. Many of these rules and expectations are provided

in writing. Others are more social and implicit, such as whether neighbors tend to stop by unannounced, or they borrow things from each other, or whether anyone cares if you have a backyard party with music. These sorts of social conventions are seldom made explicit; they evolve instead through indirect communication. Autistic individuals may need help learning these community expectations.

Even more basic, both children and adults have to realize that these sorts of community customs exist—starting with their own neighborhood, circle of family and friends, and the school playground. This concept can be taught as an "if . . . then" concept via social stories or other methods. It's important that children understand this as soon as they're cognitively able. They also need to understand that these customs are specific to different environments—what is deemed appropriate on the playground is unlikely to meet with approval in the classroom. Any educator or clinician can find opportunities to teach these concepts. For example, a reading teacher can select a book on the topic or ask a child questions about the communities to which they belong. The concept that they actually belong to a community will be foreign to many children.

Another important set of skills needed for successfully navigating any community is learning to deal with authorities. Children need to understand the purpose of police officers, the fire department, and ambulances and emergency personnel. This goes further than learning to call 911. It entails how to respond when these people talk to you or ask you questions. This is best taught through social stories and role-playing. If cognitively able, children need to know how to state their full name, age or birthday, parents' name, and address. They should have some form of identification on them. For young or verbally challenged individuals, this can be a formal ID bracelet or identification sewn into clothing. Teens and adults need a place where they routinely and consistently put their driver's license or ID card. Drivers also need to be aware that insurance and registration cards should be in their car at all times.

Few schools teach these types of daily living topics, and it may not occur to parents to make them explicit. If more than one professional is helping a child, they can together decide how to incorporate teaching these life skills into their work. In the best situation, each professional can tackle specific areas, and the others can be sure to reinforce those lessons. In situations in which the child has no team, one professional can talk with the parents to see who might be available to help. Often a grandparent, church member, retired neighbor, or even a peer can be tremendously useful.

Practical Preparation for a Vocation or Productive Activities

We set aside a separate section to discuss vocational preparation both because work (paid or unpaid) can be a major source of satisfaction for many autistic people and because we are generally failing to prepare autistic children for this critical arena. Too many otherwise capable young people leave high school without having acquired the habits necessary for successful employment or the skills needed to be part of today's workforce.

Some children with autism will remain unable to communicate or care for themselves and likely will never enter the workforce. Even these children, however, can grow into adults who can find satisfaction in creative, productive activities. Some of these individuals have specialized abilities, such as singing with perfect pitch or playing an instrument beautifully even with no training. Others can artistically replicate—often in exquisite detail—what they see. Even absent savant abilities, cognitive- and language-impaired individuals have interests that can be channeled into activities that add value and meaning to their daily lives.

Autism has historically been inaccurately equated with intellectual disability. This is partly because more severely impaired individuals are more obvious and make an impression on others. As we've recently come to regard autism as a spectrum, we've also come to better appreciate the large numbers of autistic individuals of average or above average intelligence. Studies in the last decade or so have found a wider range of intellectual functioning than previously recognized. Our capacity to prepare all autistic people for productive lives after childhood, however, hasn't yet caught up with this recent shift in perspective.

Encouraging all autistic people to find ways to express themselves and share their inner world with others is not dependent on language or intelligence as it's ordinarily measured. The abilities and interests of autistic kids often make themselves clear in very early childhood. These traits should be fostered, shaped, and included to whatever extent possible in educational and other treatment plans.

Two Examples of How Prevocational Aptitudes Can Show Up Early

Many children begin showing signs of interests and skills that can lead to lifelong pursuits even before they begin school. Some toddlers are obsessed with taking apart and successfully putting things back together. As long as they're safe, let them experiment and dismantle toys and other household items. Others show very early aptitude for drawing or painting or love to get their hands into modeling clay. Encourage them—they are learning motor and executive planning skills and gaining confidence and a sense of mastery. Some toddlers who are barely able to walk will stand in front of an easel, grasp a paintbrush, and thoroughly enjoy themselves. We profiled one such little girl in *The Loving Push* (Grandin & Moore, 2015). We showed her grinning ear to ear as she sat in front of her easel, pacifier in mouth, and still wearing pull-ups! Her mother kept her supplied with paint and paper and found ways for her to start selling simple cartoon drawings even as a child. This young woman ended up attending college to study graphic design, and she now regularly exhibits and sells her work.

Some early childhood interests go dormant but manage to reappear when a teen or young adult is searching for their place in the world. We also shared the story of Patrick in *The Loving Push*. As a toddler, Patrick's aunt noticed he gave voices to all his toys (not just the animals). She took a photo of him holding a toy in each chubby little hand, the two objects apparently having a conversation, as Patrick stared at them intently.

After high school, Patrick struggled, and he dropped out of community college after the first semester (Grandin & Moore, 2015). He floundered, and for a period of time he got way too heavily into video games. His aunt was determined to help him find a career path. She remembered how well he voiced his toys, and then one day riding in the car with her Patrick broke into a perfectly pitched rendition of "Maria" from *West Side Story*. She promptly signed him up for singing lessons. His teacher, who also did voice-overs, recognized his talent not only for singing, but also for mimicking.

Today, Patrick, who lives with his parents, has turned one room of the house into a professionally soundproofed voice-over studio with a variety of microphones. He's met and received advice from a well-known Hollywood voice-over artist and has landed a few paid jobs doing voice-overs for commercials and video games.

Keep a Child's Vocational Future in Mind With All Interventions

Educators and clinicians should always seek ways to integrate prevocational skills into lessons and treatments. Prevocational skills include all the habits necessary for successfully doing any kind of work. Even if a child never becomes employed, these skills will help them get along with others and gain a sense of self esteem.

Teaching a child positive habits is sometimes seen as less important than working on challenges, but they are just as necessary. For example, employers who hire workers with autism may be willing to adjust to many autistic characteristics. Especially if the employee isn't in a public role, employers may not care about repetitive behavior, for instance. They may not care that an employee has no interest in socializing with others. All workplaces, however, want employees who are honest, diligent, reliable, clean, and polite. These valuable traits and habits can offset traits that may cause an employer concern.

Here's an example of how a teacher can impart these values and behaviors in an elementary school setting. In addition to getting stars or other rewards for academic qualities such as good handwriting (which is no longer vital for success), a teacher can give praise and concrete awards for putting away materials or supplies as soon as requested or not talking with one's mouth open while eating lunch.

A mental health counselor can easily role-play the appropriate way to disagree with someone or how to ask for assistance effectively. Minor inappropriate behaviors are often glaring in the workplace: examples include sneezing on others, picking your nose, or belching or passing gas in front of others. Some children need to be explicitly taught not to touch private body parts in public.

Few therapists focus on these sorts of behaviors. But think about it—which is likely to cause an employee with autism more problems—picking their nose in front of their boss or not being able to get their boss's joke? Some counselors spend too much time on trying to teach or fine-tune neurotypical skills that may not be necessary in many jobs.

Schools No Longer Prepare Kids for Work in the Trades

We've done a big disservice to many autistic kids when we removed instructions in the trades from our schools. Lots of girls and boys used to learn skills that they could use to get a job after high school. They may have been unnecessarily divided by gender, but at least the kids learned how to make things, whether for the home or a job.

Plenty of kids won't go to college, but that doesn't have to limit their ability to have a satisfying, productive work life. While we hear a lot about jobs being outsourced, there are still skilled trade positions going unfilled. Numerous trade jobs currently need workers who have specialized niche training, and these positions are expected to see increasing demand. Examples include mechanical insulators, cement and concrete mason workers, extraction workers such as oil and mineral drillers, electricians, dental hygienists, paralegals, and elevator mechanics (Rusk, 2020). If our youth graduate from high school with no skills other than being great at playing video games, it's going to be hard for them to find decent paying jobs. Our autistic kids don't usually interview well, and without specific, in-demand skills, they are at a disadvantage. If we can't get trades back in the schools, then we need to have parents or other adults introduce these kids to activities that can translate into jobs.

Get kids who are visual thinkers constructing things. Help them take things apart and figure out how to put them back together. Let them spend a day observing their local mechanic or welder or electrician. These are all jobs that can be done well by some on the spectrum. No one can know what will grab a kid's interest until that child is exposed to a variety of experiences.

> *I know plenty of older, successful folks on the spectrum. Some own a business. They started with little jobs in their town and they learned a trade. That was when schools still taught welding and shop. Taking out those real-world classes has hurt our kids."*
>
> TEMPLE

Kids who love to memorize facts about their favorite topic can be guided to careers where those facts matter. High school teachers can incorporate these interests into many class assignments. If, for example, a teenager is enamored of sports statistics, let them do their American History report on how the demographics and records in sports shifted in the 20th century. A teen who loves cooking can do a Biology report on plants that are used as herbs. The first young person may end up being a sports reporter; the second could end up working in a restaurant.

Occupational or physical therapists can use real-life settings to help children with mobility and coordination. It's easy to create a mock classroom with a chair and desk. The child can learn to cross their median, for example, by designing an intervention in which they have to arrange items on their desktop in a way that requires this maneuver. They can practice several motor skills by practicing sliding their chair under the desk in a straight and quiet way. Instead of using plain blocks or other equipment for stacking exercises, an OT can just as easily use books or unbreakable kitchen items. Tailoring interventions to the child's real world provides added value.

The Importance of Early Work Experience

Many autistic children graduate from high school having had no paid or unpaid work experience. This puts them at a great disadvantage. A prospective employer wants to see that a teen has at least done some volunteer or community service. If it was unpaid, they may even value it more, because it says something about a child's values.

One study followed teens with disabilities for 2 years after graduation from high school. They found that if the child had held a paid, community-based job while in high school, they were much more likely to have post-school employment success. Other factors associated with increased odds of employment included having a higher level of self-care skills, having higher social skills, having had more household responsibilities during adolescence, and having had parents with higher expectations (Carter & Lee, 2011).

Teachers and professionals are in a position to educate parents on the importance of getting their child working outside the family. Any mental health professional or guidance counselor working with an autistic child past elementary school should include prevocational exposure in their goals. It is more productive to talk about these goals in family meetings rather than just with the child. Parents often need as much reassurance as children that work is a reasonable goal. Many parents, having understandably taken on the role of protector of their child, are anxious about pushing them into the larger world.

> *When I was a teen, I cleaned horse stalls, painted signs, helped a local seamstress, and built carpentry projects. I learned how to do work assigned by other people. That is the number one most important skill our kids have to learn."*
> TEMPLE

Meetings focused on prevocational training give mothers and fathers a place to express their worries and concerns about their child's future. With guidance, they can move from fear-based thinking to realistic discussions of what their child is capable of work-wise. Many parents get overwhelmed about their child's future because they jump to thinking about an end goal, such as a paying job, and they imagine their child failing because the child has not yet developed the skills they'll need. Parents can learn to refocus on small steps their child can successfully master at their current age that are prerequisites for later, more advanced skills.

One Example of How a Project
Can Teach Multiple Skills

Though children with autism may need extra help, many of them can participate in community or church projects or school fund-raising activities. Teachers and counselors should always include autistic children in these activities, plus encourage their parents to provide added support and guidance. In turn, the parents should let any other professionals working with their child know about the project, so it can also be incorporated into their interventions.

For example, if fifth grader Daniel and his class are selling candy bars to raise money for a field trip, this can be usefully incorporated into his general academics and skill building. Here's an ideal way this could play out and the role each of Daniel's team members could play. The team could make up a list of skills that could be increased by mixing them into Daniel's candy-selling project. Here's a list of goals and what activities team members could enact to support those goals.

GOAL: Practice planning and sequencing.

ACTIVITIES: Daniel's teacher could have him list who his buyers might be in order to estimate how many candy bars he might sell. He could also make a list of the steps he'll have to take to make these sales.

GOAL: Practice social skills.

ACTIVITIES: Daniel's parents or therapist could create a social story and then use that story as the basis for role-play in how to approach others about buying a candy bar.

GOAL: Practice gross and fine motor skills.

ACTIVITIES: Daniel's PT or OT could help him learn proper ways to maintain balance while lifting boxes of candy. They can teach him ways to get closely packed bars out of their box and how to stack them for display. Perhaps they could make some "Candy For Sale" signs together.

GOAL: Practice arithmetic.

ACTIVITIES: Daniel's teacher can help him practice counting and making change. She can help him figure out how much profit he'll make on each candy bar and how much he'll make if he sells a certain number of them. She can also teach him how to figure out how much profit he will make per hour of his work.

GOAL: Practice appropriate self-presentation.

ACTIVITIES: Parents or any professional can help Daniel choosing how to present himself to customers. They can help him select which clothes to wear. He can learn social rituals like hand shaking.

GOAL: Practice language skills.

ACTIVITIES: If Daniel has a speech and language therapist, they can work together on appropriate voice tone and volume to use while selling the candy bars. If they are doing expressive or pragmatic language exercises, they can use a sales script as the content.

GOAL: Increase self-confidence.

ACTIVITIES: If Daniel has a counselor, they can work together to decrease any anxiety he has about this project. If he doesn't have a counselor, his parents, grandparents, or any caring adult can help him identify and talk about anything he might be nervous about. They can practice deep breathing, visualize successfully interacting with a customer, and frame expectations realistically.

GOAL: Increase safety awareness.

ACTIVITIES: Almost any team member (parents included) can use this project to help Daniel be more aware of safety issues. For example, if Daniel will be going door to door selling the candy bars, he can be taught how to safely cross streets, what different traffic signals mean, and how to not go into fenced yards with dogs. Assuming an adult will be accompanying Daniel, these situations are great real world learning opportunities.

GOAL: Increase self-advocacy.

ACTIVITIES: Daniel can practice how to ask for what he wants (to sell a candy bar) and how to handle

rejection appropriately. He may be selling with
a group of children (outside a grocery store for
example), and he can practice how to handle
any conflicts or bullying that may occur, first
by speaking up and then by asking an adult for
help if necessary.

Notice how this one project incorporated all the areas of skills that we discussed at the beginning of this mindset? Almost any task can be used to practice multiple skills. Educators and other professionals can turn any project into a rich learning experience. The skill building can be spread out among various adults helping the child. With everyone on board, the child is more likely to get excited about the project, to have more opportunities to repeatedly practice skills, and to generalize and maintain them.

Summary

Children with autism need preparation for the real world. Educators, professionals, and parents should design interventions and interactions with practical applications. The most effective academic and treatment settings recognize that children have to be able to transfer and generalize the lessons they learn. All autistic children—no matter where they are on the spectrum—need tools that apply to everyday situations they will encounter in life.

Everyone working with autistic children is wise to keep the child's future in mind. Thinking ahead is vital. We do a great disservice to kids if we postpone introducing them to a variety of age-appropriate tasks and activities. We need to place as much importance on life skills as on academic proficiency.

MINDSET 7

Focus On Strengths, Not Deficits

The seventh mindset required for helping autistic children reach their fullest potential is to focus on their strengths rather than their deficits. By definition, the diagnosis of a spectrum disorder highlights challenges and the ways in which those who meet diagnostic criteria are different from the norm. While we need diagnostic criteria, effective professionals remember their primary purpose is to help us identify those who require resources. The design of interventions can naturally spring from needs related to these deficits, but the design and implementation of those interventions should be based on the child's strengths, not the deficits.

The most effective educators and clinicians don't think in terms of what they see *wrong*. They don't focus on *fixing* a child. Instead, they stick to Mindset 1—seeing the whole child and appreciating their unique qualities. This is a necessary and natural foundation for the mindset we are elaborating on in this chapter. Building on and incorporating strengths in all interventions reflects both an acceptance of each child's interests and gifts and also a respect for the individuality of each person's life.

Strength-based professionals also tend to use different language than those who are deficit-based. Clinicians and teachers who think of children in terms of potential are more likely to forego terms like *symptoms* or *deficits* and instead use words like *characteristics, features*, and *differences*. They also avoid labeling children or their behaviors as normal or abnormal. They realize that these are relative terms based on what is statistically most common in a population. They recognize that a child does not fit the cultural or biological norm, but they perceive that child as atypical rather than abnormal. Likewise, when a child does fit the norm, they refer to that child as typical, not normal. When speaking specifically of neurological functioning, they may use the terms *neurotypical, typically developing*, or *non-autistic* to refer to a child developing and functioning in sync with most children.

Using these terms is not a question of being polite or politically correct. Their use reflects a perspective that our judgments about a child's behaviors, characteristics, and ways of processing information are based on what we are accustomed to and what occurs most often. Using these terms also shows a respect for the value of each child. The terminology used in front of children and families makes a difference.

Parents, especially of newly diagnosed children, often struggle as they adjust to the new labels their child has received. While their child has not changed because of a diagnosis—they are exactly the same child they were the day before receiving a label—it can be easy to begin viewing their child differently. They may begin to consciously or unconsciously look at their child as defective. Professionals who use deficit-based language reinforce this perspective. In contrast, those who use strength-based language provide a model of acceptance, affirmation, and hope.

For example, suppose we have Lena, a 9-year-old girl who has social skill challenges that are causing problems for both her and others. At school, she has no awareness of appropriate social distance, does not know how to take turns, and gives orders to her classmates. An unskilled teacher would focus on these problems: perhaps taking away privileges when they occur, calling Lena out in front of the other children, or talking about her using labels like *bossy*.

Over time, Lena may or may not decrease her problematic behaviors. Unfortunately, the best case scenario—one in which she does in fact exhibit them less frequently—will also be one in which Lena suffers negative consequences. While unintended by her teacher, Lena has now been singled out. This has probably put even more distance between her and her classmates.

Secondly, Lena now thinks of herself as someone who gets in trouble: someone who is bossy and bad. She was probably low in confidence to start. Reprimands, public embarrassment, and labeling most likely further eroded her self-esteem. Even if the specific deficits targeted by the teacher lessened, Lena is likely to channel her frustration and unhappiness into other areas. Perhaps she will boss her peers less, but she may, for example, start to passive-aggressively refuse to turn in her homework on time.

When we primarily focus on deficits, we neglect a child's primary need. That need is to build skills. Eliminating a problem without replacing it with newly learned productive behavior does not advance a child. If no replacement behavior is taught, that child will be left with a void. They will fill that void with another behavior of their choice. You do not want to let a child choose a replacement behavior! That is the job of an adult who can base the choice on what will be most useful to the child's growth.

Children—whether on the spectrum or not—naturally want to grow. They always prefer mastery to helplessness. They want to feel confident, not inept. If educators, professionals, and parents believe this, they will come naturally to harnessing these positive desires. Children want attention, and they want to please. When children seek negative attention, it's either because they do not possess the skills to do better, or they have internalized a self-image that tells them they are unworthy of approval or praise.

In addition to targeting deficits associated with autism, the best therapists and teachers give equal time to building up a child's sense of worth and mastery. They do this by searching for and building on the child's strengths. These may not be readily apparent, but they are always present.

Look for These Conditions That Can Obscure Strengths

Lack of Motivation

A child who does not see a payoff for engaging with you or with an activity may be apathetic. Sources of motivation vary among children. You can't assume praise, rewards, or treats motivate every child. Educators and professionals should both observe and also ask parents for input about a child's specific motivators. They usually know what gets and keeps their child's attention. This is another instance in which parents can save a professional time and effort if they are involved as an active member of the team.

Lack of Energy

Many children on the spectrum suffer from sleep disruption and disturbance that leaves them sleepy and unfocused during the day. A poor diet due to food restrictions or refusal can also cause fatigue and mental fogginess. Teachers who observe children nodding off are wise to find out if either of these issues is depleting a child's energy. Remedying these problems is recommended prior to proceeding to interventions.

Lack of Physical Comfort

The high prevalence of medical conditions associated with autism make it likely that some children will be in pain or distress while they are in the classroom or therapy setting, even though they do not communicate that to anyone. Watch for signs (as outlined in Mindset 4) that a child is hurting, and address that prior to working on identification of strengths.

Lack of Emotional Well-Being

A child's interests and abilities can easily be overshadowed by anxiety, depression, or any other mental health disturbance. You are unlikely to discover a child's strengths when they are in the midst of heightened anxiety. Depression smothers a child's ability to care about their usual interests, and a depressed child cannot function at their baseline capacity. Whether academic, social, or recreational, you will not see a child's potential if they are depressed. Emotional issues must be addressed before looking for a child's strengths.

> *My anxiety was so high I couldn't concentrate enough to show my strengths.*
> *When I started medication, it made a world of difference.*
> *If kids are suffering from depression or anxiety, you have to get them help."*
> TEMPLE

Lack of Trust

A child who does not trust their teacher or therapist may refuse to share information about their interests. They may downplay their abilities—only showing a small part of their knowledge or skill. If the child doesn't seem to have a trusting relationship with a professional, parents may have clues about the problem. Consult them and ask them to give you direct, unfiltered feedback. There may be ways you are approaching or interacting with their child that are preventing you from establishing rapport and trust.

Lack of Ability to Communicate

A child with limited or no language may not be able to convey their areas of strength. They may have rich, hidden inner worlds full of knowledge and curiosity. Educators and therapists should find communication mediums that do not require or rely primarily on language so the child can demonstrate their strengths. Children with autism can sometimes best communicate their needs or ideas by diagraming, drawing, gesturing or dramatizing, or using assisted technology. Every child deserves whatever help it takes to let them connect with others.

Lack of Sensory Regulation

A child who is overwhelmed by too much sensory stimulation is just hanging on. They are not functioning anywhere near potential. You can't expect their strengths to be visible when they are shut down in order to protect themselves from adverse incoming stimuli. Fix their environment so that they can relax and center themselves. Only then can you assess for areas of strength.

How to Bring Out a Child's Strengths

Educators, parents, and professionals have to create an environment that fosters the emergence of a child's strengths. We can't expect a child to recognize or tell us about their strengths. We also can't expect strengths to develop without assistance. Adults who care about a child must intentionally and proactively create situations that develop and grow areas of strength.

There are two primary ways to bring out a child's strengths. One is to build on any observable area of heightened ability or interest. The other is to expose a child to new activities and experiences so that previously untested or unobserved strengths can show up. For example, Temple's revolutionary designs for livestock processing probably would not have happened if she hadn't been exposed to farm animals.

Any child's interests arise from exposure and that interest evolves into action only if they have the tools needed to nurture the interest. Interest alone is not enough. Here's a typical scenario: one child with inherent artistic ability is never exposed to art, so their interest is never piqued. A different child is taken to museums or just shown books with different types of art. They realize it brings them pleasure and holds their interest. Perhaps their parents observe it calms them down. Even if they discover an interest, though, without being given art supplies, they cannot put that interest into action. Even two children equally exposed to art will probably end up very differently if one is given paint and given freedom to create whatever they want, while the other can only view the art of others.

Inherent strengths need nurturing. It is the rare child, autistic or not, who has the sustained drive necessary to develop an interest into a skill. Whether a child has mathematical, social, linguistic, or artistic strengths, these strengths will probably lie dormant and not turn into skills unless an adult recognizes and helps the child channel them.

There are many ways any adult can increase the odds that a child will hone interests and inherent strengths into useful skills:

- *Get the child into new environments.* Think about environments a child has never been in. If it's a child-friendly environment, how could you arrange a visit? Could it be part of an academic lesson? Could it relate to a topic you are addressing in a child's therapy? Would parents be open to taking the child? Examples could include taking an urban child to a free art exhibit for the first time, or for a suburban or city-bound child, taking them to a farm. If the child has never been in a factory, there are many free tours they could go on.

- *Tailor new exposures to the child.* The visit does not have to fit any prescribed limits. You can leave in the middle of a tour. You can just do a drive-by visit at first. Once you get creative about how to expose kids to new things, you can come up with a multitude of free places. The child does not need to have any enthusiasm for this visit—since they've never been exposed to the activity or place before, expecting interest is too much. Just take them.

- *Have other adults show a child new things.* Both parents and professionals can do this. Parents can expose Johnnie to Uncle Bob, who plays the piano. Bob can play one of Johnnie's favorite songs or show him how to play a few keys. They can play a game of guessing which note is higher of two notes. Even if the child protested at the beginning, if their eyes light up at the sound of the music, it's all worth it. You cannot predict how a child will react

Another child might surprise you and be interested if you take them to a neighbor's house while that neighbor is baking cookies. Maybe they can help stir the batter or have the job of identifying and passing ingredients. A PT or OT can use recipes and cooking (with play dough or even mud) as an exercise in fine and gross motor skills, sensory regulation, and turn taking. Any activity can be customized to a child so that skills are worked on at the same time that new experiences are being introduced. This has much more value than using objects that don't relate to broader life activities.

> *We have to get kids out of their bedrooms and into the world. It doesn't have to cost anything— plenty of companies, factories, and workplaces will show you around. You just have to ask."*
> TEMPLE

- *Talk about people, places, and things a child has never heard of.* Routinely talk in front of a child about subjects that are new to them. Perhaps the child will show absolutely no interest—that's fine. Again, the whole idea is that no one knows what a child will find interesting, and a child cannot become intrigued by something if they don't know it exists. Mentioning new ideas and facts in front of a child applies equally to school, therapy settings, recreational settings, and at home. Don't have expectations, but if a child does show a response or ask a question, give the child as much information as they seem to want. Too little, and a budding interest may fade away. Too much, and you may bore or overwhelm them. Revisit the topic later.

For example, a reading teacher who is using a book about trains could add in her own experience riding a train. She could bring in a photo or two and a map of where her trip was. She should tailor the information she shares to the specific child. For one child, who loves to make sounds, they could listen to audio clips from an internet search of different train whistles and learn why they are used. For a child who loves designs, she could download images of various train logos and learn where the trains are from. For a child who loves animated children's movies, she could find out which children's movies contain trains and find out more about one of the trains. In each instance, she takes the child's existing interest and builds on it by introducing one more idea.

- *Stretch a child's interests into new territory.* If you can already identify a child's interest, take that topic and expand it. Use it to expose the child to related areas that may also end as interests. Also use it to introduce the child to unrelated information by linking the interest to that new data.

For example, say Owen is interested in birds. Perhaps at this time he's only interested in spotting them. Help him learn to recognize visible differences among birds or in their calls and songs. Or show him internet videos of exotic birds not found where he lives. You may or may not have a budding birder or aviary specialist, but using birds as a jumping off point lets you build other strengths. In this example, Owen's speech and language therapist might be able to use bird songs as tools in improving his auditory perception, or his OT might use patterns of birds calling to each other to teach social turn taking.

Use Interests and Strengths to Minimize Problem Behaviors

Use a Child's Interests to Replace Undesirable Behavior

Instead of working simply to eliminate a problematic behavior, a skilled professional or parent aims to replace it with a desirable one. They seek to understand not only what triggers the problem, but also what substitute behavior would calm the child. Incorporating a child's already existing interest into interventions is a strength-based approach that has shown positive effects in multiple areas of a child's life (Harrop et al., 2018).

For instance, Josh, age 5 years, has started to bite himself. His occupational therapist (or his parents, if he does not have a therapist available) needs to keep track of when the biting occurs. Then they can track three other components: what happened just before Josh bit himself, what reaction Josh or others exhibited to the biting, and Josh's subsequent behavior.

Let's say they discover there are two instances when Josh routinely bites himself. One is within 30 minutes prior to dinnertime. This happens no matter what else is happening before the meal. Another is when the neighbor's dog starts barking.

These are very different triggers—one appears most likely due to hunger or eating problems, the other seems to be a sensory issue. Still, similar concepts guide how to prevent Josh's biting. We seek to eliminate what is causing him distress if possible or to help him cope better if it can't be removed. One of the ways we can help a child cope better is to direct them to activities they care about.

For example, Josh bit himself prior to dinner. He didn't have any eating issues or GI medical problems (these have to be eliminated first, as described in Mindset 4). He wasn't especially hungry, either. It turned out he was having a hard time waiting. He could tell when dinner was being prepared and it was hard for him to tolerate the preparation phase. He wanted what he wanted now!

Josh's dad decided to build in a ritual for Josh during this half-hour period. He knew Josh loved to copy simple shapes and that he could focus on this for more than 30 minutes. So each evening, Josh's dad either found a simple object for his son to copy or he drew a simple shape himself and let Josh replicate it. One evening, for instance, he put a book in front of Josh, and his son drew a rectangle. Another evening he put a lid, and Josh drew that. Not only did these activities distract Josh from his waiting frustration, but also they gave him extra practice with fine motor skills, plus a pleasurable surprise from his father. It also fostered continued interest in drawing, something Josh had taken to naturally.

Josh also bit himself when the neighbor's dog barked loudly. He didn't like surprise sounds, so first his heightened sensitivity and anxiety had to be addressed. His mom gradually lessened his fear by systematically introducing him to dogs and barking. She started with pictures and videos and then let him meet and pet the neighbor's friendly dog. She made up what she called a barking game in which the two of them pretended to be dogs and talked to each other. This made Josh laugh and gave him a sense of control, which is fundamental when you want to reduce a child's fear. However, there was no stopping Rex, the neighbor's dog, from occasional barking, so Josh had to learn to deal with that. His mom decided to pair the barking with an activity that Josh enjoyed. Any time Rex barking was especially loud or long, she got out some paper and let Josh use special markers to draw what the bark sounded like that day. Again, this shows the use of an interest and strength (Josh was probably a year or so ahead of his peers in artistic ability) to help minimize a problem.

Using Interests and Strengths During Adolescence

The teen years are fraught with anxiety and depression for many on the spectrum. Hormonal and body changes often produce distressing mood swings. Also, non-spectrum peers are developing new interests that hold little appeal to many autistic teens. These interests tend to center on whatever is popular—clothes, brands, music, celebrities, and trending media content. Most teens with autism would like to be accepted by their peers, but they just don't care about the latest fads, and they are not apt to pick up on subtle cues about what is "in" or "out." Few are willing to adjust their clothes or interests simply to fit in. They may look at typically developing teens with a mixture of confusion and disdain.

The pain of being an outcast is real and can lead to serious mental health problems. It's vital that parents, educators, and other professionals pay close attention to teens with autism. If they show signs of regression or increased anxiety, apathy, or depression, using their interests and strengths can help them feel better.

For example, Jenny is a 15-year-old who has been retreating to her room more and more. She spends hours online playing Sudoku and other games involving numbers. Math comes easily for Jenny and she doesn't have to think or feel when she's playing. She has started to fall behind on her schoolwork.

Jenny used to have one special friend, her next-door neighbor named Brittany. The girls would watch movies together (Jenny loved science fiction and Star Trek) and enjoyed playing board games. About a year ago, Brittany started hanging out with her other friends more often and spent less time with Jenny. When she did visit, she wanted to watch a different kind of movie—it had to have "cute guys" in it or star popular celebrities. Brittany wanted to show Jenny videos of how to apply makeup and curl her hair. Jenny thought these videos were stupid.

Jenny's parents could tell that their daughter missed Brittany and was starting to get depressed. They noticed she didn't seem excited about school anymore. In fact, she seemed unhappy most days.

Jenny was fortunate. She had a wise teacher who recognized the changes in his student. Mr. Rohnert called in Jenny's parents and they brainstormed how to help. Jenny's dad mentioned that he totally understood his daughter's "disgust" with all the emphasis on "reality shows and reality life." He said he'd never fit in either. Mr. Rohnert asked what had gotten him through high school (Jenny's dad was a successful tech engineer for their county). Jenny's dad said it was his high school chess group and spending time with his own dad on weekends learning computer code.

Mr. Rohnert guessed correctly that Jenny and her father had much in common. He asked her father if he'd be willing to teach Jenny chess, and if Jenny could join the school's new chess club. He asked Jenny's mom if she could help Jenny search for online groups of teens who also enjoyed activities involving numbers or websites that provided STEM activities.

Jenny's teacher wisely realized every teen needs to be around similar peers. It doesn't matter so much whether they are on the spectrum, but it is vital that they share interests. With encouragement, autistic teens gravitate to their strengths. Look for their interests and you usually find areas they excel in. Find other teens they can join in pursuing and expanding these interests. Teachers are in a great position to help put similar teens together on projects or in after-school activities.

Reframing Deficits: Finding Their Unintended Positive Consequences

A strength-based mindset ensures we are able to appreciate all facets of a child. Educators and professionals who follow this approach reject rigid definitions of "good" and "bad" characteristics. Instead, they recognize nuance, subtleties, and neutral or positive aspects of all behaviors.

Earlier we used an example of Lena, a 9-year-old who struggles socially. We described her problematic behaviors: not knowing how to take turns, intruding into the personal space of her peers, and tending to order her classmates around. These behaviors warrant attention because they're likely to interfere in the quality of Lena's life. They also

> *Adolescence was very hard for me.*
>
> *What saved me was finding others who had similar interests. We have to get kids that think alike together."*
> TEMPLE

deserve to be examined with other goals in mind besides their elimination. If her teacher or therapist or parent wants to more fully understand Lena, several questions can be posed. Why, and when, does Lena engage in these behaviors? What goals might she have in acting these ways? Do these patterns reflect other qualities in Lena that may be positive and serve her well if they are redirected?

There is a common ingredient in these three behaviors, and depending on one's perspective, that variable can be viewed as wholly "good," "neutral," or "bad." How we define a characteristic often depends on the persons doing the observing (what their values and goals are) and the context in which the behaviors appear. For example, if an overloaded classroom teacher with an already rowdy group of students is viewing Lena, the teacher's goal of reducing classroom conflict may override all other intentions. If a parent is embarrassed by school reports that mention these behaviors, they may be too stuck in their shame or anxiety about their child to see beyond the report. If an applied behavioral analysis (ABA) therapist was taught that their only goal is to eliminate behaviors that are labeled diagnostic deficits, she may only focus on interventions aimed to quash these behaviors.

A teacher, parent, or therapist who has a whole child and strength-based mindset will notice the common ingredient in these behaviors could be thought of—in another context—as assertiveness, determination, or single-mindedness. It's possible to hold both viewpoints in mind. Lena can still be helped to learn the skills of turn taking, to understand the concept of personal space, and to balance her own wants with the desires of others. Those assisting her can also genuinely appreciate that this young girl has the ability to energize herself to get her needs met. They can see that Lena cares enough to go after what she wants. They can see the potential advantage in a child wanting to play or participate enough that she can't wait her turn. They can appreciate long-term value in her desire to be close to other children. They can even envision times when Lena's ordering others around might serve her to effect change or make things happen.

Keeping these potential upsides of Lena's actions in mind will help those working with her do more than simply extinguish them. Appreciating the positive sides of Lena's behaviors will even help them go beyond learning replacement behaviors. Teachers and others who interact with Lena will view her personality in a more positive light overall. Children pick up on how we view them. Lena will sense their shift in perspective.

It's even more powerful if the adults in Lena's life explicitly explain to her that while she must learn to wait her turn, must not invade other's personal space, and must not order others about, not only are there better alternatives, but the drives behind these behaviors can be a good thing. Adults don't need to use words like "drives" of course, but Lena can learn that her feelings of excitement, impatience, and desire for results are acceptable and under the right circumstances even useful. Many children are capable of telling you what the "good" things are about things that get them in trouble!

This is the essence of seeing the whole child and appreciating more than a label. A mindset of uncovering, legitimizing, and channeling strengths brings out a child's full potential. It also honors their unique motivators, yearnings, and traits. It captures the innate complexity of each individual.

Clearly Communicate Your View of the Child to Parents

Some parents are naturals at seeing the best in their children. For these parents, if is often frustrating and sad when teachers or others only seem to perceive their child's misbehavior. If you are an educator or clinician stuck in seeing a child through a deficit model, these parents can help shift your perspective to one more helpful to the child. If you are mired in frustration, it is time to sit down with the child's parents and ask them directly to tell you what delights them about their child. They may have stories that reshape your narrative and free you to more accurately see all facets of their child.

Other parents are themselves trapped in the deficit model. This often arises from fear of what will become of their challenged child, and they become hypervigilant in an attempt to catch all bad behavior. Ultimately, this tends to erode a child's confidence and may paradoxically increase the unwanted behavior.

These parents need your guidance. You can help them see their child through fresh eyes so they begin to attend to strengths more than weaknesses. These anxious parents often need reassurance that focusing on a child's strengths does not take away from addressing struggles or unacceptable behavior. If they see that you are helping their child on both fronts, they will be stronger advocates for their child and more involved team members.

For example, Abe, age 12 years, had been diagnosed with autism when he was in first grade. He had an applied behavioral analysis (ABA) therapist and later a special education teacher for reading. Nevertheless, he continued to struggle in school—often off in his own inner world, not hearing his teacher's questions and instructions, and forgetting what he did hear. He talked during quiet periods and frequently left his seat. A subsequent evaluation resulted in Abe receiving a second diagnosis of Attention Deficit Hyperactivity Disorder (ADHD).

His parents, already worn down emotionally and financially, felt a surge in their anxiety and helplessness. They had come to view Abe in their words as rather "lazy" and "not having any common sense." Now that an actual diagnosis was applied, they felt their son was stuck with these characteristics for life. They wondered how he would ever find a place in the world.

Unfortunately, while Abe's evaluator had done a thorough job of describing the criteria their son met in order to get this diagnosis, the evaluator had not talked to them about positive characteristics that also tend to accompany children who struggle with sustaining attention. It would never have occurred to Abe's parents to think that there even were any positive aspects to this new development.

A more helpful evaluator would have explained how Abe's brain was likely wired and how that wiring brought both gifts and challenges. The evaluator could have spelled out how children who have a hard time sustaining attention in most situations also tend to have above average ability to concentrate when the subject grabs them. He could have drawn them a simple diagram showing how their son's brain needed more fuel in the form of intense incoming stimuli before it engaged. He could have described how once that level of arousal was reached, Abe was probably able to highly attend to what he cared about. The evaluator could have elicited examples from Abe's parents so they could internalize the information.

The evaluator also could have outlined specific strengths often found in people with ADHD. He could have told them they are often able to come up with novel solutions to problems because their minds wander creatively, or that their energy can lead to success and also can enthuse and motivate others, or that their quick thinking can lead them to try new things and enjoy life more fully than a less spontaneous person.

Telling Abe's parents about all sides of their son's behaviors wouldn't change the need for Abe to get tools for channeling his attention in order to find more academic success. Looking at strengths does not negate the reality of challenges. What it does is respect all parts of a child and recognize their authentic makeup. The difference is subtle but critical. Both children and their parents take the words of a professional to heart. They should always be given full and comprehensive information which includes both challenges and possibilities. With a strength-based approach, that occurs naturally.

How Educators and Clinicians Can Focus on Strengths, Not Deficits

Example One: The Educator and André

André is a third grader who is strong in math and is passionate about the space shuttle. He struggles, however, with sensory overload and is also frequently disruptive if put into a group to work on a project. His handwriting is illegible and he turns in crumpled, torn homework. When his stress level reaches a critical point, he often starts kicking things and slapping his legs, or he leaves the classroom.

Tables 7.1–7.6 show how educators might approach André depending if they are grounded in a strength-based versus a deficit-based way of viewing students.

TABLE 7.1　André Is Highly Focused on Science and the Space Shuttle

Situation	Strength-Based Perspective of André	Deficit-Based Perspective of André
The Perspective	André is a motivated student pursuing a passion.	André is an obsessive student wasting time.
The Action	Embed André's special interest in classroom work.	Redirect André to other topics. Reprimand André.
Examples	During a learning module on the earth's water, André is assigned the task of telling the rest of the class how the space shuttle uses water.	During the earth's water module, André is assigned to a group making a map of the oceans. No consideration is given to André's lack of fine motor skill.
The Words	"I love your enthusiasm for scientific information!" "I think I can learn more about the space shuttle from you." "What a wonderful part of you, André!"	"Pay attention, we're talking about something else now." "Focus, André!" "Can't you think of anything else?"
The Effects	André feels valued, respected, and accepted. His confidence is bolstered. His mood brightens.	André feels dismissed, unimportant, and unaccepted for who he is and what he cares about. He withdraws or become aggressive. His mood deteriorates.

TABLE 7.2 André Has Horrible Handwriting

Situation	Strength-Based Perspective of André	Deficit-Based Perspective of André
The Perspective	André's brain is likely not wired for good fine motor performance.	André doesn't work hard enough on his writing. He is sloppy and needs to slow down.
The Action	Refer André to a PT to see if working on his handwriting is indicated. If not, make accommodations.	Increase focus on André's handwriting with the goal of improving it.
Examples	Allow André to print, use larger lined paper, or do homework on the computer.	Assign extra handwriting practice. Reduce points awarded on tasks if handwriting is poor.
The Words	"I know handwriting is difficult for you." "Let's find a way for you to concentrate on learning the information, not worrying about your writing."	"I know you can do better." "This is so messy!" "It's not that hard."
The Effects	André worries less. He can focus on his assignments easier. His relationship with his teacher is strengthened.	André starts to dread homework and "forgets" to turn it in. André is mad at his teacher.

TABLE 7.3 André's Homework Papers Are Often Crumpled and Torn

Situation	Strength-Based Perspective of André	Deficit-Based Perspective of André
The Perspective	André needs help with organization. Facts are more important to André than presentation.	André is careless. André is just being a boy. André doesn't try.
The Action	Assess whether organizational challenges are pervasive. Consider whether André is struggling with undiagnosed ADD/ADHD. Develop strategies to help André.	Mark André's work down if his papers are a mess. Give up expecting neater papers, yet convey to André that you expect better.
Examples	Refer André to the school psychologist for evaluation. Have his parents get him a stiff folder and have them check to see if all his papers have been put in it each evening. Make sure he puts all papers given out in the classroom into it, not just stuffed into his backpack. Consider whether André could send his work in via computer.	Make André redo his work if his papers are torn or crumpled. Roll your eyes at André when he turns in messy work.
The Words	"I want to help you find a way to keep your papers as neat as possible. I love reading your homework and don't want to miss anything because the paper is torn or crumpled."	"This is unacceptable, André." "We don't turn papers in like that!"
The Effects	André realizes his teacher wants to help. André knows neatness is important, but that his acceptance is not based on the condition of his paperwork.	André once again feels rejected and not good enough.

TABLE 7.4 André Struggles When Put into Group Situations

Situation	Strength-Based Perspective of André	Deficit-Based Perspective of André
The Perspective	André lacks either the social skills necessary to work in a group or he just prefers to work alone.	André is unfriendly. André is unpopular.
The Action	Find ways to balance individual and group work. If group projects are necessary, make accommodations that increase André's odds of success.	Continue to randomly assign André to groups. Reprimand him if he does not participate.
Examples	Pair André with another student with similar interests and cognitive abilities. Consider whether social skills training would help André. When he has to be in a larger group, define roles explicitly.	André is put in a group of peers whose interests are foreign to him. André is left on his own to figure out his role in groups.
The Words	"It seems like you prefer working alone. What are some reasons you like that better?" "If you have to work with another student, which student would you prefer?"	"Everyone has to work together. You are no different." "André, you need to join in."
The Effects	André feels understood instead of weird.	André feels even more different from his peers. His peers resent him being in their group.

TABLE 7.5 André at Times Becomes Disruptive—Throwing Things or Crying

Situation	Strength-Based Perspective of André	Deficit-Based Perspective of André
The Perspective	André is overwhelmed. André needs help regulating himself.	André is out of control. André's behaviors are odd.
The Action	Assess André's environment for clues to what has triggered him. Design and give him self-regulation tools. Give him time to calm down as a support, not a reprimand.	Give André time out as a reprimand. Send André to the principal. Fail to equip André with strategies.
Examples	Give André a choice of strategies to use for self-soothing, such as squeezing a stress ball, taking a few minutes break in the back of the room, or practicing deep breathing.	Make André sit by the teacher's desk. Use André as an example of unacceptable classroom behaviors.
The Words	"I'm here to help you." "Could you use a break?" "It's OK to cry."	"Do you need help?" "You need to learn to control yourself." "Stop crying."
The Effects	André feels supported and his baseline stress level lessens. He is more likely to turn to his teacher for assistance.	Use André as an example of unacceptable classroom behaviors.

TABLE 7.6 André Is Specifically Triggered by Sensory Stimuli

Situation	Strength-Based Perspective of André	Deficit-Based Perspective of André
The Perspective	André is neurologically very sensitive to incoming stimuli and probably struggles daily with sensory sensitivity	André's sensory sensitivity is yet another issue that sets him apart from his peers and makes it difficult to accommodate his needs.
The Action	Assess the classroom to see if there are any sensory inputs that are triggering André. Attempt to mitigate them and also to give André tools to handle any that cannot be mitigated. Make adjustments based on his specific sensitivities.	Make minor, if any adjustments and assume this is a deficit André will have to learn to live with.
Examples	Institute quiet times when lights are turned off and students practice relaxation strategies. Place André's desk in the most sensory calm area of the classroom as long as it does not separate him. Warn André if there will be additional sensory input so he is not caught off guard (e.g., construction workers, fire drills, new paint that smells).	Tell André's peers he has a "problem" with being overly sensitive to things in an attempt to keep the classroom quieter.
The Words	"Maybe we can figure out some ways to make school more comfortable." "I will try to give you a head's up anytime there is going to be a loud noise" (or similar sensory assault). "Boy, this classroom gets really hectic sometimes, doesn't it, André?"	"It's not that loud André, and you're going to have to get used to it." "Try not to focus on it." "You sure are sensitive."
The Effects	André knows his teacher cares. He is more likely to tell her about sensory challenges. He is less likely to feel judged.	André may think he is "too sensitive" and feel shame. He is unlikely to inform h his teacher when he is under sensory assault.

Example Two: The Clinician and Mia

Now aged 13 years, Mia was diagnosed with autism when she was 7 years old. The psychologist who evaluated Mia rated her as functioning at level 2 (requiring substantial support). Mia lives at home with her parents and attends her neighborhood school, where she has been placed in special education classes since second grade. Her interests (present in some form since kindergarten age) include copying designs of buildings and playing online games that involve building things or challenge her to draw designs based on dimensions given.

When Mia was first assessed, her cognitive abilities were tested via the Wechsler Intelligence Scale for Children, Revised (WISC-V). This is one of the common instruments used to assess IQ for children her age. She obtained an IQ score of 82, which placed her in the "low average" range, but only a few points higher than "very low" range. Her evaluator's report emphasized Mia's refusal to answer many questions, the use of minimal language when she did respond, her lack of eye contact, and her hand flapping. Mia's scores on the specific WISC-V subtests measuring verbal abilities fell into either very low or extremely low ranges. Her scores on subtests measuring spatial memory and the ability to manipulate designs were average. While these differences were noted, the evaluator did not attempt to use other instruments that might have further assessed these relative strengths. There was also no informal conversation or play with Mia that focused on her interests.

Mia appears to have no interest in socializing, generally rebuffs others who approach her, and rarely initiates conversation. She makes odd sounds when drawing or playing online. If interrupted during these times, she often engages in hand flapping.

Following her initial assessment, Mia was placed into special education classes for every subject except art, the one period of the day when she joins mainstreamed classmates. Her academic performance is lackluster at best. She does not complete reading assignments and does not participate in class discussions. Her teacher noticed that when the class was working on a history module that included a slide show of famous American historical buildings, Mia perked up when Monticello appeared. She began copying the drawing from the slide show and continued working on it long past its disappearance from the screen. Her teacher asked her to please pay attention, but Mia ignored him. The teacher had no expectation that Mia might be able to function at a higher level.

Table 7.7 shows how both evaluators and treating clinicians might approach Mia depending if they come from a strength-based versus a deficit-based way of viewing students.

Research on The Effects of Strength-Based Assessments

One group of researchers designed a strength-informed assessment for autistic children with little or no spoken language and a functional level of 3 (requiring very substantial support). They discovered that the children achieved cognitive levels that exceeded judgments by conventional assessments. They also found that the children's results did not necessarily match the school placements that would ordinarily be recommended for a child with those results (Courchesne et al., 2015).

When these children were assessed using the WISC-IV, only 20% of them could complete even one subtest. Many evaluators

TABLE 7.7 How Strength-Based Versus Deficit-Based Approaches to Evaluations Differ

	How Strength-Based Versus Deficit-Based Approaches to Evaluations Differ	How Strength-Based Versus Deficit-Based Approaches to Evaluations Differ
Assessment Choice	Tests are selected based on their ability to accurately measure all areas of Mia's functioning, including her strengths.	Testing follows a standard protocol. If Mia is able to even partially complete a test, it is administered.
Testing Preparation	Prior to testing, the evaluator obtains a detailed developmental history and also asks about Mia's interests and strengths.	The evaluator may or may not obtain other data prior to testing. The evaluator may administer tests first, then get Mia's history.
Views on Information Processing Differences	The evaluator does not confuse a child's ability to convey information with how much information they possess or can process.	The evaluator recognizes that differences in information processing (both in taking in data and in expressing knowledge) do not equate to differences in intelligence. The goal is to do whatever necessary to enable a child to take in, digest, and respond to the cognitive tasks given.
Other Factors Given Consideration	Mia's motivation level, her energy the day of testing, and her mood.	These factors may be noticed but are not intentionally and consistently included either in preparing a child prior to testing or in interpreting results.

Testing Methods	The format of testing is customized to elicit Mia's best performance. Additional, less commonly used tests are added to the assessment to bring out strengths. Knowing Mia's interest in visual activities and her paucity of language, the evaluator would have added tests that did not rely on language and that measured visual thinking and spatial memory. Examples might have included the Raven's Colored Progressive Matrixes board form, the Embedded Figures Test or other visual search instruments.	Testing format follows standard protocol.
Examples	Technology such as voice-assist tools may be used. Evaluators may elect to employ computers, especially laptops with touch screens. Tasks that involve motor functioning but are not directly measuring that arena are adjusted so that results reflect cognitive ability, not motor challenges.	Testing generally requires children with any verbal ability to respond with their voice. Unless a child's motor functioning is grossly impaired, they are expected to try to manipulate objects if that is part of a test. Additional formats are generally not added.

continued

TABLE 7.7 *continued*

	How Strength-Based Versus Deficit-Based Approaches to Evaluations Differ	How Strength-Based Versus Deficit-Based Approaches to Evaluations Differ
The Words	"We're going to try a lot of different things today. Some may be easy. Some will be hard. Your job is to do your best even if it is hard. You're not expected to know all the answers or be able to do everything. No kids can do everything! This will show me what interests you have and what your strengths are."	"Today we're doing a number of tests. It's very important that you answer all the questions and stay focused."
The Effect On Mia's Performance	Mia feels less pressure and is likely to be able to concentrate better as a result of lower anxiety.	Mia feels nervous about how she will do and this may impair her focus.
Evaluation Report Emphasis	Differences between subtest scores are regarded as critical to understanding how to help a child. Relatively higher scores are viewed as clues to what strengths educators and others can build on. Working Memory scores are deemed very valuable for understanding how Mia can process and retain information. This is spelled out for classroom teachers and parents so they can better understand how to use the report to help Mia.	Subtest scores are reported, but may not be elaborated on other than to say for example, that Verbal and Performance Scores showed a significant difference. Working Memory scores are routinely reported but may not be explained or elaborated on. The report is regarded is primarily a diagnostic tool, not a source of information on how to help build Mia's strengths.

	Examples of how to use this information in education, therapy, and learning life skills is included in the report.	
Downstream Effects of Assessments	Anyone reading the report gets a sense of both the challenges and strengths of Mia. Her strengths are highlighted and explained so others can know how to best use them. With this information, Mia may be channeled into classes or activities that use these gifts.	Anyone reading the report will learn more about Mia's challenges than her strengths, and may subsequently focus disproportionally on her "deficits." Placement decisions may be guided by her lowest capacities.
Impact on Mia and her Family	Interests, passions, and behaviors may be reframed as the strengths they represent. More attention may be put on fostering their development. Mia's future may be viewed with more hope and a greater sense of possibility and options.	Challenges, weak areas, and "odd" behaviors may be noticed more often. Strengths may go unrecognized. Mia's future may be viewed with more anxiety, helplessness, and hopelessness. Mia and her family may not expect as much from her, and may not expose her to many growth-producing experiences.

would have subsequently labeled these youngsters untestable and cognitively severely limited. When the researchers used the alternate measures of the Raven's Colored Progressive Matrices board form (RCPM), the Children's Embedded Figures Test (CEFT), and a visual search task, 90% of these same children could complete at least two of the three tests. Over 80% of them finished all three measures.

Moreover, these children achieved scores that converted to IQs significantly higher than they could demonstrate on traditional verbal instruments. Over half of them (56.7%) performed at levels indicating IQs of 75 or above. Another 27% of them obtained scores indicating IQs above 100, a number that marks the 50th percentile on the WISC-IV. Strikingly, 10% of these barely verbal or nonverbal children judged to need "very substantial support" scored higher than 90% of neurotypical children their age.

Clearly, children similar to those in this study would be predicted to have similar strengths. Their cognitive abilities are likely to go unrecognized, however, without strength-based assessment. Their intelligence is highly likely to be underestimated. This misperception is apt to lead to depriving them of learning tasks that further develop their true potential. If evaluators investigate, discover, and engage knowledge of an autistic child's atypical cognitive strengths, a more accurate picture will emerge. This in turn will lead to more appropriate educational placement and learning activities.

The researchers noted that their study, due to its design, might not even have captured the full abilities of these children. They point out that minimally verbal autistic children are often trained in repetitive routines (e.g., stacking items by shape) that can lead to inflexibility when these approaches are not what a task calls for.

If they have been repeatedly working on doing something one way only, then it will likely be confusing or distressing for them if a task on an assessment measure calls for a different approach.

The researchers also note that the measures they used were narrow in scope and that adding others to highlight specific abilities would show even further cognitive capability. For example, some nonverbal or minimally verbal autistic children may have interest and above-average ability in areas such as numerical manipulation or memory, receptive vocabulary, or the ability to decode text. A thorough evaluation should include tasks that let a child demonstrate their abilities in specific areas of skill.

With all children, but particularly with those whose verbal communication is impaired, it is vital that examiners challenge them adequately. If a deficit-based examiner is focused on a child's particular weaknesses, the examiner may generalize and assume that child incapable of attempting certain tasks. In fact, there is some evidence that autistic children may do better on more complex tasks or more complex versions of certain tasks.

For example, researchers have found some autistic children obtain higher scores if tested on the adult Embedded Figures Test rather than the children's version (Schlooz & Hulstijn, 2014), if given more complex versus less complex tasks of mental rotation (Soulières, Zeffiro, et al., 2011) and if given tasks more abstract than concrete (Stevenson & Gernsbacher, 2013). Finally, there is also indication that on matrix reasoning problems, more complex rather than less complex examples more fairly assess some autistic children's potential (Soulières, Dawson, et al., 2009).

Now let's examine ways therapeutic work with autistic children will reflect the viewpoint of the clinician. As shown in Table 7.8, a strength-based approach considers the whole child, with empha-

TABLE 7.8 How Strength-Based versus Deficit-Based Approaches to Therapy Differ

	Strength-Based Evaluations	Deficit-Based Evaluations
The Reliance on Language	Interventions combine all senses and modes of communication. A child's way of processing information guides intervention.	Unless a child is completely nonverbal, therapy approaches often rely primarily on language, asking children to verbalize feelings.
The Formulation of Goals	Goals focus on strengthening positive behaviors and skill building.	Goals focus on elimination of behaviors deemed inappropriate.
The Role of the Child in Setting Goals	The child's goals are considered, elicited, and respected. Goals that originate from others (e.g., teachers, parents) are framed in ways that let the child see their benefits.	Goals are automatically adopted from recommendations in evaluations or other reports. They are not generally discussed with the child.
The Therapist's View of the Child	The therapist intentionally learns about the whole child and seeks information on their interests, passions and skills—no matter what brought them to therapy.	The therapist is guided by issues defined as problematic. Other parts of the child may be neglected or minimized.
How Mia's therapy might look	The therapist uses Mia's visual interests to help her build other skills. Her enjoyment of art and design, especially of historical building, can be incorporated into helping her feel more comfortable with others. The therapist will help her find others with shared or similar interests. That is where Mia can most successfully build her skills.	The therapist may work to decrease Mia's "odd" sounds and hand flapping. The therapist is unlikely to use Mia's drawing as part of the therapy because it is already viewed as an excessive preoccupation. Mia may be given assignments involving increased socializing, but it may not be targeted to shared interests.

Specific Examples of Therapy Activities	Mia's therapist could bring in books about renowned architects or the history of architecture. At first, Mia could simply point to pages she likes. This would establish rapport and decrease anxiety. Looking at a book together also gives Mia practice tolerating close physical proximity, which is part building her social skill repertoire.	Mia's therapist might ask her questions while sitting across from her. The therapist might use pictures in some tasks, but not think to choose ones related to Mia's passions. Some illustrations used may reflect activities Mia has zero interest in.
The Use of Visual Metaphors Related to Interests	Since Mia is a visual thinker, her therapist uses this asset by incorporating it into tasks. Adding interest-related images can boost Mia's learning and recall of therapeutic goals.	The therapist relies solely on verbal interaction or uses images that have no personal meaning or interest to Mia.
The Role of "Doing"	Mia's therapist is more interested in getting this client to actually do new things as opposed to talking about them. An increase in verbal output is viewed as a natural secondary effect of Mia's increased confidence and connection to the therapist and the therapy.	Mia's therapist may focus on getting her to talk more as one of the main goals. Even if this is successful, Mia may be saying more words, but feeling less engaged. It is unlikely an increase in fluency under these conditions will generalize.
The Effects of the Talking vs. Doing Approach	Mia is more likely to start to look forward to her therapy time. She is more likely to respond to simple questions because the question relates to something she is doing and enjoying.	Mia may clam up even more from a sense of pressure. Children know when someone disapproves of how they are, and they have a natural inclination to maintain integrity by clinging to old ways and resisting change.

continued

TABLE 7.8 *continued*

	Strength-Based Evaluations	Deficit-Based Evaluations
The Role and Use of Motivators and Rewards	Mia's genuine interests are used as motivators and rewards.	Rewards and motivators may be artificial and have little to do with Mia.
The Perspective on "Fitting In"	Mia's therapist does not prioritize Mia becoming more like her peers. The therapist genuinely appreciates Mia's unique qualities and facets.	Mia's therapist may try to get her invested in interests of her typically developing peers. This will serve to marginalize Mia even more.
Effects on the Child's Mood and Motivation	Mia will appreciate her therapist's interest in her passions and skills. Her motivation for all therapeutic tasks will likely be higher. If tasks generate anxiety (which usually happens when we try new things) Mia is more likely to tolerate the anxiety if the content interests her.	Mia may think her challenges are more important than her strengths and interests. She may become discouraged and motivation may decrease.
Effects on the Child's Ability to Learn New Skills	Mia can think more clearly, learn more easily, and remember more fully when therapy goals incorporate information she cares about.	Is Mia is unmotivated or anxious, her cognitive abilities will likely be hampered. Her working memory will be less efficient.
Effects on the Family	Mia's parents will be taught to work with her interests and strengths. They may gain greater appreciation for these aspects of their child.	Mia's parents may actually focus more on her "problems" now and give her less positive reinforcement.

sis on harnessing their interests, passions, and gifts to assist their progress and growth.

A Specific Example Using Cognitive Behavioral (CBT) Therapy

Table 7.9 is a specific example of how a strength-based and a deficit-based cognitive behavioral therapist might work with Mia. Note that the particular therapeutic approach, CBT, is the same (using thoughts and behaviors to produce change). Any branch of therapy can be used in a strength- or deficit-based format. The focus on building positive outcome versus reducing problems and purposefully incorporating a child's interests and skills into therapeutic tasks is what distinguishes a strength-based approach, not the choice of theoretical orientation.

Note that the goals are different. The strength-based goal entails building a skill. The deficit-based goal entails eliminating a behavior. The tools used in the deficit model are standard positive and negative reinforcers. There is nothing inherently problematic about using these, but they often mean little to autistic children. Plus, there are other reinforcers that are much more powerful to many children with autism. These reinforcers are items or activities directly related to their unique interests and abilities.

For example, in the strength-based example below, the therapist could incorporate information about the role of foundations in architecture to increase Mia's interest and motivation for learning relaxation skills. She could show Mia photographs of famous buildings and how they were built to withstand stress. Mia could learn that people need stress-handling foundations as well and she could be helped to visualize what these might be. Mia would probably easily understand this concept and she could likely appreciate the importance of including stress-reduction tools into her daily life. She already has respect for how architects build strong structures, so this would not be too much of a stretch or a foreign concept to her. She would be more likely to practice and remember tools such as calm breathing and intentional listening when she needs to weather social storms in the future.

TABLE 7.9 Strength-Based versus Deficit-Based Mindsets within a Cognitive Behavioral Therapy Approach

Strength-Based
— **Goal:** To remain more relaxed and interested when interacting with peers.
— **Tools:** Slow and regular breathing, concentrating on what the other person is saying.
— **Method:** Incorporation of Mia's interest: Visualizing and drawing a building, with emphasis of its foundation.
— **Application:** Helping Mia remember the two tools by linking them to visual cues in the drawing. For example, the poured concrete foundation could be her breath; the walls could be her brain listening and concentrating.
Deficit-Based
— **Goal:** To eliminate hand flapping in front of other kids.
— **Tools:** Rewarding reduction in hand flapping with stars. Reducing allowed time on computer if hand flapping is not decreased.
— **Method:** The therapist verbally relays the goals and tools and may simply expect Mia to figure out a method.
— **Alternate method:** Role-playing conversations and praising Mia when she does not flap her hands.

CBT is a useful way to help children replace negative, self-defeating narratives with positive, confidence-building ones. Kids with autism often share common self-defeating views of them-

selves. Examples include: "I'm weird," "If I stay away from people, I will be safe," "I can't trust people," or "I'll never fit in and
nobody will ever like me." A strength-based clinician validates
the child's concerns, wants to learn how the child arrived at these
beliefs (some will be able to verbalize this; others will not), and
empathizes with the distress these beliefs create.

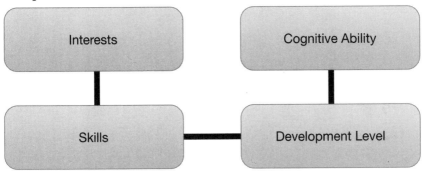

FIGURE 7.1 Strength-Based Interventions Must Be Matched To
These Characteristics of the Child

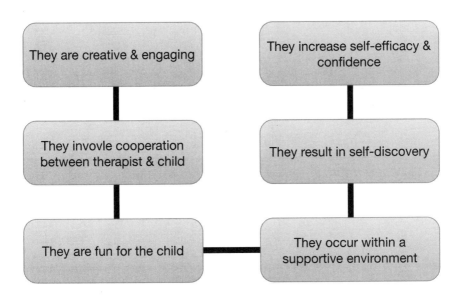

FIGURE 7.2 Primary Characteristics of Strength-Based Interventions

The therapist doesn't negate these beliefs, but instead seeks to discover times the child did not believe them. Often, these were times when the child—not surprisingly—was engaged in their special interest. This is important for the child to realize. It helps them further honor their passions and strengths. The therapist works along two parallel paths. The therapist helps the child use their interests to increase positive experiences that contradict their denigrating narratives. (If they can broaden the child's interests, there are even more opportunities to do this.) The therapist also helps the child recognize logical fallacies in their thinking and replace them with more accurate statements. Children with autism are often very responsive to this approach—perhaps more than typically developing children. Autistic children are frequently logical by nature. They embrace structure, scientific thinking, and facts. Using these traits, the therapist can engage the child in fact-finding that serves to modify inaccurate self-statements.

A Final Example: Helping Mia Increase Her Ability to Trust Appropriate People

Mia believes she can't trust people. A strength-based clinician helps her test that belief and gather real data. Mia's therapist can create experiments that teach her how to decide which people to trust and what information is appropriate to share with them. Mia can use her interest in historical buildings to experiment with finding out who is interested in her architectural drawings. Whom can she show them to and get a positive response? Who will make fun of them?

This exercise will probably generate anxiety. It should start with baby steps. Her family can be consulted to help select people. They could even choose a family member they know is not interested in the topic. The therapist, anticipating that not everyone will care about what Mia cares about, can help her prepare for negative encounters as well as more receptive ones. Role-playing (with the therapist doing most of the acting at the beginning) will help Mia rehearse short, simple statements to use in these situations.

During these more anxiety-provoking sessions, Mia's interests can be used as a powerful reward system. For example, Mia's courage in trying the experiment could be rewarded by her parents taking her on a field trip to a nearby historical building.

A child's interests can also be incorporated graphically to measure progress. In Mia's case, a building could be a useful metaphor for setting goals and noting achievements. She could choose to draw one of her favorite architectural designs. She and the therapist can compare the logical, stepwise design process of building with the similar process of building any skill. A picture will help Mia envision this.

Perhaps Mia and the therapist color in parts of the building as she progresses, starting with the foundation, then the walls, and eventually aiming for the roof and adornments.

Presenting behavioral and cognitive strategies visually is more likely to appeal to Mia than a conversation about those strategies. Using her preferred drawing and design tools (e.g., pencil, felt tip pen, templates, computer drawing programs) will further engage her. Like any child, she is more likely to remember and integrate learning when it occurs using multiple senses and during a state of attention.

As Mia makes progress, a strength-based therapist will always be sure she is aware of precisely how she has changed. This cements her progress and builds further confidence. The therapist will also show Mia how her new behavior can be generalized to other situations. For example, after completing the "Whom can I trust?" exercise, Mia could begin to investigate how to begin and end short conversations.

Summary

A strength-based evaluator or clinician helps a child by emphasizing and building on their natural interests and strengths. Challenges are given appropriate consideration, but strengths are viewed as the pathways to furthering a child's development and potential.

Strength-based evaluators learn as much as possible about a child prior to selecting specific testing instruments so that they use the tools that will elicit the most accurate picture of a child's abilities. They also prepare a child before starting any tests, so that the child is in the best position to relax, focus, and sustain motivation and attention.

Sometimes the interests of autistic children are uncommon or unusual for neurotypical children, but strength-based clinicians do not judge them negatively. Rather than viewing them as deficits or impediments to learning, they recognize these unique passions as gifts that reflect areas of cognitive strength and paths that can lead to a child reaching their full potential. Courchesne and her colleagues (2015) make an excellent point: in the typically developing child, isolated or single cognitive strengths are generally recognized and viewed worthy of development. This leads to "large eventual advantages via progressive access to more complex information and more demanding activities" (Courchesne et al., 2015).

The reports of strength-based evaluators not only fully discuss a child's interests, passions, and gifts, but also they elaborate on how these aspects can be used educationally and clinically. They give teachers, therapists, and families hope.

Strength-based clinicians incorporate creative, multisensory therapeutic approaches into their clinical work. They start with baby steps and build from there. They use a child's interests, passions, and gifts as motivators, anxiety reducers, and rewards. They amplify and make explicit these aspects of the child, so that both their client and their family can better see and appreciate them.

The clinician always helps the child use interests and strengths to solve problems. Metaphors, such as the need for foundations in both buildings and social interactions, are especially practical tools for many autistic children. By melding interests into their clinical work, the strength-based therapist's interactions with the child become intrinsically engaging rather than dull or aversive. The best strength-based therapists function not only as agents of effective change, but also of hope, resiliency, and empowerment.

We owe our children strength-based assessments and strength-based clinical interventions as the basis for fully appreciating the whole child. By working from this perspective, both educational plans and placements as well as clinical interventions will be better suited to bring out a child's true potential.

8

Work in the Growth Zone

The eighth mindset is a reminder that each child functions at their highest potential only when given the opportunity to learn and progress within their own, unique *growth zone*. Educators and clinicians who work from a whole child approach always search for this zone of optimal development. They first assess the child's internal state and their environment to be sure both are conducive to learning. Then they plan lessons or interventions to appropriately fit within each child's unique growth zone. Finally, they take steps to ensure their efforts have been successful by systematically reviewing and tracking the child's progress.

Let's define growth zone. This term refers to a set of conditions that, if met, maximize the chances that an educator or clinician will succeed in helping a child obtain desired growth. An analogy from gardening may be helpful. Gardeners consult zone maps, which indicate optimal growth zones for various plants. The maps show which areas are suited for successfully growing different plants, depending on their specific needs. Every plant has a set of conditions that promote optimal growth. You can't expect every plant to do well everywhere. They each need specific environments and conditions. If we want children to fully blossom, they, too, need to be firmly rooted in growth zones.

There are two factors that combine to create a growth zone. First, certain basic conditions must be present. For a gardener, at a minimum, these ingredients would include good soil, clean and adequate water, and enough sun. Additional gardening strategies may not be absolutely necessary for a regular garden, but to reach a true growth zone garden, they would need to be added. Including them greatly increases the odds of producing healthier, fuller growth. Examples might include using fertilizers, staking plants for support, and installing irrigation systems for consistency in watering.

The second necessary part of creating a growth zone garden is proactively planning for destructive forces that could stifle growth or destroy plants. The best gardeners know, for example, that they have to protect vulnerable crops from adverse conditions like high winds or hail. They don't plant during bad weather or when bad weather is predicted. Knowing that wind and hail will come at some point, they plan ahead. They take whatever steps they can to protect the plants, such as planting trees around the garden to serve as windbreaks and covering the garden with netting, They also have contingency plans for times they can't avoid damaging conditions. That way they aren't caught off guard. They know what steps to promptly take so that that damage is mitigated. For example, they have heat sources available as backup for freezing spells.

Children, like vulnerable garden plants, have similar needs in order for their growth to be steady, strong, and protected. Their environments must nurture and proactively protect them. Autistic children—due to sensory and information processing differences—are especially sensitive to their surroundings. Their ability to self-regulate, to take in and process data, and to store and remember that information all depend on both their internal states and the conditions of their environment.

The Four Zones of Development

As children develop, they are in one of four zones at any given time. As shown in Figure 8.1, these zones occur on a continuum, and children move back and forth among them. Our goal for each child is to discover their unique growth zone and to keep them in it as much as possible. Yet they will naturally shift from zone to zone as they encounter diverse experiences and challenges. Skilled educators and clinicians automatically notice these shifts and make appropriate adjustments that help a child move into a zone conducive to greater development.

The *fear zone* is an area with which many autistic children are all too familiar. Children generally enter this zone when they encounter surprises, sensory overload, bullying, tasks they are unprepared to tackle, or demands beyond their emotional or intellectual ability. Undiagnosed or untreated anxiety, depression, or other psychological conditions can place a child squarely within the fear zone. Being excluded, neglected, or shamed also propels a child into the fear zone.

In the fear zone, a child cannot fully process incoming information. Some children may shut down entirely, becoming almost catatonic. Brains do not function well in a state of fear. For autistic children with language processing differences, this can show up as a sudden inability to understand language—their receptive language skills stop working, and it all sounds like noise. Some

| Fear | Comfort | Learning | Growth |

FIGURE 8.1 The Four Zones of Development

kids can still hear what is being said to them, but they take a very long time to respond or cannot respond at all. Their expressive language abilities fail.

For some children, language may remain largely intact in the fear zone, but other cognitive abilities falter. Tasks they could complete the day before are suddenly beyond them. This can be mistaken by teachers or parents as poor attention or lack of motivation. A child in the fear zone simply cannot retrieve information at that moment. Once they are out of a fear zone, the information becomes accessible once again.

Children in the fear zone are emotionally unregulated. Adrenaline and cortisol levels rise, as do respiration and heart rates. None of us can think clearly or behave at our best under these conditions. Some children tend to withdraw when emotionally overwhelmed. They may curl into themselves, try to hide, or attempt to run away. Others may act out and become self-harmful by biting or scratching themselves or banging their heads. They may strike out at others. Many have meltdowns, with crying, kicking, and screaming often occurring.

Children in the fear zone are highly vulnerable. They are easily manipulated by promises of safety or comfort, and they do not have the clarity to discern when someone offers genuine help versus someone taking advantage of them. Their sensitivity to the opinions of others is heightened, and they are easily shamed. Any self-confidence they possess disappears. They want to escape their fear, but unless they are equipped with specific skills (discussed later in the chapter) they don't know how.

In addition to obvious signs that an autistic child is in the fear zone, there are also other ways some children signal they are overwhelmed. A child who is usually friendly suddenly becomes snappy. One who usually complies, resists. Another refuses to interact with peers, while another becomes intrusive and pushy around playmates. Many children in a state of fear find excuses to avoid further stimulation. For example, they may refuse to join an activity or try something new. They also may be unwilling to go somewhere or be around someone, even if it's a typically welcome setting or person.

The *comfort zone* is an area that may sound desirable but can actually hold a child back. In this zone, a child feels safe and in control. A child is usually in familiar surroundings and among familiar people in this zone. Parents, especially mothers, may be present. If the child is in an educational setting, they are generally participating in routine activities or reviewing already learned material. If they are in a clinical setting they may be playing a preferred game or telling someone about a special interest.

Parents, educators, and clinicians sometimes aim for the comfort zone as an ultimate goal for an autistic child. This approach is shortsighted and actually holds a child back. While all of us enjoy being in our comfort zone, it is also rewarding to move past it and learn new skills. Trying new activities and gaining new knowledge brings mastery and confidence. Helping all children step beyond comfort so that they too can grow is a powerful gift for children anywhere on the spectrum.

Educators and clinicians can help parents see the benefit of stretching their children past comfort. Explaining and diagramming these four zones can make the benefits clearer. A major part of parenting is to protect children, and those with kids on the spectrum have usually learned this role well. Children with autism, especially at young ages, often warrant more sheltering and buffering than typically developing peers because the world so often overwhelms them. As children get older, however, parents help their children by increasingly stepping back, so the child can develop self-protective skills. Therapists and teachers can help parents who are continuing to use protection strategies that are no longer needed. The concepts in this mindset can help a parent realize if they are actually holding their child back.

> *I see too many parents who do not stretch their children. I have mothers of fully verbal children speaking for the child. I see older children perfectly capable of things they've never been asked to do, such as paying for something themselves. If I'm talking to a mom in an airport and discover this, I'll tell her to give the child some money and have them go buy a small item from a nearby clerk. The child does it for the first time."*
>
> TEMPLE

The *learning zone* is an area in which a child is engaged in new activities or is acquiring new skills. For many autistic children, this involves some degree of anxiety, at least initially. Educators, clinicians, and parents can help a child tolerate the discomfort that may accompany the learning zone by careful attention to the child's emotional state. The goal is for a child to be attentive and motivated but not overly stimulated or frightened. Soothing a child and making necessary environmental changes may be necessary before learning can take place. A child's brain has to be "on," with a sense of expectation and cortical arousal necessary to receive, process, and store information.

To move a child from the fear or comfort zone into the learning zone may require slowing down and fine-tuning the learning environment. Each child needs professionals who have an accurate sense of that child's sensory sensitivities, emotions, and cognitive and language abilities. Skilled teachers and therapists make frequent adjustments to a child's environment as they observe changes in any of these conditions. This is easiest to do when working one on one with a child. Children working in a group may need very different settings and circumstances to achieve the learning zone. This is an ongoing challenge for classroom teachers, and the wisest among them dance (metaphorically) with each child, making necessary modifications to accommodate their needs and keep them in an able-to-learn state.

You can tell when a child is successfully in the learning zone. They become appropriately animated and involved. They deal with challenges and problems without having meltdowns or withdrawing. They are able to transfer skills they already possess to novel experiences. They show increased interest, effort, and confidence as they try out and succeed at new activities.

The *growth zone* is the step beyond the learning zone. When a child's inner state and outer environment are optimal, they are capable not only of learning but also of intentionally stretching themselves. They can seek purpose and meaning in their lives. In the growth zone, a child can set their own personal goals, beyond simply what others want for them. They can willingly embrace new experiences as part of moving toward these goals, and they have the skills to handle obstacles.

Being in the growth zone is the goal for all children on the spectrum, independent of their level of functioning. While living in the growth zone may look very different for a cognitively impaired, nonverbal child than it does for a highly verbal, intellectually gifted child, the growth zone is still the appropriate goal. We will provide concrete examples of very different children, and their lives in the growth zone, later in this chapter.

Regulation Must Come First

We've explained that a child cannot enter their growth zone if they are overwhelmed or distracted by internal distress or adverse environmental conditions. Now let's look more closely at how to achieve a balanced state and see what steps you can take to help a child with autism reach this state of regulation.

It is well known and documented that children with autism frequently have significant challenges with self-regulation. Studies comparing self-regulation capacities of children on the spectrum with typically developing peers found slower rates of adaptation, lower ability to persist on a task, less ability to focus and shift attention, and higher rates of getting distracted (Konstantareas & Stewart, 2006). An emotionally upset or physiologically unregulated autistic child will not have the resources to effectively receive, process, store, or recall information.

The autonomic nervous system is the body's control system that operates largely beyond conscious awareness. It includes heart and respiration rates, digestion, pupil response, the body's elimination functions, and other reflex actions like swallowing and vomiting. This system is the main way our bodies react to stress, and it signals a child to either fight against or flee from perceived danger.

Many autistic children have exquisitely sensitive autonomic systems. They may display chronic hyperarousal, with resting heart rates higher than their typically developing peers (Patriquin et al., 2019). This sustained biological threat response is incompatible with learning and successful growth. These kids are biologically reacting as though they are unsafe, and they cannot be expected to move out of the fear zone without assistance.

Children in this state of negative arousal can't relax enough to attend to their environment. They certainly can't adapt to environmental changes or challenges. Their systems are too busy trying to keep their body organs and systems functioning adequately. With their body working so hard preparing to defend against danger, there are no resources left to restore a calm resting state or to take on additional challenges. It's not surprising that researchers are finding growing support for a link between aberrant cardiac activity and core deficits associated with autism, such as communication and social impairment (Klusek et al., 2015).

> *We can't expect kids to learn if their amygdala is in fear mode. Lots of autistic kids spend a lot of time close to panic. Adults have to help the kids get this under control before trying any intervention of any type."*
> TEMPLE

Educators and clinicians working with autistic children are wise to assume many of these children need help regulating basic biological functions before they can learn.

Here are some steps—both basic and more involved—that all professionals and parents can take to help children be biologically prepared to benefit from school or clinical interventions:

- Assume most autistic children need this help.
- Do a quick visual check of children. Look for signs of hyperarousal, such as dilated pupils, fast breaths, frequent sighs, sweating, or flushing.
- Observe other possible indicators of a body in distress, such as frequent or sudden bathroom trips, gagging, problems swallowing, or stomach upset.
- If you observe signs of distress, consider (with parental permission) having school nurses or other qualified personnel check a child's vital signs, such as heart rate and blood pressure.
- Use basic relaxation tools in the classroom or prior to clinical interventions. These might include belly breathing, stretching, loosening a cramped posture, progressive muscle relaxation, or visualization exercises. Most children enjoy using these tools.
- Use rating scales or pictorial ratings for children to self-monitor their state of arousal. Consider using pre- and post-measures of heart rate.

If a child cannot calm their nervous system using these basic tools, consider additional resources. These might include:

- If the child is working with an OT or PT, have them regularly incorporate these exercises into their work.
- Refer the child to a cognitive behavioral therapist for more extensive practice self-regulating.
- Inform all team members of the child's struggles. All adults working with the child, including reading teach-

ers, speech therapists, aides, or others can help the child with basic breathing or relaxation exercises.

- Equip parents to help their child at home. A simple way to learn these techniques is by watching free online videos on relaxation exercises for children.
- Consider a referral to a psychiatrist familiar with autism. Some children have nervous systems so chronically or severely disrupted that they need medication to stabilize or reset their system. In addition to medication, some professionals use noninvasive vagus nerve stimulation to regulate the autonomous nervous system (Finisguerra et al., 2019).

In addition to a regulated nervous system, children need a regulated environment in order to function in either the learning or growth zone. For a child to remain calm, there must be calm around them. Sudden or loud noises, changes, or surprises will probably move a child back into an unregulated state. A sensitive nervous system will rapidly revert fight or flight status, and the autistic child will quickly retreat into a zone of fear.

Once a child is in a calm, regulated state, they then have the potential to process information successfully. Because that state is likely to fluctuate, however, working with an autistic child requires consistent attention to their degree of regulation. A sensitive educator or clinician makes frequent adjustments to help children return to greater regulation.

For example, if Clara is successfully attending to an OT exercise but becomes overwhelmed, her therapist may need to pause and simply sit quietly with her or a bit. Another child may need the lighting temporarily dimmed, or they might need to spin or flap their hands to help them return to their physiological base-line. If these activities move them toward regulation, they are coping skills, not deficits.

The Steps After Regulation

Once a child is regulated, professionals can begin educational or clinical interventions. The next immediate step is to determine the most appropriate level and content of those interventions for each individual child. Professionals with a whole child approach always customize their work to each child. They base their choice of lesson plans, activities, or therapies on the child's cognitive, developmental, and emotional level.

Much has been written about educational best practices, and it is not the intent of this book to review them in detail. A few concepts, however, have particular relevance for children on the spectrum, so we will discuss and give examples of their use.

Elementary versus Higher Mental Functions

This concept distinguishes between foundational states of the brain (elementary functions) and more sophisticated mental processes built upon them (higher mental functions). Children can only perform higher mental functions when elementary functions are in place.

There are four elementary functions: attention, sensation, perception, and memory. In order to learn a new task, children need to be able to focus on it, register the incoming stimuli or sensation, perceive that information accurately, and hold the information in mind long enough to work with it (Constable et al., 2018).

Here is an example of a child who needs help with elementary functions before moving on to higher mental functions:

Martin is 6 years old and nonverbal. He sometimes responds to the requests of others, but many times he seems not to hear those requests. He is easily overwhelmed by sound and light and responds by starting to rock. He can usually indicate his needs nonverbally, by pointing and gestures. Sometimes, though, he appears to forget how to use the gestures. At these times, he cries out. Others know he is asking for something, but they are unable to decipher his specific need.

Martin appeared to have near average intellectual abilities when he was tested by instruments designed for use with nonverbal children. He is able to carry out most age-appropriate daily tasks of living such as toileting, feeding, and picking up toys. He enjoys looking at books, playing with anything that requires assembly, and watching any videos that are even remotely related to machines.

For Martin to successfully process new information, or learn a new task, he needs help with all four elementary functions. His mother has found the best way to get his *attention* is to incorporate his interests into the new material and to give him frequent breaks. She also finds he enjoys games, so she embeds her teaching of new tasks in the context of a fun activity. Researchers have found similar results. One study found that children with autism learned fractions faster when they were taught them as a game using concrete, touchable materials (Triwahyuningntyas et al., 2020).

For Martin to register incoming data, his environment must be free of distracting stimuli, especially loud sounds or moving objects. His mother speaks slowly to Martin, and she enunciates clearly. She keeps the volume of her speech moderate and consistent. She accurately suspects that faster or louder speech results in a jumble of incomprehensible sounds for her son. She realizes he can't be expected to learn if he can't *perceive* the incoming data. When teaching him, she turns off bright overhead lights and closes the curtains to the street. She clears out a large space where they sit on the floor to learn. If Martin starts to rock or flap his hands, she stops any activity and gently joins him for a minute, simultaneously modeling deep breathing.

Martin's preferred *sensory* mode is tactile, and touching objects helps him learn. He is much more likely to remember how to do a new task if he is physically guided through it repeatedly until it becomes muscle memory.

Therefore, to teach him numbers, his mother drew oversized digits on enlarged photos of machinery. She used modeling clay to add texture to the photos and the numbers. She also gave Martin dice corresponding to the number he was learning and he was allowed to rub the indentations in the dice while he viewed the photos.

Martin's mother always uses objects to help her son remember. His *memory* function seems better if he has been able to touch objects connected to the subject matter he is learning. With repetition, his mother can later gradually fade the use of objects.

Task Scaffolding and Working One Step Up

Both of these terms refer to ways we can help a child learn new tasks more successfully. They embody the concept of providing a child specific supports appropriate to their current level of development and skills. The use of these approaches is based on the idea that a child has the best chance of growing under certain conditions. First, they need encouragement and guidance by more knowledgeable or skilled others. These more advanced individuals then present the child with information or a challenge just above, or *one step up* from their current developmental level. Finally, all teaching is presented in small, manageable bits of information, given to the child in stepwise fashion. As one bit of information is mastered, another is added, or *scaffolded*, onto the first material.

Task scaffolding and working one step up might look like this. Let's say 7-year-old Joyce wants to learn to swim. She'll be most successful if she has a teacher who is relaxed around water, is a skilled swimmer herself, and knows effective swimming instruction strategies for children. If that instructor understands how to scaffold, Joyce will first be given a very simple learning task.

However, the teacher has to know what exactly is simple for Joyce. For one child, putting their head in the water might be an easy first step. For Joyce, submerging her face may be terrifying. So the teacher needs to access Joyce's current level of development—not only in the specific arena of swimming, but also in the broader area of familiarity and comfort with water.

The teacher also needs to know Joyce's cognitive and emotional developmental level. Can Joyce understand verbal instructions? Can she regulate her breathing? At what level does she function in fine and gross motor control? Is she either generally a fearful child or specifically afraid of the water? If so, what are her specific fears?

Once the instructor knows Joyce's functional level, the teacher can scaffold onto that and then build additional skills. She'll first choose a task Joyce can already do and then add a small step to it. For example, if Joyce is afraid of putting her head into the water, her teacher respects this. She needs to finds out how high the water can go on Joyce's body before the child gets uncomfortable.

If Joyce gets scared when the water reaches the bottom of her knees, the instructor could encourage Joyce to aim for the middle of her knees. If that's easy, Joyce can move to the top of her knees, then her thighs, and so on. When the teacher gets all the way to Joyce's face, she slows down if necessary, perhaps adding additional supports at that point. These supports can take many forms. For example, the teacher could incorporate a game, add extra verbal or physical support, use a concrete tool such as goggles or a floatation doughnut for Joyce to put her head into, or modify the step and have Joyce just put one side of her face in the water.

It's fairly obvious no respectable teacher would throw Joyce in the deep end of the pool, but scaffolding is much more detailed than that. A scaffold is built uniquely to each child. It takes the child's unique challenges into consideration. It also builds on specific interests and strengths. For example, Joyce was competitive, and she loved games. She also enjoyed anime. Using anime characters as avatars, Joyce and her teacher competed for badges, as players do in a commercial game. This greatly increased Joyce's motivation, attention, and physiological regulation. As a result, she was able to learn faster and retain the swimming lessons more easily.

Effective instructions and interventions always follow the approach that helped Joyce learn to swim. Teaching aims for the zone, or region of capability, that is just one step beyond the child's present competence. Teachers who use this approach do not expect a child to skip steps in a misguided attempt to speed up learning or reaching goals. They know that doing this risks overwhelming a child and returning them to an unregulated state in which they can't learn at all. Desired outcomes for the child are based on individual needs, not their age, gender, diagnosis, or external factors such as school or clinic objectives.

> *You always work just one step past where a child is. You don't want to stretch them too far or they'll just shut down. But you have to stretch them or they won't grow."*
> TEMPLE

This type of teaching necessarily includes the guidance and direct involvement of a more experienced adult or a more knowledgeable peer. With this assistance, a child can accomplish a task they could not learn on their own. When a child is collaborating with and being supported by an attuned teacher, a variety of internal emotional and cognitive developmental processes can awaken and foster growth.

One Successful Model: Teaching at the Right Level (TaRL)

This methodology relies on organizing instruction so that it is based on a child's actual learning and development level, rather than on a prescribed syllabus. It has been shown very effective (Banerjee et al., 2017). While this is not a methodology developed specifically for autistic children, some guidelines in the approach appear well suited for children on the spectrum. We will therefore give you details of these guidelines and an example of their implementation:

- *Actively engage children:* This approach believes children's capacity for growth increases if they are encouraged to actively participate in learning. Verbal exchanges, visual demonstrations, and collaboration are provided within a supportive and structured environment. That environment is dynamic and adjusts to the child's needs and pace of growth.

- *Children are not required to sit at desks:* This guideline can be applied to settings beyond the classroom. Some children are able to learn and grow better if allowed to position themselves on the floor or a soft cushion. When children and professionals are given the flexibility to move around, this liberal use of space is believed to benefit many children's ability to attend. It seems also to foster more communication and closer bonds between the child and the teacher.

- *Foundation skills are introduced via familiar content and materials:* It is believed that children learn basics better if they can personally relate to what they are being taught. For example, if a child is at a beginning reading level, books should stick to familiar items, places, and everyday tasks. For beginning arithmetic, materials such as sticks or other simple items kids have handled before are preferable to unfamiliar materials or abstract concepts. Instructors often create their own teaching aids, which they adapt to suit their learner's needs. This is also less expensive for school districts, and parents can make these same items to use for reinforcement the teaching at home.

- *Building a child's confidence is viewed as an integral part of growth:* The TaRL approach assumes that school is daunting to many children. The methodology aims to increase each child's sense of self-efficacy and confidence by providing challenging yet achievable tasks. Teachers are expected to praise each accomplishment and practice patience while each child learns at their own pace.

- *Act on data:* Each child's current competency level is assessed before proceeding to instruction. Once teaching is underway, instructors need to know if the child possesses the specific prerequisite skills needed before attempting a more advanced learning task. When placing students into learning groups, teachers use his data to form homogeneous developmental levels among each set of children.

- *Set achievable goals:* Goals are set just above the student's current level of competency. These goals are shared with everyone working with the child.

- *Assess one on one:* This model uses oral one-on-one testing techniques to assess each child's progress. They

believe this not only yields the most accurate view
of growth, but also deepens the connection between
the teacher and the child. This is thought to result in
instructors being better informed about the child and
also to result in increasing the child's motivation.

- *Track learning:* Each child is assessed regularly, so
that progress is tracked and goals can be adjusted as
necessary.

An example of working with an autistic child by using and
building on these concepts might look like the following:

Zoey is just beginning first grade.
She was diagnosed with autism at age 4 years and has
received intensive applied behavioral analysis (ABA).
She is fully verbal, and an evaluation showed her
intellectual abilities were in the average range.

Following the guidelines of the TaRL model,
Zoey's basic academic skills were tested the first
week of school. Her level of competency in language,
reading, and arithmetic were quantified. Her ability
to understand numbers and spoken language were
on par with her peers. Her ability to recognize letters,
however, was not. She was unable to write or recognize
any letters or to match sounds to letters. She was also
unable to follow the rules of conversation, such as
listening and taking turns.

Zoey was placed in a small group of other first

graders who also lacked these foundational skills. Her teacher's first goal for Zoey was for her to be able to listen without interrupting for 1 minute (she was currently able to listen without breaking in for about 45 seconds). When this goal was met, additional time was progressively added until Zoey could listen for 3 minutes 80% of the time. This progress was tracked visually so Zoey could see it, and it was shared with her regular classroom teacher and parents.

Zoey's teacher also prioritized turn taking, believing that until Zoey improved in this area, her learning of other tasks would be undermined. They practiced turn-taking activities daily and again visually tracked progress on a colorful chart that was shared with everyone who worked with Zoey. Because she loved music, Zoey she was rewarded with an extra minute of listening time any day that she completed taking at least five successful turns during an activity. She was also orally praised when she exhibited appropriate turn taking.

Once Zoey showed progress in both listening and turn taking, her teacher then introduced her to sounds and letters. Both verbal explanations and visual aids were used. The teacher and Zoey sat on the floor and periodically got up to position letters on a felt board. They made duplicate letters so Zoey could take these and a piece of felt home to practice with her parents.

When Zoey regressed in either her ability to listen or take turns, her teacher refocused on these skills until they returned to baseline. Then they went back to the pre-reading lessons. Zoey's teacher adjusted her student's goals as needed following regularly scheduled assessments.

If Zoey had been an older child who turned in written assignments, her teacher would still implement some one-on-one assessment as part of this model. A core belief of this approach is that it's easy to disconnect from a stack of assignment papers, even if they indicate a child's need for help. Working individually with a child, and learning of their progress by engaging with them directly, is viewed as a sort of insurance against this disconnect.

Working With the Child's Type of Thinking

Autism is often described as a difference in information processing. That's a fair portrayal, but it risks implying everyone on the spectrum thinks alike (just in a different way than typically developing peers). In fact, there is a wide range of thinking styles in people with autism, and it's vital that professionals can recognize the specific style or styles of each child with whom they work. They also keep the child's thinking style in mind when considering eventual vocations. Each thinking style brings different skill sets to a child, making some vocations better fits than others would be.

Most children are wired to innately process information by only one of these styles. They often show above average ability in their natural style and below average ability in the others. Few people with autism are exceptional at more than one style, although some perform moderately at two or more (Kozhevnikov et al., 2010).

A child cannot work in the growth zone if they are expected to think or learn in a style that doesn't come naturally for them. Effective clinicians and educators adjust lessons and interventions as much as possible to accommodate each child's way of thinking. They realize that different forms of thought are real and one form of thinking is not better than another.

For younger children, presenting educational material or clinical interventions in a style that matches the student's wiring may make it more appealing or easier for them to learn. This is another way of appreciating the whole child. Learning how they process information and respecting it as simply the way they are wired honors their individuality and moves beyond an overreaching label. One thinking style is no better nor worse than another. Rather, each thinking style has benefits for particular tasks. Fitting a child's thinking style to appropriate tasks creates a good fit and an opportunity for the child to experience mastery.

> *The first thing is realizing different kinds of thinking exist. When I was young, I assumed everybody thought like me—in pictures. Since then I have learned that different minds learn and solve problems differently."*
> TEMPLE

Three main ways of thinking have been documented (Grandin, 1995). Recently, one of the ways has been further subdivided into two types (Grandin & Panek, 2013). Originally, Temple believed everyone thought the same way she did, which was by seeing the world in pictures. She has described it as having a brain similar to an internet search engine set to search for images.

This type of thinking is referred to as *visual thinking*, and it is now known that visual thinkers come in two varieties. Some, like Temple, are *photo-realistic* thinkers. These people process information in an associative manner. To form concepts, they sort pictures into categories much the way you can sort computer data into files. The pictures are the foreground; words merely serve to narrate the imagined images.

Photo-realistic thinkers are bottom-up thinkers—they take bits and pieces of visual data and combine them to form ideas and theories. Because a certain threshold of data is usually needed before the big picture concept starts to appear, children who think this way may need longer to process information because they have to generate many, many images.

Teachers who want to help photo-realistic thinkers will give them time to sort through their mind images before expecting a verbal response. They will also note how different ways of introducing information impact these thinkers. Some of these children have to see how all the little pieces fit together in order to learn and remember information. Starting with explaining a theory or umbrella concept may not work for these students.

Other visual thinkers use internal images and maps of space in order to make sense of the world and to learn. Instead of using objects (with color and shape), these *spatial visualizers* default to using location and spatial relationships to understand and learn. These children often don't see images as a whole unit; rather, they generate and analyze parts of incoming stimuli. Educators and clinicians who understand can try using charts, maps, and diagrams as a tool for growth. These thinkers are also referred to as *pattern thinkers*. Research has shown that pattern or spatial visualizers may use a mix of both text and pictures, sometimes to the same degree (Blazhenkova & Kozhevnikov, 2009).

Interestingly, we're now finding that a small group of children may have absolutely no ability to imagine visual images. This phenomenon is termed *aphantasia* and occurs in otherwise healthy people with intact visual systems. These children are, however, able to imagine spatial relationships. They rely on either their spatial memory or verbal strategies to process and retain information (Bainbridge et al., 2021).

Our educational system has historically relied on teaching through verbal methods. Images were used as supports rather than as primary learning tools. For many autistic children, this is not ideal. While educators and clinicians realize nonverbal children require alternate approaches, they may fail to appreciate that many fully verbal children also can't learn well if teachers only use verbal approaches.

The third type of information processing is *auditory thinking*. These children are good at listening and processing language. They may find it useful to repeat information, sometimes aloud, in order to remember it. The cadence or music of language may come naturally for them. They may prefer to get their information in lectures or talks, and they may do best on oral exams. These children may also be good storytellers.

Let's look at how four children, each with a different thinking style, might react to the same school assignment. First, we'll describe each child.

- Dianna is a photo-realistic thinker. She automatically generates images in her mind when people speak to her. She needs people to speak slowly in order to catch everything they say. She is literal minded and learns best with concrete examples presented visually.

- Roger is a spatial visualizer. He loves maps and diagrams. He can remember any route he has been on,
  even it if was only one time. He reminds his father
  which street to turn on when they take drives. He loves
  puzzles and can put them together faster than his peers.
  He can also complete Sudoku games with ease.
- Odessa is a verbal thinker. She loves books. She was
  a self-taught reader by the age of 4 years. She is not good
  at drawing, imagining things, or recalling images from
  memory. She does not enjoy or do well at video games that
  require spatial memory. She prefers crossword puzzles.
- Isaac is an auditory thinker. He loves to talk about his
  special interests and sometimes monopolizes conversations. He enjoys listening to docents in museums. He is
  good at mimicking voices and animal sounds. He loves
  animated children's movies.

Now let's imagine these four children are in the same sixth
grade classroom. They are working as a group on an earth science
learning module. The curriculum goal is to obtain, evaluate,
and communicate information about how the earth's surface
was formed.

If these children were working alone, or in a group composed of the same types of thinkers, their approaches to the module would be narrow and guided by their particular thinking style.

Dianna would be able to easily visualize various rocks she
has actually seen in real life or in picture books. After compiling a
large database in her mind, she could begin to generate categories
of rocks. If her teacher started out by giving a lecture on general
concepts related to geological change, Dianna might get lost.

Roger would benefit if his science book happened to contain diagrams of the processes rocks go through. A visual chart outlining sedimentation, compaction, weathering, and erosion would appeal to him. He might adapt a simple chart into a more complicated flow chart in order to better understand the process.

Odessa would find it appealing to read text explaining how the earth formed. She might skip over photos and diagrams unless she needed them to comprehend a specific part of the text that she didn't understand. She would probably highlight or underline words in the text, but it's unlikely she would draw anything to supplement her understanding.

Isaac might procrastinate reading the chapter but do a good job of listening when the teacher talked about all the types of rocks. He might sustain focus longer than his peers and his attention might heighten further when his teacher talks about ringing rocks, a type of rock that makes bell-like sounds and is used for musical instruments. His teacher might have to ask him to stop mimicking these sounds in the classroom, something he might or might not have realized he was doing.

You can see how each child working independently would miss out on perspectives that result from other ways of thinking. Different minds not only process information differently, but also they contribute different ideas and have different insights. They are turned on by different aspects of a subject.

Now let's imagine these four children working together in a group, with a skilled teacher facilitating their interaction. Let's further imagine this teacher is aware of different thinking styles and purposefully works to bring out each child's unique strengths.

In their working group, Dianna can recall details of the rocks she has seen. If other group members forget the name of a rock, she can usually supply it. She also remembers facts about each rock and she is able to visualize the processes by which rocks are formed and change.

Roger adds his flowcharts to the group, which they decide to use in their class presentation. He incorporates photos Dianna has found and pastes them at various points in the chart.

Odessa's careful reading of the text provides additional details the other students had missed. She edits the written description that accompanies Roger's flowchart and Dianna's photos.

Isaac was elected to get up in front of the class as the representative of the group. He excitedly explained their project and delighted his classmates with his animated description and replication of ringing rocks.

The group's final product received praise from their teacher, and the other students were impressed. Compared to many of the other presentations, it was more encompassing and the presentation more engrossing. The primary reason for this was simple: this group had the advantage of being composed of different kinds of minds. Each child had a unique contribution. It was a great example of how important it is to combine different thinkers and to value the input of each.

Summary

- Giving a child the opportunity to learn from within their growth zone is a central tenet of working from a whole child approach.
- Growth zones require two ingredients: a regulated child and an environment free of distracting or upsetting conditions such as sensory overload.

- Children will inevitably move back and forth among the four zones of fear, comfort, learning, and growth. Skilled professionals maintain vigilance and make necessary adjustments to help children return to the growth zone as efficiently as possible.

- Professionals and parents can avoid having a child languish and stagnate in their comfort zone by stretching the child with baby steps. Allowing a child to remain in their comfort zone deprives them of growth they will need to navigate their life successfully, no matter their level of functioning.

- Children with autism frequently have highly sensitive autonomic nervous systems, which causes significant challenges with self-regulation. They often require and benefit from additional supports such as environmental changes, relaxation techniques, or medication.

- Elementary mental functions including sensing, perceiving, attending, and remembering must be working adequately before a child can be expected to perform higher mental functions.

- Children are most likely to grow when presented with learning challenges that are just one small step above their current ability level. New learning tasks that are scaffolded onto already mastered ones have the best chances of being successful.

- Teaching children at the right level includes customizing approaches, being flexible, and frequently assessing outcome in order to make needed changes.

- Children with autism tend to have distinct styles of thinking. Knowing how a child is wired to process information helps professionals use these innate strengths to advance growth.

— Different kinds of minds working together can result in broader and deeper understanding of problems and more effective outcomes and solutions.

ADDENDUM

A Child's Growth Zone Under Trauma: The COVID-19 Pandemic Impacts and Recommendations

The COVID-19 virus and ensuing pandemic have greatly impacted children and families. All children, both typically developing and autistic, have had to adjust to major changes in their daily and academic routines. Family stress has increased, and parents may not be as emotionally grounded or physically rested as usual. Parents and children alike have experienced disruption of their usual social protocols and interactions.

Researchers have reported that children who are isolated or quarantined during pandemic diseases are more likely to develop acute stress disorders, adjustment disorders, and grief. Historically, almost one-third of children who endured isolation or quarantine met the clinical criteria for post-traumatic stress disorder (Sprang & Silman, 2013).

Children with autism have arguably been affected more intensely by the COVID-19 pandemic than have their typically developing peers. There are predictable reasons—directly related to the characteristics and impacts of autism—that these children may be more severely impacted:

- *Autistic kids need sameness and routine.* Under pandemic and quarantine conditions, that need has been impossible to meet. No matter how hard parents and professionals attempt to maintain routines, all children have seen their world change. Even tasks that used to be highly automatic may now require thought and extra steps.
- *School has been disrupted.* Children who need and are used to receiving additional academic support no longer have it. Virtual online classes cannot compare to an in-school environment, where an autistic child may be accustomed to an aide or specialized attention.
- *Children with autism process information (sensory, cognitive, and emotional) differently, and often more slowly.* Pandemic conditions heighten these differences because more information is coming in than usual. For example, there may be new odors in the child's environment, such as more cooking or cleaning smells. The barrage of new and frequently changing information and the news coverage that accompanies it can be overwhelming. At home, with more people there more of the time, there may be more noise and perhaps more clutter. This can feel especially chaotic to a child with autism.
- *Everyone's cognitive load is higher now, with new routines, decisions, and demands.* This is true for all children, but autistic kids may not have enough information processing bandwidth in reserve to absorb the added load.

- *Children with autism don't always understand and experience time the same as their typically developing peers.* Even neurotypical adults report experiencing a sense of a time warp as pandemic days blend into each other in the absence of markers usually associated with pre-pandemic daily schedules. For autistic kids, this can feel as if they have no anchor in time.

- *They often have a harder time regulating emotions, especially under stress or novel conditions.* Under conditions of high alert, tension is chronic and can lead to meltdowns and exhaustion. Whatever is anxiety-provoking or difficult for a child usually shows up as a behavior problem or as noncompliance.

- *They usually do not have as secure or broad a social network as their non-autistic peers.*

- *Their baseline anxiety is usually higher and now it is likely intensified for many reasons:* with everyone home there may be greater sensory stimuli, there are new and different transitions, their schedule has changed, and there are inevitable surprises in their daily life.

- *They may experience heightened stress or frustration related to special interests.* They may have been forced to change when or where they engage in them. With other siblings home all day, it may be harder for autistic children to isolate with their interests or protect their things from being handled by others.

- *Autistic kids often rely on rules (that they or others made up).* During the pandemic, people may be breaking these rules. The rules also keep changing, and they are different for different places.

Autistic children with sensory sensitivities (most autistic children) find masks, the standard safe garb during the pandemic, highly aversive and anxiety provoking. It can be difficult for them to tolerate masks. If they do manage to keep them on, their ability to interact or learn may be grossly compromised due to their discomfort.

Clinical services have generally either stopped or are being offered virtually. In-home care providers have been unable to go into homes as usual. Some therapists and clinics have done a commendable job of adapting services to the online world, but they simply cannot replicate in-person services. Touch is frequently part of how a child learns in physical or occupational therapy. Even speech and language therapists use touch, direct eye contact, and social space to enhance their teaching skills.

Here are our recommendations for helping autistic children stay in their growth zones during the pandemic:

Emotional Support

- Seek to understand each child's understanding and fears about the pandemic. Correct any distorted or inaccurate thinking. Put fears into realistic perspective.
- Place more attention on the child's emotions than on their behavior. Calm the child instead of reacting to the behavior.
- Help kids focus on the positive and what they can control. Review what is going well, and point out their successes. Consider developing a gratitude practice: a

regular time you either say aloud something you were grateful for that day, or a time and place to write it down or draw it.

- Engage alongside kids in stress-reducing behaviors such as deep, audible breathing; singing; listening to music; touching comforting objects or textures; playing with pets or favorite toys; stretching; or exercising.
- Watch for signs of either underarousal (e.g., boredom, apathy, fatigue, depression) or overarousal (e.g., acting out, anxiety, meltdowns) and seek ways to regulate. Sensory interventions work for both. See what you have around the house to provide regulating sensory input. For example, make it a game to see how many kitchen items can provide either sensory stimulation or calming.
- Be sure all team members working with the child understand the added stress burden resulting from the pandemic. While you may assume this is obvious, when others are under stress themselves, they can have tunnel vision about the stress of others.
- Carefully monitor both the child's and your own stress level. Kids look to adults for cues about whether they should be worried or afraid. Beware of emotional contagion in the family—kids will soak up the anxiety of parents and siblings.
- Get the child's input about which changes have impacted them the most. Prioritize finding ways to mitigate these particular changes.
- If a child is in therapy, continue it if possible either in person with social distancing or virtually.
- Recognize that a child's self esteem and sense of mastery

are vulnerable to deterioration under pandemic conditions. A child may blame themselves for not being able to rise to added demands, rather than recognizing that everyone is struggling. Let them know they are reacting in expected ways to an unexpected set of events. If parents need to work, the child may miss classes and meetings with specialists. Other parents said virtual sessions were so ineffective that they just skipped them.

- Make some reasonable plans for the future. These could include small trips or visits to parks, monuments, gardens, or other activities a child enjoys.

- Make advance plans for bad days. Have ideas on hand, including who the child can reach out to as a bad day buddy. These are friends or relatives who will lend a compassionate ear when your child is struggling. They can be other children or adults and offer support, encouragement, distraction, or perspective.

- Recognize that some autistic children, no matter know much support they are given, will be unable to adjust to the many changes they face. Some children will be angrier and more physically aggressive. They may show regression of skills gained or show new or increased self-harm. Sleep disorders may become a real problem, with downstream, daytime emotional and physical impact. Kids may try to run away. Obsessions or compulsions may show up or worsen. Some children will be completely unable to sustain attention via virtual learning. Some families will decide that virtual learning and constant redirecting is not worth the emotional toll on them or their child.

- Monitor your own emotional state and seek support where you can. Try not to get into a downward spiral of "what ifs" and catastrophizing. Kids pick up on the fears of adults. They build resilience when adults can model calmness in the face of challenge and hope in the face of loss. Children can handle knowing that things aren't the way anyone wants them to be, as long as they are reassured that there are things to look forward to and that they will have support.
- Finally, there are some autistic kids who will actually prefer virtual to classroom learning. Particularly for kids who experience bullying at school, this may be a reprieve. Others simply enjoy being on computers. Even for these children, however, there are many other novel situations to be faced, and their emotional well-being needs monitoring.

Practical Support in Daily Living

- Keep daily life as predictable, routine, and structured as possible. Set up new schedules and make them visual. Mark off days and events to give kids markers they can see.
- Give children extra opportunities throughout the day for alone time, physical activity, and special interests. Limit their exposure to the news and social media.
- Break down tasks into small steps and give kids extra support. Whenever possible, let them know what tasks and situations are coming up so they don't have surprises.
- Tell kids what you want them to do, not what you don't want them to do.

- Maintain bedtime and mealtime in the midst of other schedule changes.
- Have reasonable expectations and boundaries.
- Stay connected with friends, family, and your community. Plan some enjoyable activities in advance, even if they are small. For example, you might schedule socially distanced events such as a shared ice cream, an outdoor game, or a walk.
- Keep talking to your kids. Engage them in conversation about their special interests. With less verbal interaction coming from classroom interactions, additional interaction at home can determine whether your child regresses in their language production or skills.
- Use regular household activities to substitute for occupational or physical therapy that may have stopped. Walk up and down the stairs with kids who have motor challenges. Have them draw, so they keep getting practice holding a crayon. Make a game of trying to walk with a book on your head. Give extra hugs and touches (to children who want them) during these times together.
- Include kids even more when possible in tasks like grocery shopping, preparing food, and setting the table. Kids who are missing out on learning or practicing these skills due to disrupted therapies need compensatory help or they will likely regress.

Educational Support (Recommendations for Educators and Parents)

- For children no longer attending in-person therapies or school, explain in age-appropriate ways the reasons for this. For example, you might say this to a second grader, "School is starting (fill in the date) and some things will be the same and some will be different this year. Let's make a list of what's the same and what is new."

• Realize that anxiety affects learning, especially now. Adults need to ask kids questions to assess their anxiety level. You can't expect kids with anxiety to learn. Some kids with autism specifically don't like, and get anxious, looking at faces or eyes on screens. They may cover their eyes or ears or even start self-harming.

• Many students with autism have high distractibility. Some, if given a computer unsupervised, will minimize the classroom screen and get on a video game immediately.

• Even though everyone is under more pressure and has additional tasks, this is a time that parents and educators can connect. Parents may need to reach out to extra busy teachers though, and the teachers in turn have to make time to speak to families—to find out what their situation is, learn what challenges they're facing, and brainstorm realistic ways to keep children engaged. This may be a unique opportunity to initiate or deepen collaborative relationships. Educators who communicate interest and respect to parents, combined with practical tips, can become trusted allies.

• Teachers have to work with whatever a family's reality is. The most important needs of a child take priority. Others may have to wait. Special interests are more important than ever in harnessing a child's energy, motivation, and attention. Move instruction to what a child cares about. Writing, conversations, assignments—all can be tailored to special interests.

— Kids may naturally be even more focused now on special interests as a way to handle anxiety. Don't move kids away from these areas—it is their way to cope. Instead of changing topics, try to adapt the lesson so that it incorporates the interest. For example, if a child is obsessed with dinosaurs, instead of saying, "We're not doing dinosaurs now," instead incorporate dinosaurs into turn taking or conversation skill lessons. Even math problems can feature dinosaurs.

— Children who have IEPs and accommodations ideally need teachers and parents to find new ways to at least partially implement components of these supports. Collaboration with families is vital to learn what resources they have at home and whether parents are available and able to use them. Your goal is to find a balance between encouraging and not overwhelming already struggling parents. Some can take on extra tasks; others simply cannot. Ideally, a virtual learning addendum would be added to each student's IEP, created from input from both parents and teachers.

— The new challenges being placed on families and caretakers are immense. Teachers base instruction on applied behavioral principles and educational theory that took years to learn. Translating that to a parent or family can be difficult. It is asking a great deal of already stressed parents.

— This is a time you can't teach everything. While IEPs and the federally mandated program guaranteeing every child's right to a free appropriate public education (FAPE) still need to be implemented, educators have to choose what's most important, partly based on what families can support. For any intervention or instruction to work, parents have to be able and comfortable assisting. Parents are used to the idea that professionals implement, not them. When asked to do tasks at home that are usually carried out at school, some parents will succeed, some will try but not be able to follow through, and some simply won't make an attempt. Recognizing this reality lets educators proceed most realistically.

- Educators also need to remember that children often act one way at school and another at home. IEP components most important in the classroom may now have lower priority. New accommodations may need to be created. For example, more frequent or longer breaks may be needed to keep a virtual learner on task. Without teachers physically present, many autistic kids will feel lost. They are accustomed to them being there— providing calming touches, motivating, and encouraging them. Without these supports, children may not behave in their typical classroom manner.

- When clinicians or educators do prompt therapy with a kid who has autism, it often involves touching them. A teacher or therapist may touch their face, arm, or shoulder. Therapy is not the same when it's from a distance.

- Visual communication between professionals and parents is ideal if possible. Even brief check-ins via commonly used online options can help maintain connection and accurate exchange of information, although some of those systems are not HIPAA-compliant and should be used only as a last resort, if at all. If email is used, attachments with visual information are better for many parents than text only.

- Virtual school schedules do not have to be similar to in classroom schedules. This is the time to adapt to your child's needs. Do what works for the family and the child. Incorporate old routines as much as possible, but don't be rigid about adhering to them.

- Whatever new structure is created, keep it consistent. Routines such as hygiene, getting dressed, meals, and bedtime should become automatic. Kids need cues for these new routines: visual reminders, timers, changes in clothing (e.g., no PJs during a school day) and environment (e.g., computer use for school is always at the kitchen table, not in bed). Most children do their best work and are able to learn and attend most fully in the morning when they are fresh. Afternoons are better for less demanding activities, often ones the child engaged in prior to the pandemic.

- The focus of pandemic learning is to reinforce current skills, with introduction of new ones if possible. There are no federal guidelines, and few children will have their entire team replaced, virtually or otherwise. It's just not realistic.

- While IEP time frame requirements haven't changed, many children will experience delays in starting them. Meetings should be happening on schedule, but the way the meeting time is used may need to change. More time is needed to help parents. Lesson and interven-

tion plans ideally can be sent in advance to parents and
adjusted with parental input about the home environment and resources.

- The consultation section of IEPs takes on added priority
now. Use this time to talk to other team members and
for training parents. If a child's IEP has no specific section for consultation, add it now.

- Educators are wise to recognize how pre-pandemic disparities in school districts impact each family. Parents
in less wealthy districts are at distinct disadvantages
that are perhaps clearer now than ever before. They may
have been particularly impacted by workforce changes.
Lower paid workers may not have choices about what
shifts they are assigned, and if they need to work their
child may miss classes or meetings with specialists.
Families may not own computers or have internet
access. Less-funded districts also usually have fewer personnel, with less training, and they have more turnover.
They may have let proportionally more staff go during
the pandemic compared to better funded districts.

- Use the child's special interests and preferred activities
to focus on life skills. One aspect of the pandemic that
can be viewed as positive is that some children will now
have more time with parents, at home, to learn practical
life skills. Competency in these daily skills is the biggest
predictor of success in adulthood.

- In larger families, stress is multiplied. Multiple children
cannot access a computer at the same time. Parents
cannot be with two children, doing two different tasks,
at once. Sibling needs are not equivalent, and rival-

ries and jealousy may increase. A parent—even if they are at home—can't be expected to teach children anything if the parent is distracted by constantly putting out fires or stopping behaviors of other children in the household.

- Some children will be especially vulnerable to negative effects of added screen time during the pandemic. Be specific about what you allow. Write down and display rules: When can your child be online, for how long, and on what sites?

- Nonverbal learners are especially impacted by virtual learning. Even if a child was already using a communication system, the parent might not have been trained on it. These students will always require parents during this period. Some students can't even turn on the computer themselves, nor can they set up or operate assistive technology alone.

Therapeutic Support (Recommendations for Clinicians and Team Members)

Many of the above recommendations apply to clinicians and all types of therapists. Here are a few additional suggestions:

- Therapists such as PTs, OTs, and speech therapists benefit from having accurate information about the current home environment. They need to know how parents are coping and what resources are available. It's crucial to take stock of these fundamentals before creating protocols for at-home use. Some questions to be asked include: *What sensory issues show up at home?*

Can parents do basic logging to identify patterns, or is that asking too much? Do parents want to be trained to implement some supports? Do they have the emotional and cognitive capacity right now? Who is able to support the child? What is available at home for sensory input (e.g., toys, play structures, furniture)?

- Therapists often use their own prompts during their time with children, but parents may not be familiar with the terms their kids are used to. Can training be provided so parents understand basic concepts, coping strategies, and language cues their child already knows and uses?

- Therapists depend on feedback about a child's progress in order to change or refine interventions. Can parents provide this? Is there a simple form or questionnaire parents can complete, especially if other communication is not happening?

- Therapists need to know their state regulations for providing telehealth. What licenses are required for insurance compensations? Does the parent have to be present? What security and access protocols are required for sessions to be reimbursed? These questions need to be answered before starting any virtual programs, to avoid unexpected financial expenses to families.

Summary

Living during the COVID-19 pandemic has shifted many children into the fear zone. This, combined with the shift to at least part-time virtual learning, has created real barriers to the growth of children with autism. While most children—whether autistic or not—are struggling with virtual learning amidst the heightened anxiety around them, those on the spectrum face additional challenges.

Educators, parents, and therapists can use their knowledge of these challenges to help children in several ways. Extra emotional support is vital. Many children will also need additional help with practical tasks of daily life. Academically, expectations and teaching methods may need to be adjusted. Finally, therapists will need to increase their communication with families and assess the parents' ability to take on additional tasks. If parents are able to implement therapeutic tasks, therapists can give them tools to use at home. Therapists can also adapt interventions for virtual delivery, depending on the regulatory guidelines of their profession.

Some children with autism may flourish during their time away from the school environment, but many will stumble and fall behind.

9

Envisioning a Successful Adulthood

Learning is a lifelong process for everyone. While academic instruction often ends in the teen or early adult years, life demands we continue to gain new information and perspectives as we encounter new situations and roles. If the pandemic has taught us nothing, it should have taught us this. The skills required to navigate adulthood go far beyond classroom lessons. Unfortunately, acquiring these vital competencies is often left to chance. Society assumes that young adults will pick up these skills by observation and imitation.

Ideally, a student's individual education plans (IEPs) include detailed transition guidelines, preparatory steps, and informed visions for each child's unique future. However, this is frequently a weak part of the student's IEP. Plans often disproportionately focus on reducing perceived deficits or on building skills needed by younger children. The skills that the older autistic child or adult will need for success may be regarded as secondary or even overlooked. This chapter will discuss how educators, clinicians, and parents can better prepare autistic children, teens, and young adults to handle the unique demands they will face in adulthood.

Autistic students and teens need a great deal of direct help achieving the competencies needed to meet the different requirements of adulthood. Because they often miss social cues, autistic persons might not notice differences in what is expected of them as an adult versus a child. They're often unable to discern subtle nuances of adult social or vocational interactions. The workplace in particular can be a confusing, frustrating environment.

Adhering to Mindset 9 means remembering that autistic youth will continue, like their typically developing peers, to learn and improve over the entire course of their lifetime. Preparing for and assisting with that ongoing learning, with the goal of helping them lead successful adult lives, is a vital part of a whole child mindset.

A major difference between the student years and non-student years is there are no longer built-in teachers. The structures of lesson plans are gone, and opportunities to hone proficiencies via assignments and feedback no longer exist. As a result, autistic adults are often left on their own to figure out all the new tasks confronting them. Even if they were provided with ideal interventions during childhood, autistic individuals often still need substantial additional help as they get older.

> *Functional ratings are not the most important part of predicting adult success. A child taught life skills and appropriate planning, even if rated as severely impaired, might progress more than a less impacted child who doesn't get these interventions."*
> TEMPLE

A relevant characteristic of many on the spectrum is a reluctance to ask for this assistance. Some may not even recognize when they are in need of outside help. This combination of traits can leave a person isolated and without necessary guidance. It's critical that adults remember that people with autism, like every-one else, will always face new challenges requiring new skills. A mindset of lifelong learning and growth views autistic individuals as persons capable of continued development and of needing this extra support that is committed to them living fulfilling adult lives. Teachers and therapists with this mindset proactively prepare autistic students and clients for the time most of these children, as they age out of systems, will no longer have access to professional guides. These professionals assume no matter what the functional level of the student, with appropriate assistance each has the capacity to build and engage in a meaningful adult life.

Guidelines for Best Transition Practices

The Individuals with Disability Education Improvement Act of 2004 (IDEA) includes mandated guidelines for transition planning, beginning when the student is 16 years old. Some states require planning to begin a year or two earlier. This law also says the transition services must be based on each student's strengths, as well as on their interests. The main purpose of transition planning is to prepare youth for meaningful, successful adult lives. The student's education is viewed as the foundation for further learning, employment, and if possible, independent living. The goal is to maximize and bring into concrete form the highest potential of each person, no matter how they are capable of functioning.

All successful transition plans begin with reviewing the student's history, with a focus on specific interests, motivations, and skills. Multiple opportunities to volunteer or job shadow at sites that involve these interests give teachers and job coaches the opportunity to observe and access the student's fit and readiness. Comprehensive assessment includes noting each student's ability to apply their academic knowledge to real world settings; to manage functional living skills needed to optimize independence; and to exhibit basic employability skills, such as reliably showing up on time and maintaining appropriate hygiene.

Good transition planning also pays close attention to sensory sensitivities and how they manifest in new settings, as well as emotional reactions such as fear, anxiety, or helplessness. Transition assessments include determining what triggers bring about or escalate sensitivities or inappropriate behavior.

The best transition planning is characterized by these components:

- It is highly coordinated among educators, parents, the student, and all other team members. Outside clinicians have important input, and even if they're not ordinarily included in the IEP, this is a good time to invite them.
- It is results oriented, with specific, measurable goals discussed and then put into clear writing. Progress on each goal should be rated at regular intervals.
- Participation and competency in regular, everyday activities is seen as equally important as academic functioning.
- Each plan is realistically based on the student's strengths, needs, goals, and interests. Plans are always student centered, not program or school district centered.
- Transition planning asks two questions: What will the student need to learn while still in high school that is

good preparation for meaningful adult life? How will the
student best learn these skills?

- The best plans usually bring in outsiders who have not
been involved previously with the student. Expert transition planners think creatively and outside the box.
For example, community businesses, nonprofits and
other agencies, church and social leaders, coaches, and
extended family are all potential transition coaches and
assistants.

- For students attending college or other vocational
schools, information on disability services or other in-
house guidance should be researched ahead of time.
Appointments with these support services should be
made prior to the student starting classes.

- Transition planning is a dynamic, ongoing process. It is
experimental.
Activities and sce-
narios are tried,
and new ones are
developed depend-
ing on the results. It
is data driven. The
ratings of progress
guide plans, and
activities that are benefiting the student are continued,
while those not showing benefit are revised or eliminated.

> *School success does not
> always predict life success.
> There are many
> successful workers who
> did poorly in school
> but found a good vocational fit.
> They do their job very well."*
>
> TEMPLE

- Transition plans go far beyond focusing on current academic progress. They are forward looking and require
imagining a child's future. They are a leap of faith based
on specific knowledge of each student.

Start Early: Pave the Road for Ongoing Growth

Viewing an autistic child as more than a label naturally leads educators and clinicians to provide opportunities for building independence. This independence is based on a foundation of proficiency at each child's unique ability level in tasks of ordinary daily living. The change in regular life routines after high school is arguably greater for autistic children than for their typically developing peers. Children on the spectrum, especially those severely impacted, have had numerous supports in place during their younger years. After high school, these supports frequently are abruptly withdrawn. Even those teens who go on to vocational school or college usually get few if any programs to replace their high school supports.

Thus, while transitioning to adulthood is challenging for all teens, those with autism face major additional changes and losses during this period. Their support systems are dramatically altered. Leaving school often means leaving highly structured formats and environments. Preparing for this ahead of time is the best insurance against these children becoming overwhelmed or immobilized by these substantial changes.

Whether you are a teacher, therapist, or parent, your main goal for each child is to help them stand on their own to whatever extent they are capable. Their ability to handle real life situations (either by themselves, or by knowing how to ask for appropriate help) is not only a matter of personal satisfaction; it is also one of well-being and safety.

Every child needs adequate communication and emotional regulation skills to cope with all the novel and challenging situations they will encounter as adults. These competencies, in addition to the child's cognitive ability, will determine how easy or difficult they find adult life. Any child with an IEP should have these skills specifically outlined in their plan. The development of these skills needs to begin early, to be refined and adjusted as the child grows, and to include transition planning that anticipates the day the plan will not be in effect.

No matter how good transition planning is, each child also needs a network of adults who are available for support and guidance. This network, similar to transition planning in general, needs to be built ahead of time. You can't wait until a child graduates from high school to suddenly look around for a support team. A good network is built over time, because it takes time to build trust and to get comfortable sharing problems and fears with another person.

Just as when they were younger, adults on the spectrum benefit from having a circle of acquaintances with similar interests. This gives them people to actually do things with—not just talk about them in theory, but to go and try them out—to walk through the real steps of activities. For example, they might learn to navigate a city bus system by riding with another person who also wants

> *Parents and professionals need to stretch children and teens. They are often capable of more than adults expect. Adults who coddle students with labels hold them back from standing on their own."*
> TEMPLE

to go to the planetarium or join a group of coders on the other side of town. Or they might learn to purchase and pay for movie tickets by going to the theater with a peer who also loves science fiction films. Preparing for transitions ahead of time and building networks in advance help prevent a young adult from being overwhelmed when faced with these changes. It's easy to get over-loaded by all the new experiences a teen encounters after high school.

Proactive preparation reduces the number of times the indi-vidual will encounter a brand-new situation. Facing and figur-ing out unknown circumstances is exhausting for everyone, but especially for those on with autism. No one can prepare another person for every eventuality, but when educators, therapists, and parents join together, they can eliminate many surprises.

An Example of Growth Over a Lifetime

Even toddlers or young children can display hints of future apti-tudes and passions, yet these signals can often be missed. Many parents look back and, in hindsight, can point to signs of their adult child's propensities. The traits or interests weren't registered as important at the time. Yet if nurtured, they can lead directly or indirectly to lifelong interests or vocations. Helping a child keep a passion alive and channeling it into a meaningful part of their adult life is a tremendous gift to that person.

Tyra's journey is a good example. Now 22 years old, and diagnosed with autism and anxiety during elementary school, she started her first paying job a year ago. She works in a local bakery, where she's quickly acquiring new skills, as well as using offshoots of abilities she acquired in childhood. These skills range from technical ones related to baking to many other routine tasks, like cleaning counters, that go along with work-ing in a bakery. She has also learned to operate the espresso maker and has mastered running customer's credit cards. Socially, she is honing her skills, using scripts her employer recommended, plus experimenting with spontaneous interactions with coworkers.

This chapter of Tyra's life did not magically or suddenly come into being. A lifetime of small, progressive steps prepared her to be ready to move into, handle, and find meaning and a good fit in the bakery. While this type of guided, stepwise development is important for typically developing children also, it is crucial for those on the spectrum. Neurotypical children have better executive skills than those with autism. Typically developing children are more likely to self-initiate, to experiment with diverse interests, and to make their own plans for the future. Autistic children often stagnate if they are not given explicit exposure to opportunities and instruction in life skills. Without adult guidance, structure, and encouragement, inertia is a pervasive problem among autistic teens.

Let's consider some of Tyra's early childhood interests and behaviors that were her first steps:

- She loved being in the kitchen when her mother was preparing food.
- She loved the aroma of most foods and happily sniffed many of them before she ate them.
- Tyra wanted to help her mother in the kitchen, and she was enlisted to do whatever was age appropriate from the time she could stand. She started by handing stirring spoons to her mother, and Tyra learned to identify basic utensils at any early age. She was allowed and encouraged to play "cooking" with real utensils, with the exception of sharp knives.
- By age 4 years, Tyra was practicing some steps of

making simple cookies. She was allowed to insert chocolate chips into their centers and to decorate them with sprinkles.

- Once Tyra was able to read, her mother and her teacher found children's books having to do with food and cooking. Tyra struggled with reading, but these were her favorite books and held her attention the longest. They helped her improve her reading.

- Tyra's mom held a cookie competition when her daughter was 6 years old. She assisted Tyra in making sugar cookies that they divided into small batches, adding a different flavor or spice to each. Tyra enjoyed discerning differences in flavors and finding words to describe them.

- Tyra's OT used cooking and baking-related materials whenever possible. For example, Tyra learned to improve her balance by carrying baking sheets and reaching for items off shelves. She refined her hand-eye coordination by filling measuring cups and spoons. Her fine motor control got better as she worked with play dough to make pretend cookies and candies. Her overall muscle tone improved from all of these activities.

- Tyra's mom decided to teach a children's baking class for a small group of neighborhood children. This gave Tyra a chance to be with other children in a comfortable setting (her kitchen) and with no surprises. Unstructured play activities were difficult for Tyra, so this informal class, with each child given an easy task, gave her an opportunity to get more comfortable around peers. A few of the children discovered they shared Tyra's interest, so the mothers of those kids organized a cooking club. The girls and boys met twice a month—rotating homes—and experimented with simple recipes. Tyra looked forward to these Saturday activities. This also helped her get more comfortable being in other people's houses.

- As Tyra entered middle school, her teachers let her apply her interests to the assigned learning modules whenever possible. For example, when each student had to write a short paper on Colonial America, Tyra wrote about food production and preparation during that time.

- At the age of 16 years, Tyra and her mom started volunteering at a local soup kitchen. She learned how to appropriately interact with the clients and other volunteers and also learned what was involved in preparing large quantities of food.

- Tyra often made a cake or cookies on the weekends. Tyra's mom found several neighbors who welcomed purchasing her daughter's baked goods. Tyra learned how to keep simple records of her costs and profits.

- As part of her IEP, an unpaid internship was arranged for Tyra during her senior year of high school. She assisted in a restaurant, doing prep work and preparing dessert trays.

- Tyra had no interest in being a full-time college student, and many courses would have been difficult or unrealistic for her. She did sign up for a food preparation class at a local community college and completed that successfully.

This example shows how many progressive steps—both socially and academically—can be part of learning and honing skills that develop into lifelong activities or vocations.

While not all young adults follow a straight path into the work world, those who do benefit from confidence and readiness built on a many-footed foundation. Tyra's employer has offered to teach her more skills if she stays at her job. Tyra looks forward to this, wanting to learn cake decorating and how to bake specialty items. Her boss has noticed that Tyra has a good eye for design and can imagine her helping with window decoration at some point. Finally, because Tyra is good at making lists and following rules, she and her employer have even discussed the possibility of her training new employees.

Blips on the Learning Curve: How to Help When Transitions Overwhelm

Some young adults with autism become overwhelmed by the new demands of life after high school. When this happens, educators, clinicians, and parents can step in and make necessary adjustments to the young person's situation. The young person themself might not have adequate insight into either what is stressing them or what they need in order to regroup and move forward. Perspectives from outsiders are crucial during this transition period. The following are two examples of individuals who stumbled, one a young man who wanted to attend college, and one a young woman with cognitive impairments that precluded her from living independently.

Keith was accepted into a college 2 hours away from his home. While both he and his parents were nervous about this big change, they believed he could navigate it successfully. He had done well academically throughout school, and his social skills had improved during his teen years. He wanted to study engineering and selected his college based on their program in that major.

Within a month, however, Keith was struggling. He couldn't articulate his difficulties, but his mood had become somber, and he said he wanted to drop out. He had nothing positive to say about college.

This is a common scenario. The individual has an all-or-nothing response (in Keith's case his solution is to quit college entirely). They are reticent or unable to explain their struggles. And they do not know how to reach out for help or support. Fortunately, Keith's parents were neither shocked nor defeated by their son's situation. They had anticipated that college might prove daunting for Keith, but they had agreed to support him while he gave it a try. Keith had declined the services of the on-campus office of disability services, and they felt powerless to force him. He selected his own courses and was resistant to recommendations to lighten his first semester load.

Now Keith had to face the fact they he needed additional support. This embarrassed him. His parents asked his older brother, whom Keith looked up to, to join them for a family meeting. They talked about the pros and cons of using disability services. They helped Keith appreciate the logic and wisdom of taking advantage of these supports. They proceeded to set up an appointment with a member of the college's student office of disabilities. Keith's parents attended the meeting with him.

The counselor helped Keith identify the main causes of his struggles. This overwhelmed young man was experiencing a great deal of anxiety that related to two primary factors. First, Keith had no plan for how to structure his study time. He had managed in his high school classes both because they were less advanced and also because his family had a homework routine that provided structure. Keith no longer had that and hadn't created a substitute. The counselor helped him realize that he wouldn't be able to master his more difficult classes without one. They set another appointment to jointly create a study plan.

Second, Keith had several courses with in-classroom timed, written final exams. This terrified him. During high school, his teachers had known about his autism and his slower processing speed. They had given him extra time on his tests, and when possible, let him write essays at home or take oral exams. It hadn't occurred to Keith that he might be able to get similar accommodations at college, so he hadn't asked for them.

The counselor scheduled an assessment for Keith. It had been many years since his last evaluation, and the counselor wanted an accurate measure of his current working memory and processing speed. With that information, he planned to help Keith build appropriate testing accommodations into his classes. This was a tremendous relief for Keith (and his parents).

The counselor also came up with some other suggestions. He often worked with students on the spectrum, so he anticipated several additional areas that were likely causing Keith stress. He knew that college is very different from living at home, and practical tasks other students may handle with ease can overwhelm a student with autism or poor executive functioning. He also knew that many tasks that the student technically knew how to do wouldn't get done because parents were the ones who had always kept the calendar and given their teenagers reminders.

For example, when the counselor asked Keith about how he was doing with his laundry, Keith admitted he actually had not washed his clothes in the month he'd been on campus. He was anxious both about how to operate an unfamiliar washer and dryer, and also nervous about going into a loud, often busy area where other students tended to socialize while doing their laundry.

By asking other questions, the counselor discovered Keith was skipping some meals, and instead eating out of the coin-operated soda and candy machines. It turned out this had started after Keith got disoriented and lost on his way to the cafeteria, which was in another building across campus. Instead of asking for directions, he turned around, found his way back to his room, and ate chips and cheese sticks for dinner that night.

The counselor paired up Keith with a peer advisor. This student was also on the spectrum, but was a senior who had achieved mastery of the areas that were inundating Keith with anxiety. The peer advisor went with Keith to wash a load of laundry. He also helped him draw a map to the cafeteria, just in case he ever got lost again. He made sure Keith knew where other important campus facilities were as well, such as the student health center, the library, and a quiet corner of an on-campus park that few students used. He gave Keith his cell phone number and checked in by text at least once a week.

Ideally, these measures could have been put in place prior to Keith's first day at college, but they usually aren't. As a result, many students with autism will find themselves overwhelmed during their first semester at college, or their first month living independently, or their first month on a new job. If these glitches are viewed as common blips on the learning curve, instead of failures, adults can help the young person regroup and develop needed supports. Then their lifelong learning can get back on track and continue.

The second example of a young adult with autism becoming overwhelmed by the new demands of life after high school involves a young woman with cognitive impairments that precluded her from living independently.

Ruthie graduated from high school a year ago. Her learning occurred in a self-contained classroom alongside students with special needs. Her teachers made educational, social, and emotional accommodations, but she still struggled. It was difficult for her to remember more than the simplest instructions. She was easily overwhelmed by noise, sudden movements, or novelty. Ruthie was often unable to get her words out and used a speech generating device most days.

After graduating, Ruthie at first seemed calmer, but within months her agitation increased. She was bored, restless, and lonely. Ruthie had enjoyed the companionship of classmates. Now she spent most of the day alone in her room, watching the same few videos over and over. Her father was employed outside the home, her one sibling was away at college, and her mother worked from home as a technical writer in order to supervise Ruthie.

Family stress was high. Ruthie's mother felt guilty she didn't spend more time with her daughter, but the family needed her income and her job required long hours. By the time Ruthie's father got home it was late, both parents were tired, and Ruthie was often irritable to the point of meltdown. The family talked with Ruthie about her moving to a group home and were surprised she seemed excited by the prospect.

Ruthie's parents had no idea how difficult it was to find a suitable group home. Most had long waiting lists, and some seemed inadequately staffed. Once they made the decision, though, the move seemed urgent, and Ruthie asked every day when she could see her "new room". Her parents felt increasingly desperate and when they heard of an opening in a home 3 hours away, they took it.

Ruthie was in a good mood on the drive to the group home and she loved her new room with its big window and colorful curtains. Her parents left feeling relief mixed with sadness. The group home administrator called a week later to tell them it was not working out.

Transitioning to a supported living environment too often follows the trajectory that Ruthie and her family experienced.

Deciding whether a teen or adult child with autism should move from the family home into a supervised group setting is usually emotionally draining, and sometimes excruciatingly painful. Too often it is done under pressure from both escalating parental stress and deteriorating child behavior.

Fortunately, Ruthie's parents did not immediately give up on the idea of Ruthie living in a supported community. They met with the administrator to learn why it wasn't working out, and solicited Ruthie's input as well. They also decided to join a support group for parents of autistic teens and young adults.

In their meeting with the administrator they learned that Ruthie was having daily meltdowns and had twice hit another resident, once hard enough to knock her down. They were able to talk with one staff member, but got the impression she barely knew Ruthie.

The biggest surprise came when they talked with Ruthie. They found out that she had thought she was going to a sort of camp, like she had one summer. It turns out her aggression had occurred when a resident corrected her. She had panicked but hadn't been able to find the words to explain her fear.

Ruthie's parents brought her home and regrouped. They learned more about community living options, both from reading and from their support group. They had several talks with Ruthie and let her list pros and cons of living out of the family home. They jointly decided to take whatever amount of time necessary to prepare for any move.

During that time they read articles and blogs and learned from both professionals and parents who had been in their situation. They decided the following factors were most important in maximizing Ruthie's success in a supported living environment.

- They wanted a group home with a good reputation and testimonials, no significant safety or other violations, good staff retention, and a staff/resident ratio that met recommended guidelines.
- They decided that they wanted the group home to be as close as possible to their home.
- They visited each facility that met their criteria, met with both administration and staff, and talked to other residents. Ruthie went with them.
- When they found a program they liked, they arranged for Ruthie to go back and attend a few social activities plus one overnight stay.
- They wrote up a bulleted page of Ruthie's needs and preferences. They gave a copy to the administrator but also had a copy attached to her bedroom door so all staff, especially those substituting for regulars, would have the information. The page included a list of their daughter's triggers, what helped when she was upset, and what words and phrases either escalated or calmed her.
- They also wrote up a list of skills they thought Ruthie would need in her new environment and prioritized which she needed to become more competent in. Each parent spent some time on the weekends helping their daughter in these areas, and they found a college student who helped her 2 nights a week. They worked on skills including how to ask questions about new things Ruthie might not understand, and how to calm herself if she woke up at night and was afraid.
- Together with Ruthie, they made a list of new activities and opportunities likely to be encountered in her

new environment. They asked Ruthie which of these she looked forward to the most and put stars by those. Ruthie looked forward to checking off the stars each time she tried one of these experiences.

- The family also talked about how any change can be hard and how it takes time. They made sure Ruthie understood she would have difficult days and that they would too. They made plans for handling the tough days with concrete strategies like phone calls, texts, and letting staff know.

As in the previous example of Keith and his family, Ruthie and her family encountered unexpected challenges as their young adult with autism navigated life after high school. While each path was different, both families experienced common obstacles and learned similar lessons.

Both came to appreciate the need for extensive preparation before a young adult with autism can attempt to find their way in a new environment. They developed a greater respect for the support of others who had traveled comparable journeys. They gained a more realistic sense of how long it can take to adjust, and how many surprises can arise during that period. Perhaps most importantly, they discovered that setbacks are not failures.

How High Schools Can Better Prepare Students

Young adults are more successful after graduation if they had the opportunity to practice basic tasks of daily living at school as well as at home. Likewise, if they enter the workforce, they are more successful there if high school provided skill building directly related to their vocation interests, as well as basic workplace etiquette. We believe the majority of today's high schools are failing to prepare their students, and we have suggestions to help improve the prospects for autistic youth.

When Temple grew up, several factors in her environment helped her succeed. Some had to do with her mother, her aunt, and specific teachers. Others, however, were more systemic, and had to do with how society viewed individual differences. Children were not routinely tested or labeled when Temple was a student, and they were not singled out for specialized instruction. While many children who grew up in those years suffered as a result of not being diagnosed, Temple believes there was also an upside to the days before labeling.

When children are labeled and others overly focus on that label, the child can be viewed through the lens of a *disability mentality*. When that happens, others perceive them too narrowly and overlook possibilities and opportunities. Throughout this book, we have stressed the importance of a whole child mindset. This mindset should continue during transition planning and into adulthood, so that autistic youth continue learning at their full capacity and are given access to diverse experiences.

Mindset becomes especially pertinent when autistic teenagers, educators, and families begin to think about what kind of job the student can hold. Their vision of what's possible will be shaped by their mindset and their beliefs about an autistic person's capabilities. If the teen's identity, or the adult's perspective, is rooted primarily in the label of autism or a disability mentality, then interests and talents become secondary. Teachers and parents may presume the student can't handle challenging tasks or jobs, and the teen may not appreciate their own potential.

When Temple was a high school student, schools provided classes intended to prepare students for traditional skills. These classes were gender segregated. Boys automatically attended shop class. Some schools had further specialized options, like welding, or electrical training, or woodworking. Girls routinely took home economics, where they learned to prepare nutritious meals and to mend torn clothes and do basic sewing. While moving away from gender stereotypes is a positive shift, we have to replace these classes with other ways of teaching these skills.

Now that schools no longer provide these classes, many children never learn the skills. They might not learn to cook their own meals, or sew a button back on a shirt, or use simple tools like screwdrivers or hammers. As a result, while they may be cognitively able to live independently (or with a roommate), they are incapable of hanging a picture, cooking a balanced meal, or tightening a loose cabinet handle.

Equally important, they might never discover they enjoy some of these activities. Plenty of older carpenters, welders, electricians, and other skilled tradespeople got into those jobs because they were exposed to them in high school. Some percentage of these individuals were probably on the spectrum, but they were never identified or labeled. They may have been regarded as shy, socially avoidant, or awkward, but the quality of their work was all that mattered when it came to finding a job and earning an income. They were not held back or defined by diagnoses or labels.

Today, in the absence of these traditional classes (and many others, like choir, art, and band, which also have been removed from many schools), students only learn these skills if they have a relative or mentor to teach them. Without the basics of trade skills, they are unlikely to get the exposure to pique their interest.

Students who might have become great skilled tradespeople are falling by the wayside.

Companies cannot find enough workers, even though many autistic individuals are well suited to the trades and could fill these jobs if they were exposed and trained.

Our Suggestions:

- Expose kids to different job sites. Let them watch someone actually doing a job. You never know what will interest them.
- Remember how each child processes information, and investigate what kinds of jobs benefit from those types of thinkers. Some kids with different cognitive styles gravitate to college courses that use their natural style (Blazhenkova & Kozhevnikov, 2009), but others need someone to explicitly steer them there.
- Show kids how their interests and skills translate into vocations. Describe for them what different tradespeople actually do. A teen who likes to build things needs to know about the vast diversity of opportunities in the building, designing, and engineering trades.
- Make sure to inform kids of less common or more specialized occupations to which they can apply their natural interests and talents. For example, a teen interested and talented in drawing comic strips might only think about comic books or newspaper panels or strips. Yet children's books, greeting card companies, creative teams working in screen media, corporate design groups, and technical manual printers also use these sorts of illustrators.

Here are two contrasting examples of how exposure and planning make a difference as a teenager moves through adolescence into adulthood:

Wesley always loved to take things apart and put them back together. He did this with his toys and with small household items. His high school had no classes that gave him an opportunity to apply this interest or hone this skill. No one in his environment stepped in to encourage him to find ways to channel his interest. No one even linked Wesley's behavior with potential jobs.

Wesley's education consisted of mostly regular classes, with a specialized reading class and some social skills training. He was diagnosed with autism and had an IEP, but there was scant attention put on vocational training and none that targeted his skill manipulating and repairing things.

Also, Wesley's school, like most these days, did not offer driver's education classes. His parents offered to enroll him in a private driving school, but Wesley wasn't motivated. He figured his parents took him everywhere he wanted to go, so he didn't see the need. His parents were nervous about his capacity to drive, so they didn't push the issue.

After graduation, Wesley couldn't find a job. He hadn't liked school much and had no interest in further education. He finally got hired busing tables in a restaurant, but he never enjoyed it. It didn't challenge him, and the environment was actually noxious to him. He was overwhelmed by the mix of food smells and by all the conversations going on around him. He was always anxious. Wesley eventually quit and then spent his time watching movies and playing video games.

Wesley forgot about his interest in repairing things. He lived with his parents, because he couldn't afford to live on his own. His parents were considering having him apply for disability.

Contrast this with Jeremy:

Jeremy also loved taking things apart and putting them together. He first exhibited this interest as a preschooler, when he repeatedly took apart, then reassembled, the cars of his toy train. His parents got him some library books about trains, and Jeremy's interest broadened. He memorized the names of the various parts of trains and started learning where different train companies traveled and what goods they carried.

As his parents and team members started thinking about Jeremy's life after high school, they reviewed his interests and strengths. He hadn't spent much time recently on trains, although he had incorporated the topic of rail systems into a few school projects, because he had never lost interest in them.

Jeremy's father was a self-taught handyman, and he started having his son be his helper on small projects from the time Jeremy was a pre-teen. He taught him to use basic tools, demonstrated how to measure and weigh things, and showed him how to make sense of instruments such as pressure gauges. His father also had him read instruction manuals and then explain what he'd read. Jeremy's ability to understand these manuals increased dramatically after a few months of this sort of practice.

Jeremy wasn't particularly confident in his abilities, but his parents believed he could achieve independence if he found the right job, learned to either drive or use public transportation, and mastered basic daily tasks such as shopping, simple cooking, and handling money. Each parent, along with an older sibling, helped Jeremy learn these skills. It took him longer than his typically developing peers to get his license, but when he did, he was a careful, safe driver.

Jeremy's father went online and found a local railroad club. Most of the members were older, retired men. They were happy to have Jeremy join them. One gentleman, a former conductor and model train collector, became Jeremy's mentor. The mentor took him to visit a train museum, went with him on a ride on an old steam-powered train, and took him to a rail yard.

Jeremy's confidence grew and his friendship with this gentleman solidified. Together, they took on the role of co-historians for the club, which meant they were responsible for acquiring, organizing, and labeling documents about trains and parts from old trains. Jeremy learned a great deal about the inner workings of a railway system.

Jeremy and his father started to research what sorts of jobs existed that had to do with trains. Jeremy didn't think he wanted one that required dealing with the public. He was more interested in a hands-on, technical role. When they learned about signal maintainers, the people who service electrical parts of passenger or freight trains or subways, Jeremy said he thought he would enjoy this kind of job.

Now 18 years old, Jeremy was finishing up his senior year of high school. His father found him a volunteer job with Habitat for Humanity, an organization that builds homes for people. This let his son observe electricians at work and also get used to being part of a team of laborers. After a couple of building projects, his father asked one of the volunteer electricians if Jeremy could tag along and be his helper on other projects. The man agreed, and this was the beginning of Jeremy learning basic circuitry.

> *Sometimes, you have to get past HR. Don't demand things. Rather, explain that 'accommodating me is not going to be hard, and here's how you can do it.' Tell them, 'Try me for 2 weeks with no pay. It's a free trial.'"*
>
> TEMPLE

After high school, Jeremy enrolled in some electrical circuitry classes at his local community college. His research had told him that most signal maintainers do not have college educations and that the entry level job was an assistant maintainer. He also found online classes offered by railway associations.

It took Jeremy several years to complete enough courses to apply for a job. He lived at home in the meantime, continued to volunteer with Habitat for Humanity, and continued to be active in the railroad club. He put together a portfolio of his volunteer projects, his club work, and his projects with his electrical mentor. He also had several members of the club write letters of recommendation for his first job.

Jeremy competed against many applicants for that job, but he secured it. His technical skills were not superior to the other applicants, and his social skills were actually less refined, but he impressed the manager who interviewed him. It was clear that Jeremy was genuinely passionate about trains and he had built a good foundation of general knowledge and specialized skill. The manager figured Jeremy would be a stable, motivated employee who could be trained to master any tasks he hadn't yet learned.

Lifelong Learning of Social and Interpersonal Skills

Reaching adulthood brings the opportunity and challenge of new social and interpersonal relationships. As we've said throughout this book, each individual is unique, and the goals and desire of autistic individuals are as varied as their typical peers. Some young men and women want to build new friendships after high school; others aren't particularly interested. Some young adults on the spectrum very much want to date and might hope to marry and have a family, while others don't envision these roles in their futures.

No matter what specific interpersonal goals a person has, adult social demands are usually more puzzling and difficult that the demands of childhood. One reason is that parents, who used to organize, facilitate, and supervise social events, may no longer assume these roles. Second, without the structure of high school or another formal program, young adults are left to find and build their own day-to-day social life.

Finally, most autistic individuals have received little or no guidance on how to navigate the romantic or intimate arenas. While typically developing peers may have been getting practice by dating and attending dances, parties, or concerts, those with autism often missed these activities. Those wanting to include romance in their lives are usually at best far behind their typical peers and often have no skills at all.

How to Help Prepare for Adult Social and Interpersonal Situations

Dating

- Ask students if they want to date, have romantic relationships, or eventually live with or marry a partner.
- Mental health counselors can proactively bring up the subject of dating. Waiting for clients to discuss it may mean it never gets talked about due to discomfort.

- Assess current skill levels by asking basic questions. For example: How would you ask someone out? How do you begin conversation on a date? How do you select where to go or what to do on a first date? How do you end a date? How do you ask for a second date, or how do you let someone know you do not want to continue dating?

- Individuals who have few skills will need direct coaching. Role-playing is a great way for clinicians to assess a teen's current skill level and then to build new proficiencies as needed. Parents and siblings often make excellent coaches as well, and can independently or in partnership with a therapist use role-playing to practice dating scenarios. Clinicians can incorporate anxiety-reduction tools into the coaching and role-playing.

- Consider helping students identify potential people to ask out. Teachers often have insight into which students other students are attracted to and which students share similar interests.

- Shared interests are always the primary factor to consider. They give structure to time spent together and provide fodder for conversation.

> *I was never interested in dating or a romantic relationship.*
> *But friendships are important. They need to be based on shared interests. Get past the labels, and just spend time with people who like the things you do."*
> TEMPLE

- Simple scripts are useful. Examples include how to introduce yourself, how to ask the other person questions, and how to end a date or ask to see the person another time. There are also many short videos online that illustrate introduction tips and protocol.

- Teens and young adults need realistic perspectives on dating and romance. They need to know that not all of their social or romantic overtures will succeed, no matter how well practiced or delivered. It is important they realize this is true for all people whether they have autism or not. Understanding that getting dates and finding a partner is logically dependent in part on how many attempts they make is helpful in preventing discouragement.

- Young adults benefit from reviewing dates and interactions to reflect on what they enjoyed and what they would like to do different in the future.

Interpersonal Relationships at Work

- As with dating, first ask what each person wants from work relationships. While some individuals might hope to find friends in the workplace, others might want to keep to themselves and just do the job.

- Assess each person's level of awareness of appropriate work interactions. For example, you could ask these questions: Is there a difference between an employee's relationship with their boss and their coworkers? What sorts of things are appropriate to talk about with coworkers? What topics are not appropriate?

- How does a person let a coworker know they can't talk right now because they are busy?

- How does a person give feedback to coworkers?

- As with dating, specific guidelines can be given for various situations and practiced through role-playing. For example, one scenario could be how to handle a coworker who asks personal questions the autistic person doesn't want to answer. Another might be what to do if a coworker is gossiping about the boss and wants to know what they think. How would the autistic person respond?

- Young adults on the spectrum should know general workplace rules about interactions. For example, they need to know off-color jokes are not okay, nor are comments about a person's race, religion, gender, or age.

- They also need to know that not all rules are written down, and just because a behavior is not explicitly prohibited in workplace manuals does not make it permissible. For example, they need to know that touching coworkers without their permission (unless it's a job where this is part of a task) can be both offensive and against the law.

- Young adults often work with others on joint work projects and need guidance on navigating these interactions. For example, they need to know how to make suggestions, how to provide both positive and negative feedback, how to delegate, and how to share both workload and credit.

- If the young adult wants to pursue a friendship with a coworker, do they have the necessary tools? For example, would they recognize subtle signs of a shared interest in friendship versus lack of interest? Do they have scripts for asking a coworker to meet outside the workplace, say for a cup of coffee? Again, these are appropriate situations to role-play in advance.

Learning Workplace Interpersonal Skills:
An Example From Temple

When I was just starting out in the workplace, I didn't know how to be diplomatic. A manager helped me. Once I was working, it wasn't medical or psychology professionals who helped, it was other workers—contractors and engineers.

For example, one instance happened when I was in an early internship job. It was in 1974, and I was in my early 20s and right out of college. One day on the job, I criticized one of the welders. I said his work looked like pigeon do-do. Well, the manager took me into his private office and talked to me. He was calm, and told me I had to apologize. I had to go find the welder down in the plant cafeteria, and tell him I was sorry.

It wasn't a matter of the quality of his work. It was simply that you can't tell people their work is stupid and you can't use rude language. It's not diplomatic, and being diplomatic is a necessary skill if you want to be successful in the workplace. It's necessary just to keep your job.

Informal Adult Social Interactions

- In some ways, these do not differ much from adolescent interactions, but the young adult is likely to encounter new sorts of interactions as their world expands. For example, they may be interacting with new groups of people now, such as store clerks, or delivery persons, or wait staff, or medical professionals. They are more likely now to be alone during these interactions, without a parent to guide them.

- As with dating and workplace interactions, begin by getting a sense of the person's knowledge of appropriate rules for these settings. For example, do they know how much personal information is generally okay to share with a clerk or waiter? Do they know what to say if they need to call and make a medical appointment? Again, role-playing ahead of time—while it can't cover all situations—can greatly improve the young adult's success and comfort level.

- Many adults on the spectrum have difficulty knowing how to be supportive of others. This isn't usually a lack of empathy. It's a result of having a hard time discerning what is helpful to people. For example, if the roommate of a young adult on the spectrum loses their job, that young person might not know what to say to the roommate and thus says nothing. What looks like disregard for the feelings of another person is really lack of skill in offering sympathy or understanding.

- Some people on the spectrum are excellent at noticing mistakes. They can spot errors in what people say or do. Linear, logical thinking can lead to a quick recognition of omissions, faulty reasoning, or missing data. They might not have the skills to provide constructive feedback and might instead only point out the inaccuracy, with no awareness of the impact on others. This can also give others the impression that they are always negative.

- Consider teaching boundaries and scripts that keep the young adult safe. For example, every young adult living independently needs to be able to call for emergency help. They need to know when it's okay to answer the door and when it's unadvisable. They need to know what information is appropriate to give out over the phone to a stranger. They need to know how to respond to strangers who approach them on the street or in a public place. They need scripts to use if someone asks makes a request to them, like asking for money or a ride.

- Young adults need interpersonal skills they can use when gathered in settings of shared interest. For example, if a person attends a group related to their hobby, do they know how to introduce themselves and get to know someone they find interesting? As with other interpersonal situations, trusted adults can help the young adult by repeatedly role-playing these scenarios.

Learning Interpersonal Skills:
An Example From Temple

I've had to learn how to give feedback appropriately. By nature, I simply point out what is wrong. That seems the logical thing to do. But Tom, an older, gray-haired engineer in his fifties, helped me learn a lesson about that when I was in my 20s. He told me that it's more important to tell people my ideas for improving or fixing things, rather than tell them all the mistakes I notice. Tom told me I was much too negative. He said I wouldn't get others to listen to me if I didn't offer something positive. He had an important lesson to teach me. I took his advice and totally changed how I presented my ideas. Young people need to learn from the generation before them. You don't automatically know everything even if you think you do.

Help Instill Resiliency and Confidence

Young adults, whether on the spectrum or not, often battle insecurities and anxiety as they embark on greater independence and new environments. Part of setting the stage for successful lifelong learning is helping students, clients, and children to build confidence and excitement about their futures. As autistic children reach late adolescence, educators and clinicians often step out of their lives, but a mentor's influence can continue past the years of physical presence. Here are some suggestions for leaving gifts of hope that can sustain young adult in their more difficult moments.

- A tangible reminder of you and your support can be a touchstone for a young person. A photo of the two of you, a letter about your journey together, or a simple card with a heartfelt inspirational quote is something the person can return to time and again.
- For students who enjoy or are motivated by auditory experiences, consider taping a short message to them. If they have a phone, this can be a voice mail they don't

erase. It could be a short poem or song you write about them. It could be as simple as you reading a motivational saying. A very useful going away gift for some students is a relaxation tape.

- For those who love tactile sensations, consider a parting gift of something they can touch. So that it has added meaning, choose an object that directly relates to one of the student's interests. (For example, one student may love a stuffed animal, but for another that would be uninteresting or embarrassing). A handheld relaxation device like a squeeze ball or three-dimensional puzzle might be a good fit. Get online and get creative!

- Some students may enjoy a book that relates to their interest, or they may appreciate a book of stories about adults who worked in that area. Memoirs may interest some, while others will not see what another person's life has to do with theirs. Before making a selection, check with those who know the student best.

- Have a final experience or outing with your student or client. Document it with photos or written reminders. This can be very simple—going for a coffee or a walk. Doing something outside your usual activities together is a transition itself and marks the beginning of a new chapter.

- Share your own experiences navigating transitions, but only if the student seems interested. If the client or student can't relate, you risk turning off the student, who may not be able to identify with you in this way.

- Remind your student that no one, including adults, is perfect. It's helpful for them to hear (even if it's been said before) that we all make mistakes. Ideally, young adults embarking on their next chapter know it's enough to keep learning, to keep trying, and to keep stretching themselves. If they can internalize these goals, they can shape their world so it is the best possible fit for their unique self.

Summary

Mindset 9—that all children need help envisioning and preparing for lifelong learning—completes the circle of guidelines for successfully navigating autism. Children with autism are never too young for the adults working with them to think about each child's future. All interventions are more valuable if they are tailored to life skills the child will need in order to reach their fullest potential.

Remembering that each autistic child is unique—Mindset 1—again underlies the most impactful help that child receives. Recognizing and applying their specific interests and abilities, both academically and socially, builds confidence and motivation and begins to shape their path to eventual adulthood. A child learns and grows the most when they are exposed to a wide range of topics and activities. That's when they can stumble on or refine interests that may last them a lifetime.

With this exposure, encouragement, and the opportunity to try new things, autistic children can blossom. They will learn resilience by making mistakes and trying once again. They'll learn skills needed to maintain a job or get along with others if provided with lots of opportunities to practice ordinary, real life interactions, manners, and chores.

Parents, clinicians, and educators help determine the breath and depth of a child's world. Children who have received the gift of being fully perceived as unique, valuable, and contributing members of society are in the best position to reach their highest adult potential.

I have seven rules for successful adulthood:

Follow your passion, and learn everything you can about it.

Live life.

Be yourself, but you have to fit in a little.

Develop your talents.

Perfect is not possible.

Work hard.

Never stop learning."

TEMPLE

We hope the mindsets presented in this book guide you to embrace and enact each chapter's suggestions. All children, whether autistic or typically developing, depend on adults. No child navigates the path to adulthood alone. Educators, parents, and clinicians are role models, energizers, and lodestars. These are the gifts we can give each child.

REFERENCES

Abel, E., Kim, S. Y., Kellerman, A. M., & Brodhead, M. T. (2017). Recommendations for identifying sleep problems and treatment resources for Children with Autism Spectrum Disorder. *Behavior Analysis in Practice, 10*(3), 261–269.

Able, H., Sreckovic, M. A., Schultz, T. R., Garwood, J., & Sherman, J. (2014). Views from the trenches: Teacher and student supports needed for full inclusion of students with ASD. *Teacher Education and Special Education: The Journal of the Teacher Education Division of the Council for Exceptional Children, 38*(1), 44–57.

Aldinger, K. A., Lane, C. J., Veenstra-Vanderweele, J., & Levitt, P. (2015). Patterns of risk for multiple co-occurring medical conditions replicate across distinct cohorts of children with autism spectrum disorder. *Autism Research, 8*(6), 771–81.

AETTrainingHubs. (2016). Retrieved July 08, 2020, from https://www .aettraininghubs.org.uk/wp-content/uploads2016/01/AET_ CompetencyFramework_22012016.pdf

Al-Ayadhi, L. Y., & Mostafa, G. A., (2012). Elevated serum levels of interleukin-17A in children with autism. *Journal of Neuroinflammation, 9*(158), 1–6. https://doi.org/ 10.1186/1742-2094-9-158

Alvares, G. A., Dawson, P. A., Dissanayake, C., Eapen, V., Gratten, J., Grove, R., Henders, A., Heussler, H., Lawson, L., Masi, A, Raymond, E., Rose, F., Wallace, L., Wray, N. R., & Whitehouse, A. J. (2018). Study protocol for the Australian autism biobank: An international resource to advance autism discovery research. *BMC Pediatrics, 18*(1), 284. https://doi.org:10.1186/s12887-018-1255-z

American Psychiatric Association. (2013). *Diagnostic and statistical manual of mental disorders* (5th ed.). https://doi.org/10.1176/appi. books.9780890425596.

Bainbridge, W. A., Pounder, Z., Eardley, A. F., & Baker, C. I. (2021). Quantifying Aphantasia through drawing: Those without visual imagery show deficits in object but not spatial memory. *Cortex*, *135*, 159–172. https://doi.org/10.1016/j.cortex.2020.11.014.

Banerjee, A., Banerji, R., Berry, J., Duflo, E., Kannan, H., Mukerji, S., Shotland, M., & Walton, M. (2017). From proof of concept to scalable policies: Challenges and solutions, with an application. *Journal of Economic Perspectives, 31*(4), 73–102.

Baribeau, D. A., Dupuis, A., Paton, T. A., Hammill, C., Scherer, S. W., Schachar, R. J., Arnold, P. D., Szatmari, P., Nicolson, R., Georgiades, S., Crosbie, J., Brian, J., Iaboni, A., Kushki, A., Lerch, J. P., & Anagnostou, E. (2019). Structural neuroimaging correlates of social deficits are similar in autism spectrum disorder and attention-deficit/hyperactivity disorder: Analysis from the POND Network. *Translational Psychiatry, 9*(1), 72. https://doi.org/10.10 38/s41398-019-0382-0

Bearss, K., Johnson, C., Smith, T., Lecavalier, L., Swiezy, N., Aman, M., McAdam, D. B., Butter, E., Stillitano, C., Minshawi., N., Sukhodolsky, D. G., Mruzek, D. W., Turner, K., Neal, T., Hallett, V., Mulick, J. A., Green, B., Handen, B., Deng, Y., . . . Scahill, L. (2015). Effect of parent training vs parent education on behavioral problems in children with autism spectrum disorder: A randomized clinical trial. *Journal of the American Medical Association, 313*(15), 1524–1533.

Belardinelli, C., Raza, M., & Taneli, T. (2016). Comorbid behavioral problems and psychiatric disorders in autism spectrum disorders. *Journal of Childhood & Developmental Disorders, 2*(11). https://doi .org/10.4172/2472-1786.100019

Berg, K. L., Shui, C.-S., Acharya, K., Stolbach, B. C., & Small, M. E. (2016). Disparities in adversity among children with autism spectrum disorder: A population-based study. *Developmental Medicine and Child Neurology, 58*(11), 1124–1131.

Black, C., Kaye, J. A., & Jick, H. (2002). Relation of childhood gastrointestinal disorders to autism: Nested case–control study using data from the UK General Practice Research Database. *British Medical Journal, 325*(7361), 419–421.

Blackwell, W. H., Sheppard, M. E., Lehr, D., & Huang, S. (2017). Examining pre-service teacher candidates' sources and levels of knowledge about autism spectrum disorders. *Journal of Human Services: Training, Research, and Practice, 2*(2), Article 4.

Blazhenkova, O., & Kozhevnikov, M. (2009). The new object-spatial-verbal cognitive style model: Theory and measurement. *Applied Cognitive Psychology, 23*(5), 638–663. https://doi.org/10.1002/acp.1473

Bleil Walters, J., Hughes, T. L., Sutton, L. R., Marshall, S. N., Crothers, L. M., Lehman, C., Paserba, D., Talkington, V., Taormina, R., & Huang, A. (2013). Maltreatment and depression in adolescent sexual offenders with an autism spectrum disorder. *Journal of Child Sexual Abuse, 22*(1), 72–89.

Brenner, J., Pan, Z., Mazefsky, C., Smith, K. A., Gabriels, R., Siegel, M., . . . for the Autism and Developmental Disorders Inpatient Research Collaborative (ADDIRC). (2018). Behavioral symptoms of reported abuse in children and adolescents with autism spectrum disorder in inpatient settings. *Journal of Autism and Developmental Disorders, 48*(11), 3727–3735. https://doi.org/10.1007/s10803-017-3183-4

Buie, T., Campbell, D. B., Fuchs, G. J., 3rd, Furuta, G. T., Levy, J., Vandewater, J., Whitaker, A. H., Atkins, D., Bauman, M. L., Beaudet, A. L., Carr, E. G., Gershon, M. D., Hyman, S. L., Jirapinyo, P., Jyonouchi, H., Kooros, K., Kushak, R., Levitt, P., Levy, S. E., . . . Winter, H. (2010). Evaluation, diagnosis, and treatment of gastrointestinal disorders in individuals with ASDs: A consensus report. *Pediatrics, 125*(Suppl. 1), S1–S18. httpss://doi.org/10.1542/peds.2009-1878C

Busby, R., Ingram, R., Bowron, R., Oliver, J., & Lyons, B. (2012). Teaching elementary children with autism: Addressing teaching challenges and pre-service needs. *Rural Educator, 33*(2), 27–35.

Capal, J. K., Macklin, E. A., Lu, F., & Barnes, G. (2020). Factors associataed with seizure onset in children with autism spectrum disorder. *Pediatrics, 145*(4, Suppl. 1), S117–S125. https://doi.org/10.1542/peds .2019-1895O

Carissimi, C., Laudadio, I., Palone, F., Fulci, V., Cesi, V., Cardona, F., Alfonsi, C., Cucchiara, S., Isoldi, S., & Stronati, L. (2019). Functional analysis of gut microbiota and immunoinflammation in children with autism spectrum disorders. *Digestive and Liver Disease, 51*(10), 1366–1374. httpss://doi.org/10.1016/j.dld.2019.06.006

Carter, E. W., & Lee, G. (2012). Preparing transition-age students with high-functioning autism spectrum disorders for meaningful work. *Psychology in the Schools, 49*(10), 988–1000.

Chaidez, V., Hansen, R. L., & Hertz-Picciotto, I. (2014). Gastrointestinal problems in children with autism, developmental delays or typical development. *Journal of Autism and Developmental Disorders, 44*(5),117–27.

Chen, Y. H., Rodgers, J., & McConachie, H. (2009). Restricted and repetitive behavior, sensory processing and cognitive style in children with autism spectrum disorders. *Journal of Autism and Developmental Disorders, 39*(4), 635–642.

Chervin, R. D., Hedger, K., Dillon, J. E., & Pituch, K. J., (2000). Pediatric Sleep Questionnaire (PSQ): Validity and reliability of scales for sleep-disordered breathing, snoring, sleepiness, and behavioral problems. *Sleep Medicine, 1*(1), 21–32.

Constable, M. D., Pratt, J., & Welsh, T. N. (2018). "Two minds don't blink alike": The attentional blink does not occur in a joint context. *Frontiers in Psychology, 9*, 1714. https://doi.org/10.3389/fpsyg.2018 .01714

Copeland, W. E., Keeler, G., Angold, A., & Costello, E. J. (2007). Traumatic events and posttraumatic stress in childhood. *Archives of General Psychiatry, 64*(5), 577–584.

Cortese, S., Wang, F., Angriman, M., Masi, G., & Bruni, O. (2020). Sleep disorders in children and adolescents with autism spectrum disorder: Diagnosis, epidemiology, and management. *Central Nervous*

System Drugs, 34, 415–423. https://doi.org/10.1007/s40263-020 -00710-y

Costello, E. J., Egger, H. L., & Angold, A. (2005). The developmental epidemiology of anxiety disorders: Phenomenology, prevalence, and comorbidity. *Child and Adolescent Psychiatric Clinics of North America, 14*(4), 631–648.

Courchesne, V., Meilleur, A. A., Poulin-Lord, M. P., Dawson, M., & Soulières, I. (2015). Autistic children at risk of being underestimated: School-based pilot study of a strength-informed assessment. *Molecular Autism, 6*(1), 12. https://doi.org/10.1186/s13229-015-0006-3

Crane, L., Batty, R., Adeyinka, H., Goddard, L., Henry, L. A., & Hill, E. L. (2018). Autism diagnosis in the United Kingdom: Perspectives of autistic adult, parents and professionals. *Journal of Autism and Developmental Disorders, 48*(11), 3761–3772.

Crane, L., Chester, J., Goddard, L., Henry, L. A., & Hill, E. L. (2016). Experiences of autism diagnosis: A survey of over 1000 parents in the United Kingdom. *Autism: The International Journal of Research and Practice, 20*(2), 153–162.

Croen, L. A., Zerbo, O., Qian, Y., Massolo, M. L., Rich, S., Sidney, S., & Kripke, C. (2015). The health status of adults on the autism spectrum. *Autism, 19*(7), 814–823.

Cummings, J. R., Lynch, F. L., Rust, K. C., Coleman, K. J., Madden, J. M., Owen-Smith, A. A., Yau, V. M., Qian, Y., Pearson, K. A., Crawford, P. M., Massolo, M. L., Quinn, V. P., & Croen, L. A. (2016). Health services utilization among children with and without autism spectrum disorders. *Journal of Autism and Developmental Disorders, 46*(3), 910–920. https://doi.org/10.1007/s10803-015-2634-z

Damore, S. J., & Murray, C. (2009). Urban elementary school teachers' perspectives regarding collaborative teaching practices. *Remedial and Special Education, 30*(4), 234–244.

Dan, Z., Mao, X., Liu, Q., Guo, M., Zhuang, Y., Liu, Z., Chen, K., Chen, J., Xu, R., Tang, J., Qin, L., Gu, B., Liu, K., Su, C., Zhang, F., Xia, Y., Hu, Z., & Liu, X. (2020). Altered gut microbial profile is associated with abnormal metabolism activity of autism spectrum disorder. *Gut Microbes, 11*(5), 1246–1267.

Davidovitch, M., Levit-Binnun, N., & Golan, D. (2015). Late diagnosis of autism spectrum disorder after initial negative assessment by a multidisciplinary team. *Journal of Developmental and Behavioral Pediatrics, 36*(4), 227–234.

De Bruin, E. I., Ferdinand, R. F., Meester, S., de Nijs, P. F., & Verheij, F. (2007). High rates of psychiatric co-morbidity in PDD-NOS. *Journal of Autism and Developmental Disorders, 37*(5), 877–886.

Doshi-Velez, F., Ge, Y., & Kohane, I. (2014). Comorbidity clusters in autism spectrum disorders: An electronic health record time-series analysis. *Pediatrics, 133*(1), e54–e63. httpss://doi.org/10.1542/peds.2013-0819

Eriksson, S. H. (2011). Epilepsy and sleep. *Current Opinions in Neurology, 24*(2), 171–176.

Ferguson, B. J., Dovgan, K., Takahashi, N., & Beversdorf, D. Q. (2019). The relationship among gastrointestinal symptoms, problem behaviors, and internalizing symptoms in children and adolescents with autism spectrum disorder. *Frontiers in Psychiatry, 10*, 194. httpss://doi.org/10.3389/fpsyt.2019.00194

Finisguerra, A., Borgatti, R., & Urgesi, C. (2019). Non-invasive brain stimulation for the rehabilitation of children and adolescents with neurodevelopmental disorders: A systematic review. *Frontiers in Psychology, 10*, Article 135. https://doi.org/10.3389/fpsyg.2019.00135

Frenette, P., Dodds, L., & MacPherson, K. (2013). Factors affecting the age at diagnosis of autism spectrum disorders in Nova Scotia, Canada. *Autism, 17*(2), 184–195.

Fulceri, F., Morelli, M., Santocchi, E., Cena, H., Del Biano, T., Narzisi, A., Calderon, S., S., & Muratori, F. (2016). Gastrointestinal symptoms and behavioral problems in preschoolers with autism spectrum disorder. *Digestive and Liver Disease, 48*(3), 248–254.

Gillberg, C., Billstedt, E., Sundh, V., & Gillberg, I.C. (2010). Mortality in autism: A prospective longitudinal community-based study. *Journal of Autism and Developmental Disorders, 40*(3), 352–357.

Grandin, Temple. (1995). *Thinking in pictures: And other reports from my life with autism.* New York: Vintage Books.

Grandin, T., & Moore, D. (2015). *The loving push: How parents and professionals can help spectrum kids become successful adults.* Future Horizons.

Grandin, T., & Panek, R. (2013). *The autistic brain: Helping different kinds of minds succeed.* Boston: Houghton Mifflin Harcourt.

Green, J., & Garg, S. (2018). Annual research review: The state of autism intervention science: Process, target psychological and biological mechanisms and future prospects. *Journal of Child Psychology and Psychiatry, 59*(4), 424– 443.

Groden, J., Diller, A., Bausman, M., Velicer, W., Norman, G., & Cautela, J. (2001). The development of a stress survey schedule for persons with autism and other developmental disabilities. *Journal of Autism and Developmental Disorders, 31*(2), 207–217.

Harrop, C., Jones, D., Zheng, S., Nowell, S., Boyd, B. A., & Sasson, N. (2018). Circumscribed interests and attention in autism: The role of biological sex. *Journal of Autism and Developmental Disorders, 11*(9), 1264–1275.

Hedley, D., & Uljarević, M. (2018). Systematic review of suicide in autism spectrum disorder: Current trends and implications. *Current Developmental Disorder Reports, 5*(1), 65–76.

Hirvikoski, T., Mittendorfer-Rutz, E., Boman, M., Larsson, H., Lichtenstein, P., & Bölte, S. (2016). Premature mortality in autism spectrum disorder. *British Journal of Psychiatry, 208*(3), 232–238.

Hoch, J. D. & Youssef, A. M. (2020). Predictors of trauma exposure and trauma diagnoses for children with autism and developmental disorders served in a community mental health clinic. *Journal of Autism and Developmental Disorders, 50*(2), 634–649.

Hoffman, C. D., Sweeney, D. P., Lopez-Wagner, M., Hodge, D., Nam, C. Y., & Botts, B. H. (2008). Children with autism: Sleep problems and mothers' stress. *Focus on Autism and Other Developmental Disabilities, 23*(3), 155–165.

Holingue, C., Newill, C., Lee, L. C., Pasricha, P. J., & Fallin, M. D. (2018). Gastrointestinal symptoms in autism spectrum disorder: A review of the literature on ascertainment and prevalence. *Autism Research, 11*(1), 24–36.

Hollocks, M. J., Lerh, J. W., Magiati, I., Meiser-Stedman, R., & Brugha, T. S. (2019). Anxiety and depression in adults with autism spectrum disorder: A systematic review and meta-analysis. *Psychological Medicine, 49*(4), 559–572.

Hoover, D. W., & Kaufman, J. (2018). Adverse childhood experiences in children with autism spectrum disorder. *Current Opinion in Psychiatry, 31*(2), 128–132. https://doi.org/10.1097/YCO.0000000000000390

Hoover, D. W., & Romero, E. M. G. (2019). The Interactive Trauma Scale: A web-based measure for children with autism. *Journal of Autism and Developmental Disorders, 49*(4), 1686–1692.

Houghton, R., Ong, R. C., & Bolognani, F. (2017). Psychiatric comorbidities and use of psychotropic medications in people with autism spectrum disorder in the United States. *Autism Research, 10*(12), 2037–2047.

Hudson, C. C., Hall, L., & Harkness, K. L. (2019). Prevalence of depressive disorders in individuals with autism spectrum disorder: A meta-analysis. *Journal of Abnormal Child Psychology, 47*(1), 165–175.

Humphreys, J. S., Gringras, P., Blairaa, P. S., Scott, N., Hendersonn, J., Fleming, P. J., & Emond, A. M. (2014). Sleep patterns in children with autistic spectrum disorders: A prospective cohort study. *Archives of Disease in Children, 99*(2), 114–118.

Irwin, M. R., Olmstead, R., & Carroll, J. E. (2016). Sleep disturbance, sleep duration, and inflammation: A systematic review and meta-analysis of cohort studies and experimental sleep deprivation. *Biological Psychiatry, 80*(1), 40–52.

Isaksen, J., Bryn, V., Diseth, T. H., Heiberg, A., Schjølberg, S., & Skjeldal, O. H. (2013). Children with autism spectrum disorders – the importance of medical investigations. *European Journal of Paediatric Neurology, 17*, 68–76. https://doi.org/10.1016/j.ejpn.2012.08.004

Jaber, M. A. (2011). Dental caries experience, oral health status and treatment needs of dental patients with autism. *Journal of Applied Oral Science, 19*(3), 212–217.

Jónsdóttir, S. L., Saemundsen, E., & Antonsdóttir, I. S. (2011). Children diagnosed with autism spectrum disorder before or after the age of 6 years. *Research in Autism Spectrum Disorders, 5*(1), 175–184.

Joshi, G., Faraone, S. V., Wozniak, J., Petty, C., Fried, R., Galdo, M., Furtak, S. L., McDermott, K., Epstien, C., Walker, R., Caron, A., Feinberg, L., & Biederman, J. (2014). Examining the clinical correlates of autism spectrum disorder in youth by ascertainment source. *Journal of Autism and Developmental Disorders, 44*(9), 2117–2126.

Jussila, K., Junttila, M., Kielinen, M., Ebeling, H., Joshkitt, L, Moilanen, I., & Mattila, M. L. (2020). Sensory abnormality and quantitative autism traits in children with and without autism spectrum disorder in epidemiological population. *Journal of Autism and Developmental Disorders. 50*, 180–188. https://doi.org/10.1007/s10803-019 -04237-0

Kalyva, E., Kyriazi, M., Vargiami, E., & Zafeiriou, D. I. (2016). A review of co-occurrence of autism spectrum disorder and Tourette syndrome. *Research in Autism Spectrum Disorders, 24*(2), 39–51.

Kentrou, V., de Veld, D. M., Mataw, K., & Begeer, S. (2018). Delayed autism spectrum disorder recognition in children and adolescents previously diagnosed with attention-deficit/hyperactivity disorder. *Autism, 23*(4), 1065–1072.

Keogh, R., & Pearson, J. (2018). The blind mind: No sensory visual imagery in aphantasia. *Cortex, 105*, 53–60. https://doi.org/10.1016/j.cortex .2017.10.012

Kerns, C. M., Newschaffer, C. J., & Berkowitz, S. J. (2015). Traumatic childhood events and autism spectrum disorder. *Journal of Autism and Developmental Disorders, 45*(11), 3475–3486.

Klehm, M. (2014). The effects of teacher beliefs on teaching practices and achievement of students with disabilities. *Teacher Education and Special Education, 37*(3), 216–240.

Klusek, J., Roberts, J. E., & Losh, M. (2015). Cardiac autonomic regulation in autism and Fragile X syndrome: A review. *Psychological Bulletin, 141*(1), 141–175. https://doi.org/10.1037/a0038237

Kohane, I. S., McMurry, A., Weber, G., MacFadden, D., Rappaport, L., Kunkel, L., Bickel, J., Wattanasin, N., Spence, S., Murphy, S., & Churchill, S. (2012). The co-morbidity burden of children and young adults with autism spectrum disorders. *PloS One, 7*(4), e33224. httpss://doi.org/10.1371/journal.pone.0033224

Konstantareas, M. M., & Stewart, K. (2006). Affect regulation and temperament in children with autism spectrum disorder. *Journal of Autism and Developmental Disorders, 36*(2), 143–154. https://doi.org/10.1007/s10803-005-0051-4

Kozhevnikov, M., Blazhenkova, O., & Becker, M. (2010). Trade-off in object versus spatial visualization abilities: Restriction in the development of visual-processing resources. *Psychonomic Bulletin & Review 17*, 29–35. https://doi.org/10.3758/PBR.17.1.29

Kreiser, N. L., & White, S. W. (2015). ASD Traits and co-occurring psychopathology: The moderating role of gender. *Journal of Autism and Developmental Disorders, 45*(12), 3932–3938.

Lai, M. C., Kassee, C., Besney, R., Bonato, S., Hull, L., Mandy, W., Szatmari, P., & Ameis, S. H. (2019). Prevalence of co-occurring mental health diagnoses in the autism population: A systematic review and meta-analysis. *The Lancet: Psychiatry, 6*(10), 819–829. https://doi.org/10.1016/S2215-0366(19)30289-5

Lefter, R., Ciobica, A., Timofte, D., Stanciu, C., & Trifan, A. (2020). A descriptive review on the prevalence of gastrointestinal disturbances and their multiple associations in autism spectrum disorder. *Medicina, 56*(1), 11. https://doi:10.3390/medicina56010011

Liu, X., Hubbard, J. A., Fabes, R. A., & Adam, J. B. (2006). Sleep disturbance and correlates of children with autism spectrum disorders. *Child Psychiatry Human Development, 37*, 179–191. httpss://doi.org/10.1007/s10578-006-0028-3

Loveland, K. A., Pearson, D. A., Tunali-Kotoski, B., Ortegon, J., &

Gibbs, M. C. (2001). Judgments of social appropriateness by children and adolescents with autism. *Journal of Autism and Developmental Disorders, 31*(4) 367–376.

Lugo-Marín, J., Magán-Maganto, M., Rivero-Santana, A., Cuéllar-Pompa, L., Alviani, M., Jenaro-Río, C., Diez, E., & Canal-Bedia, R. (2019). Prevalence of psychiatric disorders in adults with autism spectrum disorder: A systematic review and meta-analysis. *Research in Autism Spectrum Disorders, 59*(3), 22–33.

Lukmanji, S., Manji, S. A., Kadhim, S., Sauro, K. M., Wirrell, E. C., Kwon, C. S., & Jetté, N. (2019). The co-occurrence of epilepsy and autism: A systematic review. *Epilepsy & Behavior, 98*(Pt A), 238–248. https://doi.org/10.1016/j.yebeh.2019.07.037

Maclean, M. J., Sims, S., Bower, C., Leonard, H., Stanley, F. J., & O'Donnell, M. (2017). Maltreatment risk among children with disabilities. *Pediatrics, 139*(4), e20161817. https://doi.org/10.1542/peds.2016-1817

Maïano, C., Normand, C. L., Salvas, M., Moullec, G., & Aimé, A. (2016). Prevalence of school bullying among youth with autism spectrum disorders: A systematic review and meta-analysis. *Autism Research, 9*(6), 601–615. https://doi.org/10.1002/aur.1568

Malow, B. A., Byars, K., Johnson, K., Weiss, S., Bernal, P., Goldman, S. E., Panzer, R., Coury, D. L., & Glaze, D. G. (2012). A practice pathway for the identification, evaluation, and management of insomnia in children and adolescents with autism spectrum disorders. *Pediatrics, 130*(Suppl. 2), 106–124. https://doi.org/10.1542/peds.2012-0900I

Mannion, A., & Leader, G. (2014). Gastrointestinal symptoms in autism spectrum disorder: A literature review. *Review Journal of Autism Developmental Disorders, 1*, 11–17. https://doi.org/10.1007/s40489-013-0007-0

Mannion, A., & Leader, G. (2016). An investigation of comorbid psychological disorders, sleep problems, gastrointestinal symptoms and epilepsy in children and adolescents with autism spectrum disorder: A two year follow-up. *Research in Autism Spectrum Disorders, 22*, 20–33. https://doi.org/10.1016/j.rasd.2015.11.002

Margolis, K. G., Buie, T. M., Turner, J. B., Silberman, A. E., Feldman, J. F., Murray, K. F., McSwiggan-Hardin, M., Levy, J., Bauman, M. L., Veenstra-Vanderweele, J., Whitaker, A. H., & Winter, H. S. (2019). Development of a brief parent-report screen for common gastrointestinal disorders in autism spectrum disorder. *Journal of Autism Developmental Disorders, 49*(1), 349–362.

Marin, J. L., Rodríguez-Franco, M. A., Chugani, V. M., Maganto, M. M., Villoria, E. D. & Bedia, R. C. (2018). Prevalence of schizophrenia spectrum disorders in average-IQ adults with autism spectrum disorders: A meta-analysis. *Journal of Autism and Developmental Disorders, 48*(1), 239–250.

Maski, K. P., & Kothare, S. V. (2013). Sleep deprivation and neurobehavioral functioning in children. *International Journal of Psychophysiology, 89*(2), 259–264.

Mason, D., Ingham, B., Urbanowicz, A., Michael, C., Birtles, H., Woodbury-Smith, M., Brown, T., James, I., Scarlett, C., Nicolaidis, C., Parr, J.R. (2019). A systematic review of what barriers and facilitators prevent and enable physical healthcare services access for autistic adults. *Journal of Autism Developmental Disorders, 49*(8), 3387–3400.

Matsuo, M., Maeda, T., Sasaki, K., Ishii, K., & Hamasaki, Y. (2010). Frequent association of autism spectrum disorder in patients with childhood onset epilepsy. *Brain Development, 32*(9), 759–763.

May, T., Brignell, A., Hawi, Z., Brereton, A., Tonge, B., Bellgrove, M. A., & Rinehart, N. (2018). Trends in the overlap of autism spectrum disorder and attention deficit hyperactivity disorder: Prevalence, clinical management, language and genetics. *Current Developmental Disorder Reports, 5*(1), 49–57.

Mayes, S. D., Gorman, A. A., Hillwig-Garcia, J., & Syed, E. (2013). Suicide ideation and attempts in children with autism. *Research in Autism Spectrum Disorders, 7*(1), 109–119. https://doi:10.1016/j.rasd.2012 .07.009

Mazefsky, C. A., Kao, J., & Oswald, D. P. (2011). Preliminary evidence suggesting caution in the use of psychiatric self-report measures with adolescents with high-functioning autism spectrum disorders. *Research in Autism Spectrum Disorders, 5*(1), 164–174.

Mazurek, M. O., Vasa, R. A., Kalb, L. G., Kanne, S. M., Rosenberg, D., Keefer, A., Murray, D. S., Freedman, B., & Lowery, L. A. (2013). Anxiety, sensory over-responsivity, and gastrointestinal problems in children with autism spectrum disorders. *Journal of Abnormal Child Psychology, 41*(1), 165–76.

McCray, E. D., & McHatton, P. A. (2011). "Less afraid to have them in my classroom": Understanding pre-service general educators' perceptions about inclusion. *Teacher Education Quarterly, 38*(4), 135–155.

Meera, S. S., Kaipa, R., Thomas, J., & Shivashankar, N. (2013). Brief report: An unusual manifestation of diagnostic overshadowing of pervasive developmental disorder—not otherwise specified: A five year longitudinal case study. *Journal of Autism and Developmental Disorders, 43*(6), 1491–1494.

Mehtar, M., & Mukaddes, N. M. (2011). Posttraumatic stress disorder in individuals with diagnosis of autistic spectrum disorders. *Research in Autism Spectrum Disorders, 5*(1), 539–546.

Mevissen, L., Didden, R., Korzilius, H., & de Jongh, A. (2016). Assessing posttraumatic stress disorder in children with mild to borderline intellectual disabilities. *European Journal of Psychotraumatology, 7*, 29786. https://doi.org/10.3402/ejpt.v7.29786

Miano, S., & Ferri, R. (2010). Epidemiology and management of insomnia in children with autistic spectrum disorders. *Pediatric Drugs, 12*(4), 75–84.

Miodovnik, A., Harstad, E., & Sideridis, G. (2015). Timing of the diagnosis of attention-deficit/hyperactivity disorder and autism spectrum disorder. *Pediatrics, 136*(4), 830–837.

Mosner, M. G., Kinard, J. L., Shah, J. S., McWeeny, S., Greene, R. K., Lowery, S. C., Mazefshy, C. A., & Dichter, G. S. (2019). Rates of co-occurring psychiatric disorders in autism spectrum disorder using the Mini International Neuropsychiatric Interview. *Journal of Autism*

Developmental Disorders, 49, 3819–3832. https://doi.org/10.1007/s10803-019-04090-1

Mouridsen, S. E., Brønnum-Hansen, H., Rich, B., & Isager, T. (2008). Mortality and causes of death in autism spectrum disorders: An update. *Autism, 12*(4), 403–414.

Mouridsen, S. E., Rich, B., & Isager, T. (2011). A longitudinal study of epilepsy and other central nervous system diseases in individuals with and without a history of infantile autism. *Brain Development, 33*(5), 361–366.

Mulligan, J., MacCulloch, R., Good, B., & Nicholas, D. B. (2012). Transparency, hope, and empowerment: A model for partnering with parents of a child with autism spectrum disorder at diagnosis and beyond. *Social Work in Mental Health, 10*(4), 311–330.

Muskens, J. B., Velders, F. P. & Staal, W. G. (2017). Medical comorbidities in children and adolescents with autism spectrum disorders and attention deficit hyperactivity disorders: A systematic review. *European Child Adolescent Psychiatry, 26*(9), 1093–1103.

Neumeyer, A. M., Anixt, J., Chan, J., Perrin, J. M., Murray, D., Coury, D. L., Bennett, A., Farmer, J., & Parker, R. A. (2019). Identifying associations among co-occurring medical conditions in children with autism spectrum disorders. *Academy of Pediatrics. 19*(3), 300–306.

Nickel, K., Maier, S., Endres, D., Joos, A., Maier, V., Tebartz, L., van Elst, A., & Zeeck, A. (2019). Systematic review: Overlap between eating, autism spectrum, and attention-deficit/hyperactivity disorder. *Frontiers of Psychiatry, 10*, 708. https://doi.org/10.3389/fpsyt.2019.00708

Nordahl, C. W., Iosif, A., Young, G., Hechtman, A., Heath, B., Lee, J., Libero, B., Reinhardt, V. P., Winder-Patel, D., Amaral, D., Rogers, S., Solomon, M. & Ozanoff, S. (2020). High psychopathology subgroup in young children with autism: Associations with biological sex and amygdala volume. *Journal of the American Academy of Child & Adolescent Psychiatry, 133*(1), 54–63.

O'Brien, L. M., & Gozal, D. (2004). Neurocognitive dysfunction and sleep in children: From rodents to man. *Pediatric Clinics, 51*(1), 187–202.

Owens, J. A., Spirito, A., & McGuinn, M. (2000). The Children's Sleep Habits Questionnaire (CSHQ): Psychometric properties of a survey instrument for school-aged children. *Sleep, 23*(8), 1043–1051.

Pacheva, I., Ivanov, I., Yordanova, R., Gaberova, K., Galabova, F., Panova, M., Petkova, A., Timova, E., & Sotkova, I. (2019). Epilepsy in children with autistic spectrum disorder. *Children (Basel), 6*(2), 15. httpss://doi.org/10.3390/children6020015

Palese, A., Conforto, L., Meloni, F., Bordei, V., Domenighini, A., Bulfone, E., Grassetti, L., & Gonella, S. (2020, April 20). Assessing pain in children with autism spectrum disorders: Findings from a preliminary validation study. *Scandanavian Journal of Caring Sciences.* https://doi.org/10.1111/scs.12857

Patriquin, M.A., Hartwig, E.M., Friedman, B.H., Porges, S.W., & Scarpa, A. (2019). Autonomic response in autism spectrum disorder: Relationship to social and cognitive functioning. *Biological Psychology, 145,* 185–197. Https://doi: 10.1016/j.biopsycho.2019.05.004.

Penmetsa, C., Penmetcha, S., & Namineni, S. (2019). Role of Dental Discomfort Questionnaire-Based Approach in recognition of symptomatic expressions due to dental pain in children with autism spectrum disorders. *Contemporary Clinical Dentistry, 10*(3), 446–451.

Pickles, A., Le Couteur, A., Leadbitter, K., Salomone, E., Cole-Fletcher, R., Tobin, H., & Green, J. (2016). Parent-mediated social communication therapy for young children with autism (PACT): Long-term follow-up of a randomised controlled trial. *The Lancet, 388*(10059), 2501–2509.

Pinto, R., Rijsdijk, F., Ronald, A., Asherton, P., & Kuntsi, J. (2016). The genetic overlap of attention-deficit/hyperactivity disorder and autistic-like traits: An investigation of individual symptom scales and cognitive markers. *Journal of Abnormal Child Psychology, 44,* 335–345. https://doi.org/10.1007/s10802-015-0037-4

Plomin, R., & Kovas, Y. (2005). Generalist genes and learning disabilities. *Psychology Bulletin. 131*(4), 592–617.

Potter, C. (2017). "I received a leaflet and that is all": Father experiences of a diagnosis of autism. *British Journal of Learning Disabilities, 45*(2), 95–105.

Richa, S., Fahed, M., Khoury, E., & Mishara, B. (2014). Suicide in autism spectrum disorders. *Archives of Suicide Research, 18*(4), 327–339.

Richard, A. E., Scheffer, I. E., & Wilson, S. J. (2017). Features of the broader autism phenotype in people with epilepsy support shared mechanisms between epilepsy and autism spectrum disorder. *Neuroscience and Biobehavioral Reviews, 75*, 203–233. httpss://doi.org/10.1016/j.neubiorev.2016.12.036

Richdale, A. L., & Schreck, K. A. (2009). Sleep problems in autism spectrum disorders: Prevalence, nature and possible biopsychosocial aetiologies. *Sleep Medicine Review, 13*(6), 403–411.

Robertson, C. E. & Baron-Cohen, S. (2017). Sensory perception in autism. *Nature Reviews Neuroscience, 18*(11), 671–684.

Rose, D. R., Yang, H., Careaga, M., Angkustsir, K., Van de Water, J., & Ashwood, P. (2020). T cell populations in children with autism spectrum disorder and co-morbid gastrointestinal symptoms. *Brain, Behavior, and Immunity – Health, 2.* 100042. https://doi.org/10.1016/j.bbih.2020.100042

Rumball, F. (2019). A systematic review of the assessment and treatment of posttraumatic stress disorder in individuals with autism spectrum disorders. *Review Journal of Autism and Developmental Disorders,* 6(3), 294–324

Russell, E., & Sofronoff, K. (2005). Anxiety and social worries in children with Asperger syndrome. *Australian and New Zealand Journal of Psychiatry, 39*(7), 633–638.

Salazar, F., Baird, G., Chandler, S., Tseng, E., O'Sullivan, T., Howlin, P., Pickles, A., & Simonoff, E. (2015). Co-occurring psychiatric disorders in preschool and elementary school-aged children with autism spectrum disorder. *Journal of Autism Developmental Disorders,* 45(8), 2283–2294.

Schlooz, W. A., & Hulstijn, W. (2014). Boys with autism spectrum disorders show superior performance on the adult Embedded Figures Test. *Research in Autism Spectrum Disorders, 8*(1), 1–7.

Schriber, R. A., Robins, R. W., & Solomon, M. (2014). Personality and self-insight in individuals with autism spectrum disorder. *Journal of Personality and Social Psychology, 106*(1), 112–130. https://doi.org/10.1037/a0034950

Segall, M., & Campbell, J. (2012). Factors relating to education professionals' classroom practices for the inclusion of students with autism spectrum disorders. *Research in Autism Spectrum Disorders, 6*(3), 1156–1167.

Shattuck, P. T., Durkin, M., & Maenner, M. (2009). Timing of identification among children with an autism spectrum disorder: Findings from a population-based surveillance study. *Journal of the American Academy of Child and Adolescent Psychiatry 48*(5), 474–483.

Shavelle, R. M., Strauss, D. J., & Pickett, J. (2001). Causes of death in autism. *Journal of Autism Developmental Disorders, 31*, 69–76. https://doi.org/10.1023/A:1013247011483

Sheehan, D. V., Sheehan, K. H., Shytle, R. D., Janavs, J., Bannon, Y., Rogers, J. E., Milo, K. M., Stock, S. L., & Wilkinson, B. (2010). Reliability and validity of the Mini International Neuropsychiatric Interview for Children and Adolescents (MINI-KID). *Journal of Clinical Psychiatry, 71*(3), 313–326.

Siklos, S., & Kerns, K. (2007). Assessing the diagnostic experiences of a small sample of parents of children with autism spectrum disorder. *Research in Developmental Disabilities, 28*(1) 9–22.

Simonoff, E., Pickles, A., Charman, T., Chandler, S., Loucas, T., & Baird, G. (2008). Psychiatric disorders in children with autism spectrum disorders: prevalence, comorbidity, and associated factors in a population-derived sample. *Journal of the American Academy of Child and Adolescent Psychiatry, 47*(8), 921–929.

Snell-Rood, C., Ruble, L., Kleinert, H., McGrew, J. H., Adams, M., Rodgers, A., Odom, J., Wong, W. H., Yu, Y. (2020). Stakeholder perspectives on transition planning, implementation, and outcomes for students with autism spectrum disorder. *Autism, 24*(5), 1164–1176. https://doi.org/10.1177/1362361319894827

Solomon, M., Miller, M., Taylor, S. L., Hinshaw, S. P., & Carter, C. S. (2012). Autism symptoms and internalizing psychopathology in girls and boys with autism spectrum disorders. *Journal of Autism and Developmental Disorders, 42*(1), 48–59.

Souders, M. C., Zavodny, S., Eriksen, W., Sinko, R., Connell, J., Kerns, C., Schaaf, R., & Pinto-Martin, J. (2017). Sleep in children with autism spectrum disorder. *Current Psychiatry Reports, 19*(6), 34.

Soulières, I., Dawson, M., Samson, F., Barbeau, E. B., Sahyoun, C. P., Strangman, G. E., Zeffiro, T. A., & Mottron, L. (2009). Enhanced visual processing contributes to matrix reasoning in autism. *Human Brain Mapping, 30*(12), 4082–4107. https://doi.org/10.1002/hbm.20831

Soulières, I., Zeffiro, T. A., Girard, M. L., & Mottron, L. (2011). Enhanced mental image mapping in autism. *Neuropsychologia, 49*(5), 848–857. https://doi.org/10.1016/j.neuropsychologia.2011.01.027

Sprang, G., & Silman, M. (2013). Posttraumatic stress disorder in parents and youth after health-related disasters. *Disaster Medicine and Public Health Preparedness, 7*(1), 105–110. https://doi.org/10.1017/dmp.2013.22

Stevenson, J. L., & Gernsbacher, M. A. (2013). Abstract spatial reasoning as an autistic strength. *PloS One, 8*(3), e59329. https://doi.org/10.1371/journal.pone.0059329

Strasser, L., Downes, M., Kung, J., Cross, J. H., & De Haan, M. (2018). Prevalence and risk factors for autism spectrum disorder in epilepsy: A systematic review and meta-analysis. *Developmental Medical Child Neurology, 60*(1),19–29.

Taylor, S. J. C., Pinnock, H., Epiphaniou, E., Pearce, G., Parke, H. L., Schwappach, A., Purushotham, N., Jacob, S., Griffiths, C. J., Greenhalgh, T., & Sheikh, A. (2014). A rapid synthesis of the evidence on interventions supporting self-management for people with long-term conditions: PRISMS – Practical systematic Review of Self-Management Support for long-term conditions. *NIHR Journals*

Library(Health Services and Delivery Research, 2, 53). https://doi
.org/10.3310/hsdr02530

Thomas, S., Hovinga, M. E., Rai, D., & Lee, B. K. (2017). Brief report: Prevalence of co-occurring epilepsy and autism spectrum disorder: The U.S. National Survey of Children's Health 2011–2012. *Journal of Autism Developmental Disorders, 47*(1), 224–229.

Triwahyuningtyas, D., Hudha, A. M. N., Tyas, D. A., Widiaty, I., Nandiyanto, A., Permanasari, A., & Hamidah, I. (2020). Teaching basic mathematics and technology to elementary students with autism. *Journal of Engineering Science and Technology, 15*(3), 1589–1595.

Turk, J., Bax, M., Williams, C., Amin, P., Eriksson, M., & Gillberg, C. (2009). Autism spectrum disorder in children with and without epilepsy: Impact on social functioning and communication. *Acta Paediatrica, 98*(4), 675–681.

Tye, C., Runicles, A. K., Whitehouse, A., & Alvares, G. A. (2019). Characterizing the interplay between autism spectrum disorder and comorbid medical conditions: An integrative review. *Frontiers in Psychiatry, 9,* 751. https://doi.org/10.3389/fpsyt.2018.00751

Valicenti-McDermott, M., McVicar, K., Rapin, I., Wershil, B. K., Cohen, H., & Shinnar, S. (2006). Frequency of gastrointestinal symptoms in children with autistic spectrum disorders and association with family history of autoimmune disease. *Journal of Developmental and Behavioral Pediatrics, 27*(2 Suppl.), S128–S136.

Valenti, M., Ciprietti, T., Di Egidio, C., Gabrielli, M., Masedu, F., Tomassini, A. R., & Sorge, G. (2012). Adaptive response of children and adolescents with autism to the 2009 earthquake in L'Aquila, Italy. *Journal of Autism and Developmental Disorders, 42*(6), 954–960.

van Steensel, F. J. A., Bögels, S. M., and Perrin, S. (2011). Anxiety disorders in children and adolescents with autistic spectrum disorders: A meta-analysis. *Clinical Child and Family Psychology Review, 14*(3), 302–317.

Vannucchi, G., Masi, G., Toni, C., Dell'Osso, L., Erfurth, A., & Perugi, G. (2014). Bipolar disorder in adults with Asperger›s Syndrome: A sys-

tematic review. *Journal of Affective Disorders, 168*, 151–160. https://
doi.org/10.1016/j.jad.2014.06.042

Wiggins, L. D., Robins, D. L., Bakeman, R., & Adamson, L. B. (2009). Brief
report: Sensory abnormalities as distinguishing symptoms of autism
spectrum disorders in young children. *Journal of Autism and Developmental Disorders, 39*(7), 1087–1091.

Wigham, S., Taylor, J., & Hatton, C. (2014). A prospective study of the relationship between adverse life events and trauma in adults with mild
to moderate intellectual disabilities. *Journal of Intellectual Disability Research, 58*(12), 1131–1140.

Zablotsky, B., Bramlett, M. D., & Blumberg, S. J. (2017). The co-occurrence
of autism spectrum disorder in children with ADHD. *Journal of
Attention Disorders, 24*(1) 94–103.

Zeedyk, S. M., Rodriguez, G., Tipton, L. A., Baker, B. L., & Blacher, J. (2014).
Bullying of youth with autism spectrum disorder, intellectual disability, or typical development: Victim and parent perspectives.
Research in Autism Spectrum Disorders, 8(9), 1173–1183. https://
doi.org/10.1016/j.rasd.2014.06.001.

Zheng, A., Zheng, P., Zou, X. (2018). Association between schizophrenia
and autism spectrum disorder: A systematic review and meta-analysis. *Autism Research, 11*(8) 1110–1119.

INDEX

elementary *vs.* higher mental
functions in, 245–47
factors impacting, 235–36
regulation prior to entering,
241–45
steps after regulation, 245–50
TaRL, 250–55
task scaffolding, 248–50
under trauma, 263–77. *see also
under* COVID-19
working with child's type of
thinking, 255–61. *see also
under* thinking styles
gut microbes, 131

Health Insurance Portability and
Accountability Act (HIPAA),
74, 86
high schools
guidelines for better preparation
for students, 298–306
HIPAA. *see* Health Insurance
Portability and Accountability
Act (HIPAA)
hobby skills, 170
home chores, 168–69
home living skills, 167–69
Hudson, C.C., 145
hygiene activities, 165–66

IDEA. *see* Individuals with
Disability Education
Improvement Act (IDEA)
"ideas worth spreading," 32
IEPs. *see* individualized education
plans (IEPs)
immune abnormalities, 129
immune dysfunction, 129
immune response, 35
impaired face recognition
autism and epilepsy associated
with, 126

impairment(s)
DSM-5 on, 29
incoming stimuli
processing of, 36
individualized education plans
(IEPs), 14, 99–100, 163–64,
272–75
components of, 279
Individuals with Disability
Education Improvement Act
(IDEA), 281
infantile spasms
autism following, 125
inflammation
generalized increase in, 122
inflammatory responses
abnormal, 131
information
background *vs.* foreground,
116
contextual, 17
gathering ahead of time, 17–18
information processing
background *vs.* foreground,
116
checklist questions for
evaluators, 68–69
COVID-19 impact on, 264
insomnia, 135–39
intellect
autism and, 64
intellectual disability(ies)
autism associated with, 126
autism inaccurately equated with,
178
epilepsy in autistic adults with
severe, 125, 126
interest(s)
during adolescence, 201–4
case examples, 200–3
checklist questions for
evaluators, 25, 71

ABOUT THE AUTHORS

Dr. Temple Grandin is one of the world's most respected experts in the fields of autism and animal behavior and livestock handling. As a toddler, she had speech delays as well as other signs of severe autism. Many hours of speech therapy and intensive training ultimately enabled Temple to speak. Mentoring by a high school science teacher and exposure to her aunt's ranch in Arizona motivated her to pursue a career as a scientist and livestock equipment designer. She is a prolific speaker, internationally best-selling author, and Professor of Animal Science at Colorado State University. In 2020 she was honored as a Top Ten College Professor in America. In 2010, Time 100, an annual list of the 100 most influential people in the world, named her in the "Heroes" category. She was also the subject of the Emmy- and Golden Globe-winning semi-biographical film *Temple Grandin*.

Dr. Debra Moore is a psychologist who has worked extensively with children, teens, and adults on the autism spectrum. She believes in therapy approaches that focus on strengths and interests, recognize the individual differences of each client, and foster confidence and potential. She was the Founder and Director of Fall Creek Counseling Associates, a practice that served the greater Sacramento area and was an approved teaching site for psychologists in training. Now retired from active practice, she devotes her time to volunteering and writing. She contributed to *The Nine Degrees of Autism* (2015), and authored "Internet and Gaming Addiction in Youth on the Autism Spectrum: A Particularly Vulnerable Population" in *Internet Addiction in Children and Adolescents* (2017). This is her second project with Dr. Temple Grandin, coauthoring *The Loving Push: How Parents and Professionals Can Help Spectrum Kids Become Successful Adults* in 2016. She resides in Rappahannock County, Virginia.